Tarot Fun

By Paul Foster Case

and Wade Coleman

Edited by Wade Coleman

Copyright 2019 by Wade Coleman

Upon my death, this book enters the Public Domain

December 2020 edition

Foreward

Paul Foster Case in 1937, copyrighted *Tarot Fundamentals*. Writing styles have changed, and many students find his work difficult to read.

I edited Case's lessons to conform to a modern writing style. When possible, I changed pronouns to be gender-neutral. That is, changing "he" to "the individual," "we," or "you."

In the last 100 years, humanities' understanding of the Hebrew letters has progressed. I rewrote much of the information on the Hebrew letters. Also, I translated the Thirty-two Paths of Wisdom from Hebrew into English. It is in the Appendix.

Whenever possible, I cited sources. Dr. Case would write something like, "ancient text on the subject says," or "Kabbalists say." What Case is usually referencing is the *Sepher Yetzirah*. I don't know why he didn't cite the book.

Transliteration

Transliteration is the spelling of Hebrew words in English. Depending on the author, Tiphareth, the 6th sphere of the Tree of Life can be Tiferet.

The 2nd Sephirah is Chokmah or Hokmah.

And Cabala can be Qabalah, Kabala, and Kabbala.

Why?

In Hebrew, Qof or Qoph is ק. It sounds like English **K, C** or **Q**. Depending on the author, Qabalah can be spelled with either of these letters.

Also, Cheth (ח) sounds different if it's in the beginning or end of the word.

For example, Chokmah (2nd sephiroth) is spelled חכמה. At the beginning of a word, Cheth is a "throaty H," as my Hebrew teacher describes it. It's an "H" sound with your throat slightly closed. Therefore Chokmah can be spelled Hokmah.

At the end of a word, Cheth is a guttural stop, as the Scottish lo**ck**. Therefore the word Ruach (רוח) ends in a guttural H and is usually transliterated as a **ch**.

I vary the spelling the transliteration of words not to confuse the reader but to get you familiar with the spellings you will encounter in your studies.

OBTW.

Hebrew is written right to left. I recommend everyone take a beginning Hebrew class. For personal study, I recommend the *First Hebrew Primer* by Ethelyn Simon, Irene Resnikoff and Linda Motzkin.

HIGHLIGHTS OF TAROT; by Paul Foster Case.
Registered in the name of School of Ageless Wisdom, Inc.,
under AA 71739 following publication June 4, 1931.
Renewed under R 235814, April 30, 1959, by Mrs. Paul
Foster Case, as widow of the author.

Facts of registration for the other work listed in your request are reported
as follows:

TAROT FUNDAMENTALS; by Paul Foster Case. V. 1-4. Registered in
the name of Paul Foster Case, under AA 239500 following publication
June 2, 1937. No renewal found.

Deborah Lloyd
Senior Copyright Research Specialist
Records Research & Certification Section

Enclosures:
Remitter's credit card receipt
Circulars 15, 15a, 22

Table of Contents

Chapter 1   The Object of Tarot Practice   8

Chapter 2   The Symbolism of Numbers   14

Chapter 3   The Life-Power   21

Chapter 4   More About the Life-Power   36

Chapter 5   Selfconsciousness   45

Chapter 6   The Magician   53

Chapter 7   Subconsciousness   63

Chapter 8   The High Priestess   72

Chapter 9   Creative Imagination   80

Chapter 10   The Empress   88

Chapter 11   Reason   95

Chapter 12   The Emperor   104

Chapter 13   Intuition   115

Chapter 14   The Hierophant   129

Chapter 15   Discrimination   135

Chapter 16   The Lovers   144

Chapter 17   Receptive – Will   150

Chapter 18   The Chariot   159

Chapter 19	The Serpent Power	174
Chapter 20	Strength	183
Chapter 21	Response	195
Chapter 22	The Hermit	203
Chapter 23	Rotation	213
Chapter 24	The Wheel of Fortune	221
Chapter 25	Action – Equilibrium	234
Chapter 26	Justice	242
Chapter 27	Reversal	249
Chapter 28	The Hanged Man	258
Chapter 29	Transformation	265
Chapter 30	Death	272
Chapter 31	Verification	279
Chapter 32	Temperance	287
Chapter 33	Bondage	297
Chapter 34	The Devil	309
Chapter 35	Awakening	315
Chapter 36	The Tower	322

Chapter 37   Revelation   331

Chapter 38   The Star   340

Chapter 39   Organization   350

Chapter 40   The Moon   357

Chapter 41   Regeneration   364

Chapter 42   The Sun   372

Chapter 43   Realization   383

Chapter 44   Judgment   391

Chapter 45   Cosmic Consciousness   402

Chapter 46   The World   410

Chapter 47   A Month of Tarot Practice   422

Chapter 48   Proficiency Test   434

Appendix 1   Tarot Correspondences   436

Appendix 2   32 Paths in Hebrew   443

Appendix 3   Hebrew Letter Names   488

Appendix 4   Cube Figures   490

TAROT FUNDAMENTALS

Chapter 1

THE OBJECT OF TAROT PRACTICE

If you stop for a moment to consider the chain of circumstances which led to your reading these words, you will discover one primary motive— your desire for enlightenment. Even if you approach this study with skepticism, your interest is evidence of your spiritual urge to seek the light.

This light-seeking impulse is the first requirement for success with Tarot. This, and a strong determination to persist in the step-by-step mastery of the work explained in the course will enable you to make the most of your study.

You reading this chapter is proof that you are ready for Tarot study because nothing ever happens by accident. One fundamental principle of Ageless Wisdom is that when a pupil is prepared, his instruction will be forthcoming.

This course on *Tarot Fundamentals* will show you how to use the Tarot Keys for evoking thought. Thus you will bring to the surface of your consciousness the principles of practical occultism which lie hid in the hearts of all humanity.

Knowledge of this truth is innate in every human being but is not available for use until the knowledge is brought into the light of consciousness.

Over the portals of ancient temples was the motto, *Know Thyself.* For the same reason, it is written: "Seek ye first the kingdom of God," and, "The kingdom of God is within you."

The Tarot Keys do not put something into your consciousness. They call forth what is already there. Rich symbolism and ingenious construction make the Tarot one of the best education instruments because the Tarot draws out the wisdom hidden within you.

The practical instruction of this course will help you develop an intelligent grasp of these Keys' meanings. Into your hands will be put clues that will enable you to use Tarot to gain an in-depth understanding of the laws of life. However, you must follow these clues yourself. Then, Tarot will bring out the knowledge within you, which is more important to you than anything else.

To each prospector in this inexhaustible mine of Ageless Wisdom. No matter how high maybe his source of information, no one may say truthfully, "This is the full and final meaning of Tarot."

There can be no final explanation. No student will ever exhaust the possibilities of the Tarot's symbolic alphabet, any more than one person can exhaust the possibilities of a language.

However, there is a particular manner in which to approach the study of these Keys, as there are tunnels that lead to the heart of the mine. In the earlier part of this course, you will be provided with a map or plan.

Then you must enter the mine of Tarot yourself, and dig out your peculiar treasure. You begin by mastering the elements of the esoteric language of symbols in which the mysteries of the Tarot has been preserved. Every chapter in this course will enable you to make positive progress.

Pay particular attention to every detail of the procedure. *Follow the instruction*, just as given. Whatever you are told to do, you can carry it out with a clear conscience, and in the sure conviction, it will be for your good.

As the results of your practice begin to make themselves manifest, you will be agreeably surprised by the changes effected in your personality. You will find yourself developing a greater ability to concentrate. Your perceptions will be sharpened, which will broaden your comprehension of yourself and the meaning of your various experiences.

Mere perusal of the chapters will be almost useless. Determine to devote a period to this work every day. Then you may expect the best results, "Out of nothing, nothing cometh." Therefore, prepare yourself to enter into the spirit of Tarot *practice*.

Do not delude yourself into believing you lack time for this work. It is absurd to say you have no time for the most important thing in your life. Your spiritual growth is more worthy of consideration than anything else. You probably prove this every day of your life by seeking continually for greater enlightenment.

You read books. You talk to people about it. You attend lectures and meetings. Fifteen minutes devoted to Tarot study every day can promote your growth more than hours of other activities. The one part of your day you cannot afford to miss is your Tarot period.

Your first practical exercise will be to commit to memory the eleven statements *of The Pattern on the Trestleboard*, which is enclosed with this chapter. These are the words of one of the great leaders of the Inner School. They are based on an ancient esoteric text. Commit the *Trestleboard* to memory in the following manner. Read the entire *Pattern* several times from beginning to end. Do not attempt to learn it a little at a time. Persist until you succeed in committing the *whole*. Then fix it by writing out the *Pattern*. Use an ink pen, not a pencil.

This is the easiest and quickest way to memorize. Take care to use it for this first practice. Then you will have made a correct beginning in learning how to organize your conscious processes.

This is a *pattern*, not a boastful declaration of personal attainment. The truth it speaks is about the SELF, the cosmic Life-power behind and above all personal activity. It is said to be "on the trestleboard," because in the old term from the building crafts. A trestleboard is a sort of table, on which are laid plans for the workmen's guidance.

Say the *Pattern on the Trestleboard* every morning on rising and every night before going to sleep. Be sure you do this, whether you like it or not. Guard against automatic, parrot-like repetitions.

Think about the meaning of every sentence. Make this same effort every time you recite the Pattern. It will aid you to discover the deeper meanings.

The next chapter will help you gain more insight into the truths behind these eleven sentences. The key is found in the numbering of the statements. As preparation, get a notebook.

Then think over what you have read, and jot down any ideas. As you proceed with your daily study, continue to use the notebook. Make the entries short, but make them, and date them.

This notebook is your occult diary. Every scientific researcher keeps records. You must do the same. This book will be of great value in your later work. Do not neglect this step. Otherwise, it will be to defeat one primary purpose of this instruction.

Use it at every regular study period, and make an entry then, even if you must record a failure to work at the time scheduled. You will find that its contents have other uses, as time goes on, KEEP IT IN A SECURE PLACE, AND DO NOT SHOW IT TO ANYONE.

This week, spend your study periods as follows:

1. Memorize the *Pattern on the Trestleboard*. When you have it by heart, always begin a study period by reciting it.

2. Read this chapter through, slowly and if possible, read it aloud.

3. Use the rest of the time to look over your Tarot Keys. You cannot be too familiar with them.

If any Key seems particularly attractive to you, make a note of it in your diary, along with the reason, if you have one. If you dislike any particular Key, note that and your reason. If a Key suggests an idea, however vague, record it.

In the third chapter, you begin coloring your Tarot Keys. By coloring the Keys, you infuse them with part of your nature and become linked to you. The work demands attention, which will impress the details of the Tarot Keys into your memory. It builds the pattern into your brain cells.

Making the Tarot Keys part of your very flesh and blood must be your Aim. It is what makes all the subtler and more potent utilization of this alphabet of Ageless Wisdom.

You are not aiming primarily at making your Keys works of art. Do them as well as you can. Whatever skill you develop in using paints and brushes will be useful for other projects.

Tarot on the table, or in a bookcase, is just a set of pictures printed on the pasteboard. Tarot built into your brain is a living instrument through which you can contact sources of knowledge and power more significant than you realize now. Coloring your Keys builds this *inside* Tarot quicker and better than anything else.

The Pattern on the Trestleboard

This Is Truth About The Self

0. All the Power that ever was or will be is here now.

1. I am a center of expression for the Primal Will-to-Good, which eternally creates and sustains the Universe.

2. Through me, its unfailing Wisdom takes form in thought and word.

3. Filled with Understanding of its perfect law, I am guided, moment by moment, along the path of liberation.

4. From the exhaustless riches of its Limitless Substance, I draw all things needful, both spiritual and material.

5. I recognize the manifestation of the Undeviating Justice in all the circumstances of my life.

6. In all things, great and small, I see the Beauty of the Divine Expression.

7. Living from that Will, supported by its unfailing Wisdom and Understanding, mine is the Victorious Life.

8. I look forward with confidence to the perfect realization of the Eternal Splendor of the Limitless Light.

9. In thought and word and deed, I rest my life, from day to day, upon the sure Foundation of Eternal Being.

10. The Kingdom of Spirit is embodied in my flesh.

Chapter 2

THE SYMBOLISM OF NUMBERS

Number symbols represent truths inherent in all things and manifest in all phenomena. The science of numbers is the foundation of every other department of human knowledge. Resolve to master the elements presented in this chapter. Thus you will prepare your mind to understand the principles and laws that will bring you into harmony with the rhythms of the cosmic life.

Let no imaginary dislike for mathematics deter you from entering into this study. You do not need an aptitude for mathematics. Set to work, and you can master the main points in a short time. Then practice will make you proficient in the various applications of these principles.

From 0 to 9, the numeral symbols represent successive stages in the cyclic Life-power's self-expression, whether on the grand scale of the cosmos or the smaller personal unfoldment level. The order in the numeral series reflects an order which prevails throughout creation.

The Master Builder has ordered all things by number, measure, and weight. Everywhere the properties of number are manifest, in the whirling of electrons within an atom, the arrangement of parts in a living body. Thus a famous relativist said: "Number is one of the few things in the universe which is not relative."

This chapter gives you the underlying meanings of the numeral symbols. As you proceed with your studies, you will gather more information about numbers and their significance.

Upon first reading, some of the numerical attributions may not seem apparent. A few may even strike you as being far-fetched or arbitrary. Do not let this disturb you. You are learning number symbols because they are based on initiates' secret language to transmit their knowledge from generation to generation. You must know their traditional interpretations of numbers to understand the esoteric language of the mysteries. No satisfactory substitute for this language has been devised. Two initiates may carry on a long conversation using symbols, even though neither knows a word of the other's native tongue. With a few lines and figures, an adept can express more meaning than he could pack into pages of words.

When you have memorized this numeral system's basic ideas, you will begin to see the connections between them and others related to them. In this chapter, the key concepts are printed in capitals at the beginning of the attributions paragraph. The other meanings follow. An essential part of your mental training is to trace the associations that join the key-words to the others in the same paragraph. Be sure you do this.

In Chapter 1, you learned a connection between the numbers and The Pattern's corresponding sentences *on the Trestleboard*. In the Pattern's key-words, there is a sense in which every key*word may be taken as the name of the corresponding number.*

MEANINGS OF THE NUMERAL SIGNS

0. NO-THING – Super-consciousness. The undifferentiated *Power* preceding all manifestation; absence of quantity, quality, or mass; freedom from every limitation; changelessness; the unknown, immeasurable, unfathomable, infinite, eternal Source, the Rootless Root of all creation; the sacred ellipse representing the endless line of Eternity; the Cosmic Egg.

1. BEGINNING – Self-consciousness. First in the numeral series, because 0 stands for that which precedes manifestation, and is therefore not included in any sequence; inception; initiation; the *Primal Will*; selection; unity; singleness; individuality; attention; one-pointedness; concentration; the definite or manifest, as contrasted with the indefinable Source.

2. DUPLICATION – Subconsciousness. Repetition; Wisdom and Science; opposition; polarity; antithesis; succession; sequence; continuation; diffusion; separation; radiation; subordination; dependence.

3. MULTIPLICATION; increase; growth; augmentation; expansion; amplification; extension; productiveness; fecundity; generation; the response of subconscious mental activity to self-conscious impulse, in the production of mental images; hence, *Understanding*.

4. ORDER; system; regulation; management; supervision; control; authority; command; dominance; the classifying activity of self-consciousness, induced by the multiplication of mental images produced by the response of subconscious mental activity of self-conscious impulse; the Cosmic Order considered as the underlying substance manifested in every form; *Reason*.

5. MEDIATION (an idea suggested because 5 is the middle term in the series from 1 to 9); adaptation; intervention; adjustment; hence *Justice*; accommodation; reconciliation; the result of the classifying activities symbolized by 4; subconscious elaboration of those classifications, and the formation of deductions therefrom. Projected into the field of self-conscious awareness, these deductions are what are termed *Intuitions*.

6. RECIPROCATION; interchange; correlation; response; coordination; cooperation; correspondence; harmony; concord; equilibration; symmetry; *Beauty*.

7. EQUILIBRIUM (the application of the laws of symmetry and reciprocation); *mastery*; poise; rest; conquest; peace; safety; security; art; *victory*.

8. RHYTHM; periodicity; alternation; vibration; pulsation; flux and reflux; involution and evolution; education; culture; the response of subconsciousness to everything symbolized by 7.

9. CONCLUSION (literally, "closing together," which implies the union of elements which are separate until the conclusion is reached, and has particular reference to meanings Key 9, The Hermit). Goal; end; completion; fulfillment; attainment; the final result of the process symbolized by the series of digits; perfection; adeptship; the mystical "three times three" of Freemasons, and of other societies which preserve some vestiges of the ancient mysteries.

The meaning of a number consisting of two or more digits may be determined by combining each symbol's ideas. Always begin with the number on the right-side. Thus the number 10 combines the concepts of 0 and 1. One (1) is the *agency* expressing the *power* represented by 0. Furthermore, since 10 follows 9, it implies that nine stands for a conclusion, which only refers to a single manifestation cycle.

The completion of a cycle is always a return to the Eternal No-Thing – 0. However, 0 is essentially changeless in its inherent nature because the Eternal Source is eternally a self-manifesting power. Consequently, a new cycle begins as soon as the preceding cycle ends.

Therefore 10 symbolizes the eternal creativeness of the Life-power, the incessant whirling forth of the Primal Will's self-expression, the ever-turning wheel of manifestation (see Key 10, The Wheel of Fortune). This makes ten the number of embodiment, the Kingdom, and Law in action. Because 10 is also a feminine symbol (0) with a masculine (1).

Memorize the numbers and the key-words in capitals. Put aside ten pages of your diary. Head each page with one of the numeral signs and its key-word. Then copy each paragraph on the meaning of the numeral symbols. *This is important*. To copy anything is to make it yours far more than merely reading it.

Whenever you get an idea about the meaning of a number, note it in your diary. If you come upon anything in your reading, copy it under its appropriate heading.

At present, do not go in quest of numerical information. Do not consult other texts on numbers to fill the pages of your diary. Only make write down notes and ideas which come to you from your inner consciousness.

WHAT YOU NEED WILL COME TO YOU and without special effort. You will be amazed at the amount of information that flows your way, as if by magic. The **magic is the hidden force of subconsciousness**, as explained in *SEVEN STEPS*. In time, this section on numbers will become a valuable item in your reference library.

A good practice is looking up dictionary definitions of the numbers from 0 to 9 and *every word in the ten paragraphs of explanation given in this chapter*. This will make you realize that the esoteric science of numbers is part of human thought's fundamental structure. You will gain a great deal of insight from this exercise.

During your study period, arrange your Tarot Keys thus:

			0			
1	2	3	4	5	6	7
8	9	10	11	12	13	14
15	16	17	18	19	20	21

Examine the tableau, paying particular attention to the numbers of the Keys. Try to connect them with the pictures. In Keys 10 to 21, try to work out the numbers' meanings from what you have learned concerning the ten symbols.

Transcribe your findings and speculations into your notebook. Do this, no matter how trivial or vague your first attempts may seem. You must make a beginning. These first endeavors to formulate ideas for yourself are like seeds that will bear good fruit.

In the prior arrangement of the Tarot Keys, the zero card is above the others to indicate that No-number, to which it corresponds, is logically superior to, and precedes, the idea of *beginning* represented by 1. Zero (0) is also separated from the other number symbols because it is not really in the sequence of manifested appearances.

However far the series may be extended, the number always comes to a final member of that particular series, beyond the No-Thing. Between any two numbers in a series, *nothing* intervenes. Thus the zero Key of Tarot represents:

1. What precedes the series;

2. What follows it;

3. The place of mediator between any two consecutive members of the series.

When he published his intentionally incorrect attribution of the Tarot Keys to the Hebrew letters, Eliphas Levi placed the zero Key between those numbered 20 and 21.

For your information,

1. The top row of Keys refers to POWERS or POTENTIALITIES of consciousness.

2. The middle row of Keys are symbols of LAWS or AGENCIES.

3. The Keys in the bottom row represent CONDITIONS or EFFECTS.

Thus Key 1 is the power that works through the agency of Key 8 to modify conditions or effects symbolized by Key 15.

In this tableau, ten pairs of Keys balance numerically through 11, the Key named Justice, a symbol of equilibrium. Thus 11 is one-half the sum of any two numbers placed diametrically opposite in the tableau, such as 1 and 21, 9 and 13, 6 and 16, and so on. Key 11 is both the arithmetical and the geometrical center, or mean, between the two Keys in each of these ten pairs.

CHAPTER 3

THE LIFE-POWER

Before reading this chapter, the first thing to do is to place Key 0, The Fool, before you. Observe every detail so that you can make a mental reference to it as you read the chapter.

Follow an orderly procedure in your examination of the Key. Begin with the Hebrew letter Aleph (א) in the lower right-hand corner. Then consider the meaning of the title. Then look at the number and mentally review the definitions you learned from the preceding chapter.

After this, inspect the picture. Begin at the upper right-hand corner, work progressively through the design, from right to left and from top to bottom.

Except for four Tarot Keys (16, 17, 18, 19), the observer right corresponds to the south. The left is north. The background is east. The foreground is west. Remember this because it is a clue to the meanings of many Tarot symbols.

The background usually contains details that refer to states or causes of manifestation, *preceding* what is represented by the details in the foreground. The foreground often shows the symbols that directly relate to the meanings of the letter, title, and number of the Key. Details placed in the middle distance often symbolize agencies intervening between what is suggested by the symbols in the background and what is represented by those in the foreground.

The Absolute

Key 0 represents how the Absolute presents itself to the minds of the wise. The Absolute is THAT concerning which nothing may be positively affirmed. We cannot define it because it transcends our finite comprehension. We may *call* it the Rootless Root of all being or the Causeless Cause of all that is, but these are just words. Words can point the mind towards the Absolute but cannot define it. Speculation into the Absolute's essential nature is futile. It's more practical if we turn our thoughts towards contemplation of how the Absolute manifests itself.

Many names that have been assigned to the manifestation are Life-power.

1. The One Force.

2. Limitless Light. L.V.X – Light in Extension.

3. The One Thing.

4. The Primal Will.

Learn these names. They designate the force you use in every thought, feeling, and action. Gaining a better understanding of this force's nature and possibilities is the primary object of this instruction. *Your advancement will be measured strictly by your growing comprehension of the real meaning of these terms.*

The first symbol of the Life-power is 0. Review *now* the list of meanings. Do so mentally, if you can. If not,

> NO-THING – Super-consciousness. The undifferentiated *Power* preceding all manifestation; absence of quantity, quality, or mass; freedom from every limitation; changelessness; the unknown, immeasurable, unfathomable, infinite, eternal Source, the Rootless Root of all creation; the sacred ellipse representing the endless line of Eternity; the Cosmic Egg.

The Life-power is NO-THING. It is *nothing* we can define, *nothing* we can measure. Yet it IS, and it is limitless.

Zero (0) looks like an egg, and an egg contains potencies of growth and development. A living body is formed inside the shell of an egg and then hatched from it. Everything in the universe is brought into embodiment *within* the Cosmic Egg of the Life -power. When this manifestation is perfected, and only then, it becomes possible to achieve the ultimate liberation, which is union with the Absolute itself.

But this attainment is far beyond our immediate objective. Right now, the task at hand is to make the *best possible use of the potencies of the Life-power, within the limits of the Ring-Pass-Not* symbolized by the zero sign.

The Life-power has within it *all possibilities*. All manifestation, every object, every force in the universe, is an adaptation of the one Life-power. Because its possibilities are truly limitless, it may be specialized in any form of expression the human mind can conceive. Many extraordinary results are achieved by purely mental means.

Because Life-power is the force behind growth and development, it is the *cultural* power. The attribution of Aleph intimates this to this Key.

Aleph - א

Aleph is the sign for air and breath. It's one of the three mother letters and is attributed to the element Air. Air is the agency through which the power of our sun's solar rays is carried to earth. Additionally, the Air of the earth's atmosphere filters and steps down the energy so that the living creatures can utilize it without causing harm.

The letter name Aleph (אלף) means *bull* or *ox*. Oxen are domesticated cattle that are trained to wear a yoke and pull a plow. They were the motive-power in the early civilizations. Oxen plow fields, thresh grain and carry burdens. Agriculture is the basis of civilization. Hence the ox represents the power at work in an activity whereby humans use the forces surrounding them and adapt them to realize their purposes.

Oxen are symbols of the taming of natural forces. Therefore Aleph (א) is a symbol of creative energy and the vital principle of living creatures. This vital principle comes to us in physical form as the radiant energy of the sun.

The Life-power is not an abstraction that is far removed from our everyday life. We make contact with it everywhere, in every form. Our senses reveal it to us physically as light and heat from the sun. Science has confirmed the truth of the ancient intuition that solar energy is the basis of physical existence.

Just as sunlight is electromagnetic radiation, so is everything else composed of electromagnetic vibrations. Man's tools for recording these vibrations have a relatively narrow range, even though it extends far beyond physical sensation limits.

However, human personality does register the higher vibrations of cosmic radiation. Human personality in an instrument that has possibilities far beyond what most persons realize. To make these potentials of human powers, the personality must be rightly adjusted and, in a sense, *completed.*

The untrained personality is like a delicate precision tool, and some of the higher functions of the organism require us to bring about actual alterations of structure. This is the purpose of occult training.

The human personality's primary function is to give free expression to the highest potencies of the Life-power. Through your spiritual practices, you will discover that the power of the cosmic order *works with us* in our efforts to reach higher stages of unfoldment.

Why?

"The purpose of Earth and earthly life is awakening of the souls of men. Earthly conditions can serve no other end." – *Egyptian Bronzebook*, Book of Morals, and Precepts 3:31.

Recall statements 0, 1, and 2 in *The Pattern on the Trestleboard.*

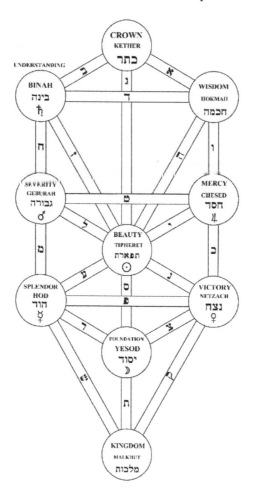

The 11th *Path* is the Shining Consciousness (connecting Kether to Hokmah). It is truly the essence of the veil which arranges the sequence of the stars. It (הוא) assigns the Paths their relationships. And (it) stands before the Cause of Causes.

The Cause of Causes is a title of Kether, the Crown – the 1st Path. Also, the divine name of Kether is Hu (הוא). The Sphere of the Zodiac is assigned to Hokmah. On the Tree of Life, Aleph (א) is the veil that stands between Kether and Hokmah.

And so we begin your training by telling you the most important form taken by the Life-power is radiant energy. This power is literally in every breath you take. You must learn to control it by learning how to breathe. Just learn to make a really *deep* breath, which fills your lungs, by giving full play to the abdominal muscles during the act of inhalation.

You do not have to *pull in* the breath. Atmospheric pressure takes care of that. You simply have to expand your diaphragm, and the air will rush into your lungs.

Do not try any forcible expansion of the chest. Let the muscles just below the ribs do most of the work. Done properly, you will feel the expansion in the small of your back, the sides, and in front of the body.

Keep in mind the picture of the air penetrating every part of the lungs to provide your bloodstream with the oxygen it needs. At first, it takes watchful attention to make breathing deep and regular. Consistent practice will establish you in good habits of breathing.

Do not make an effort to keep up deep breathing all day long. When you arise in the morning, take four deep breaths, with just as complete exhalation before each one as you can manage without any sense of strain. Remember to exhale before taking the first of these four breaths.

During the day, repeat your four breaths at noon, just before the evening meal, and just before going to bed. For the rest of the day, you need only to recall from time to time that each breath is filled with Life-power.

Your subconsciousness will attend automatically to the establishment of the proper rhythmic breathing. Don't try any trick exercises, such as are found in some books. Most of these breathing stunts have no practical value. The few that work are also dangerous unless practiced under the supervision of a skilled teacher.

Listen to your breathing. It should be practically inaudible. If your breathing exercises are noisy, they are wrong. The remedy is to slow down the alternate expansion and contraction of the abdominal muscles.

Adhere strictly to the rule of observing four periods for taking the deepest possible breaths. Observe these religiously. The rest of the time, let your subconsciousness do the work. It will if you make up your mind by your specific intention. If you are suddenly upset by something, stop for four deep breaths before thinking, saying, or doing anything.

The Fool

The only way we can conceive of the Absolute is in terms of our own experience. Therefore the Fool is drawn as a human.

The importance of breath is shown in the symbolism of the Fool. The noun "fool," moreover, is derived from the Latin *follis*, meaning "a bag of wind," and to this day, we call a noisy, silly person a "windbag." *Follis* also means "bellows," an instrument that uses air to stir up a fire. This is precisely the office of our lungs.

The Tarot title for the Life-power is ingenious. It tells us what we need to know, and at the same time, throws the idly curious and superficial dabblers off the track. A clue to what Tarot means by "Fool" is the saying: "The wisdom of God is foolishness with men." Because this is true, the wise men found in every generation, who gain knowledge of the Life-power, are often called madmen or fools by their less enlightened brethren.

Thus the title of Key 0 hints at a state of consciousness that psychologists term abnormal or even pathological because they do not understand it. Those who do comprehend its significance call this state super-consciousness, or cosmic consciousness.

To enter into this state of consciousness is to arrive at a profound understanding of the cosmic order, and at the same time, to become aware of the real significance of what it is to be a human being. This attainment is the ultimate objective of your Tarot study.

Do not look for miracles. Your study and practice will help you organize your personality forces to become an adequate instrument for the expression of super-consciousness and the exercise of powers that belong to this higher level of awareness.

The Fool's Headdress

In manifestation, energy (also symbolized by the traveler's fair hair) is temporarily limited by living organisms. Of these, the vegetable kingdom, represented by the green wreath, is the most advanced in the order of evolution. The red feather represents the Animal Kingdom.

The Direction North-West

The Life-power is forever young, forever in the morning of its might, forever on the verge of the abyss of manifestation. It always faces unknown possibilities of self-expression, transcending any height it may have reached.

Hence the Fool faces toward the North-West (a direction associated with initiation and with the beginning of new enterprises). He looks toward a peak above and beyond his present situation.

The Yellow Background

The yellow tint in the background of the picture is a symbol for Air. The Hebrew word for *Air* and *breath, spirit, mind, intellect, passion* is *Ruach* (רוח). Almost every language man employs air, wind, or breathing to designate life and *conscious* energy. Hence the importance of learning to breathe.

The White Sun

The Fool is a personal representation of the Life-power. However, the wise know that behind seeming individual is an impersonal force that animates everything. The white sun is the Central Sun. It represents the limitless energy that powers every star and, in turn, radiates the Life-power to their planets.

יהוה – IHVH

The white inner garment is embroidered dimly in the collar with the Hebrew Letters IHVH (יהוה). This is the name of God associated with Tiphareth and means, *That which was is and shall be.*

The Outer Robe

His inner robe stands for the dazzling white light of perfect wisdom. It is concealed by the black coat of ignorance, lined with the red of passion and physical force.

This outer garment is embroidered with floral decoration, but the design is a solar orb containing eight red spokes. This symbolizes the whirling motion, which brings the universe into manifestation.

The Girdle with 12 Beads

The coat encircled by a girdle consisting of twelve units, of which seven are showing. The girdle symbolizes time. As the girdle must be removed before the coat may be taken off, so is it impossible to overcome ignorance and passion until man frees his consciousness from the limitations imposed by the belief in the reality of time. **No single symbol in the Tarot is more important than this.**

The girdle is *artificial*, made by humanity, and not a product of nature. This means that man's conception of time is a manufactured product, a device of man's creative imagination. It is a most useful invention when rightly employed, but when it is abused, as it is by most persons, it becomes a prolific source of error.

The Mountains

The mountains in the background represent abstract mathematical conceptions that are behind all knowledge of reality. These conceptions seem cold and uninteresting to many. However, the melting ice and snow on the peaks feed the streams, making fertile the valleys below. Ageless Wisdom principles feed your consciousness and make fertile mental imagery, thus transforming your whole life.

The Dog

The little dog represents intellect, the reasoning mind, which functions at the personal level. In some of the older versions of Key 0, the dog bites the Fool's leg. When the Tarot was invented, the intellectual consciousness of humanity, distorted by centuries of wrong thinking, was actively hostile to spiritual philosophy and did all it could to impede the progress of higher truths

In our version, the dog is friendly, to intimate that even the lower intellect of humans has become the companion, rather than the higher knowledge's adversary. Today the human intellect goes with super-consciousness on the great spiritual adventure, but it is, nevertheless, at a lower level and must have super-consciousness for its master.

Practical Instruction

During your practice this week, read this chapter once every day. Pay close attention to any details which may seem obscure, and endeavor to think through them. Read slowly and preferably out loud. This will help you take in the full meaning. Make notes. Writing information by hand will aid you to retain the information.

Remember to take four deep breaths four times a day.

Coloring Instruction

This week you begin to color Key 0, The Fool. Depending on your skillset, you may use watercolors, acrylic, or colored pencils. A black and white deck of Paul Foster Case's Tarot Keys is available at the Builder's the Adytum website or Amazon.

Also, I recommend purchasing *The Book of Tokens*. These books have a colored version of the deck, which will help you in coloring your deck.

Color only one card at a time, and wait for the instructions in the chapters. Begin by reading the directions straight through. Before applying color to any card, try to visualize how it will look when it is finished. This is a practical exercise of great value. It tends to clarify and make definite your mental imagery. It also intensifies the suggestive power of the Keys. Be sure to do it before coloring any Key.

APPLY THE COLORS IS THE ORDER GIVEN FOR EACH KEY, especially using watercolors or acrylic. Long experience has determined this order because of the qualities of the coloring material used. For instance, we recommend that you wait until last to apply the red because it runs easily. Consequently, if applied too soon, it may run into a color you are applying next to it and spoil your work.

To give a lifelike appearance to the checks of the human figures, use a diluted red solution. A diluted brown with a trace of orange over the eyes enhances the appearance. But we recommend that you do not try this unless you are sure you can do it skillfully.

Blond hair is yellow, with a little brown added. You can tell how much brown to add by testing on white paper.

The Keys can be made more striking if you use white, but this is opaque color and difficult to do without covering up the black lines.

By following these directions carefully, you should be well pleased with the results. Let us suggest again that you *read the instructions* for each card carefully before applying any color. In this way, you will avoid coloring portions, which should be left blank for another color. Experience has taught us that this precaution is *very necessary*.

Key 0 – THE FOOL Coloring Instructions

YELLOW: Background, circles on the garment (but not flame in the top circle), shoes.

GREEN: Trefoils surrounding circles on the outer garment and other tendril-like figures. (Not belt.) Leaves on rose, wreath around his head.

VIOLET: Mountains. (Use a somewhat diluted solution since they are distant mountains. The peaks are snow-capped, so do not paint where snow is to be.)

BROWN: Eagle on the wallet; precipice in the foreground, where Fool stands.

WHITE: Sun, inner garment, dog, rose, eye on the flap of wallet, mountain peaks.

FLESH: Hands and face. (Since it is obvious where flesh color should be used, we shall not indicate it hereafter. There are two places where it should not be used - the angel's hands and face on Key 6 and the human figure on Key 20.)

BLONDE: The Fool's hair.

CITRINE: The Fool's hose. Citrine is a yellowish-green, secured by a mixture of orange and green. This is the only place where it is used.

GOLD: Star on the shoulder: girdle; knob on staff.

SILVER: Moon on the shoulder.

RED: Feather; lining of the outer garment where it shows at sleeves; spokes of wheels; flame in the top circle on the coat; wallet (except eagle and eye).

Keep the symbolic interpretation of each detail in mind as you color it. Then your set of Keys is completed, do not permit others to handle them, or even see them.

The one exception to this is that you may show your work to another student if, by so doing, you can help him. Even so, your Keys should be handled by no one but yourself.

They are part of your equipment and should only be used by you and not for selfish reasons. This will ensure that only your subtle emanations will be impressed upon the Tarot keys.

Chapter 4

MORE ABOUT THE LIFE-POWER

Now that you have colored the first Tarot Key, you can better understand the symbolism's details.

The white sun behind The Fool is in the upper right-hand corner of the design. Notice in Keys 10 and 21 this place is occupied by the head of an eagle, a symbol of Scorpio (♏).

Scorpio is assigned to the reproductive functions of the human body. Hence, the sun indicates that the One Force typified by the Fool is related to living organisms' generative power. On its practical side, our work has much to do with the control and adaptation of this force, usually expressed in reproduction.

The White Sun as Kether

The white sun is a reference to the Primal Will. On Tree of Life, the first manifestation of the Life-power, corresponding to the statement numbered 1, in *The Pattern on the Trestleboard*. Kether means meaning Crown. From proceeds, a descending path corresponding to the letter Aleph (א) and the Fool.

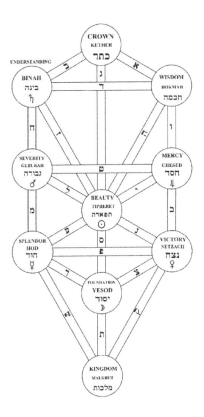

This suggests the cultural or social power represented by Aleph and Key 0 is identical with the Primal Will. It precedes from that Will when a cycle of manifestation begins.

Furthermore, since the sun's position is the same as Scorpio in Key 10 and 21, the Sun is the source of sexual energy. The white sun means sexual energy is a manifestation of the Primal Will to Good.

Everything is a manifestation of Kether. The manifested universe is not something made by the Life-power cut out of some material other than itself. Instead, it is the Life-power projection into the relative conditions of time and space as we know them.

The universe is of the same essential nature as the Life-power. It is the expression of an idea in the Universal Mind. This idea is what is meant by the creative Word or Logos. Hence even the exoteric Christian creed speaks of the Logos as "begotten, not made."

37

The Fool's Headdress

The green wreath encircling the Fool's hair symbolizes that plants' green leaves bind sunlight, just as the wreath binds the Fool's yellow hair. Capturing sunbeams, and binding them into an organic form, is the work of the chlorophyll, which is the green coloring of plants. This is what makes green vegetables so valuable for food. They constitute one of the essential forms in which the Life-power puts itself at your disposal. See that you eat enough of them.

The feather rising from the wreath is a wing-feather of an eagle. It represents animal life, a step higher in the scale of organism than the vegetable kingdom. It is red, the color of desire and action. The only genuine aspiration is the desire to *be something*, the desire to express some particular form of the Life-power *in action. What do you desire to be and do?*

The Fool's Wand

The wand over the Fool's shoulder, like a yardstick, suggests the idea of measurement. It indicates the need for careful study of the forces indicated by what the Life-power has already accomplished. We cannot measure the Life-power itself, or ever plumb the depth of that limitless ocean of possibilities. Our measurement must be of things already accomplished. Hence the Fool brings his wand with him from the lower levels whence he has ascended to the height shown in this picture. A wand is associated with magic. And the magic begins with the analysis or evaluation of conditions that are now present. The present is the result of past activity. All successful calculation of probable outcomes requires accurate estimation of past activities of the Life-power.

The most important thing to measure is our place in the universe. According to the Bible, the full measure of a man is:

"Yet you made them only a little lower than God and crowned them with glory and honor. You have given him dominion over the works of your hands; you have put all things under his feet." – Psalm 8: 5 & 6.

OBTW.

The Egyptian Bronzebook has this to say about humanity.

"I am a God of understanding and compassion. If a man cries out to Me, in genuine stress and suffering, we will not go unrelieved and uncomforted. Yet, understand that suffering and sorrow are the lot of man that he may become Man-god." – Book of Gleanings, 2:15.

"Man is the heir to divinity, and the road to divinity is spirituality. Man cannot become spiritual except through his efforts and striving. He cannot achieve it by being led by the hand or through fear of punishment, nor by greed through anticipation of reward. He who enters into his heritage of divinity will be no weakling; he will have trodden a hard and stony path." – Book of Gleanings 15:46

With those words of encouragement, back to the Tarot lesson.

In Hermetic philosophy, the emphasis is on the correct estimation and use of powers within humanity. These are powers partly physical and partly super-physical. Hermetic science is aware of realities beyond physical form and force limits yet employs careful observation like scientists to analyze the physical plane.

The Wallet on the Wand

The wand is black because it represents hidden powers. Whenever we take our measure truly, a secret force in human personality is made manifest. Our knowledge of this helps us correctly measure our environment, which would be inaccurate if we did not consider the hidden force.

The wallet suspended from the wand is a symbol of the powers of subconsciousness, which depend upon the self-conscious ability of analysis and calculation. The primary power of subconsciousness is memory, and memory is primarily reproductive. Hence the wallet adorned with a flying eagle refers (1) to aspiration, as having its roots in subconscious desires, and (2) to reproductive forces associated with the eagle Scorpio.

The eagle is also the bird of Zeus or Jupiter, King of the birds; it suggests dominance over Air's element attributed to Aleph (א) in the *Sepher Yetzirah*.

On the flap of the wallet is an open eye. It is the All-seeing Eye of Freemasonry and the Egyptian Eye of Horus. The Eye placed in a delta or triangle on the reverse side of the Great Seal of the United States. The aspect of Horus associated with the Eye is Hoor-pa-Kraat, (Harpocrates), the god of silence. He is a child seated on a lotus in Egyptian hieroglyphics, holding his forefinger on his lips. He is the "younger Horus," god of the morning sun, which shines above the traveler in this Tarot Key.

In Egyptian mythology, the younger Horus had *seven* aspects or forms. Keep this in mind, for in subsequent chapters, you will learn that the Life-power has seven principle phases of manifestation through human personality.

The Eye of Horus is placed on the wallet's flap, in the position usually occupied by a lock. It means, SIGHT IS WHAT UNLOCKS BOTH CONSCIOUS AND SUBCONSCIOUS POWERS. The way we look at ourselves and life determines whether we are mere puppets of subconsciousness or masters of its hidden powers.

Ten dots, representing stitches, are on the flap of the wallet. They symbolize ten fundamental aspects of the Life-power, and the corresponding statements numbered from 1 to 10 in *The Pattern on the Trestleboard* and the Tree of Life.

The White Rose

The rose represents desire. Its thorns symbolize pain. Its bloom typifies beauty and joy. Like the sun, it is white to intimate that we may align it with the Primal Will through the desire nature's right cultivation. Then our desires will be conscious expressions of underlying tendencies in the cosmic order. We control and cultivate the desire nature to enjoy the beauty it can bring us without suffering the pains resulting from misuse. Therefore the rose is a cultivated flower, and the youth carries it joyously, without pricking his fingers with its thorns.

The Fool's Outer Garment

The eight-pointed star on the Fool's shoulder symbolizes the sun, and the crescent near it represents the Moon. Sun and Moon have many meanings: the developments of ideas of manifestations of action and reaction between the solar, or electric, and the lunar, or magnetic, currents of the Great Magical Agent, L.V.X.

On the Fool's breast is a yellow circle enclosing a triple-flame. It represents the One Force as light and fire. This symbol refers to the One Force's formless state before the beginning of a cycle of manifestation.

The wheel or circle with 8-spokes is a symbol for pure Spirit and the Quintessence or Fifth Essence. In some respects, the Quintessence is similar to what Hindus call Akasha.

Seven trefoils surround the wheels, or 3-lobed clovers represent the seven basic modes of activity associated with the seven alchemical metals or interior stars (chakras). The trefoils are green, which is associated with immortality. They show the eternal phases of the Life-power's activity.

One wheel contains the letter Shin (ש) and is associated with Key 20, Judgment. Shin is the mother letter of Fire. It is a symbol of the fiery Life-breath and the spiritual energy which brings all things into manifestation.

The Valley Below

The abyss which yawns at the Fool's feet is in contrast to the height whereon he stands. It symbolizes "that which is below," It is nature, the relative, the phenomenon or effect, in contrast to Spirit, the Absolute, the noumenon[1] or cause. At the bottom of the abyss are a valley, the scene of labor, activity, struggle, and competition, which contrasts to the ideas of superiority and supremacy suggested by the Fool's position on the mountain top.

The valley is what the Chinese philosopher, Lao-tze, calls the Mother-Deep, the Hindus term Prakriti, the Supreme Spirit's mysterious power. Because the valley in the field of experience corresponds to ideas related second sphere on the Tree of Life, Hokmah, Wisdom, note that the Path of the Aleph (א) ends at Chokmah.

In practical psychology, the abyss represents subconsciousness. The metaphor for this plane of consciousness is "depths."

The traveler is on the verge of descending. Thus the picture shows the Supreme Spirit, or super-conscious aspect of the Life-power, as are think of it before the beginning of a cycle of self-expression. The wanderer is unafraid because he knows his descent cannot injure him. Furthermore, he is aware that he will undoubtedly raise himself to the greater height toward which he directs his eager gaze.

Summary

This picture represents the limitless force, which is the central reality of every human life. It's what you mean when you say, "I AM." It is an image of the *Something in you* which sees far beyond the seeming limitations of your present circumstances.

That something has brought you this far on your journey toward supreme attainment. That something makes you want to succeed. It makes you want better health. That something makes you want better circumstances.

Because it knows itself perfectly, knows how limitless are its possibilities, how irresistible its powers, how boundless its opportunities, *that Something in you will not let you alone.* Though you may seem to be at the end of your resources, it urges you to press on. Though you may be past middle life, it knows itself to be forever young and knocks importunately at the inner door of your mind. The Life-power in the very core of your being is a power which knows nothing of age, defeat, or ill-health. It is a power that has worked miracles of healing repeatedly, transformed disaster into victory, lack into abundance, and sorrow into joy.

The Fool is a picture of the limitless power of your own inner, spiritual, super-conscious life. To get more of that power into expression, you must begin by thoroughly impressing your subconsciousness with this image of that One Force.

The method is simple. Just *look* at this picture five minutes every morning during the week and five minutes every evening. Remember, SIGHT is the power that locks and unlocks the wallet of subconscious forces. When you do this, look at the details of the design, one after another. Simple as it is, this exercise will transfer the picture from the printed Key to the cells of your brain. Then the Key will become an integral part of your personality and make it part of your flesh and blood.

This is a great secret in the practical use of Tarot. Until you have built the Tarot Keys into yourself, they do not exert their maximum power.

When you have done so, they will evoke latent forces from within, and your direction of these forces will change your whole life.

Continue to use the *Pattern*. Keep up your regular practice periods. Pay particular attention to your notebook. Even if an entry is only a word or two, record the ideas which come to you as you work with the Tarot Keys. This practice period should include a five-minute examination of the Fool.

[1] Noumenon

A thing as it is in itself, as distinct from a thing as it is knowable by the senses through phenomenal attributes.

In metaphysics, the noumenon is a *theorized object* or *event* independent of human sense or perception. The term noumenon is generally used when contrasted with, or relating to, the term phenomenon. The latter refers to anything that can be apprehended by or is an object of the senses. Modern philosophy has generally been skeptical of the possibility of knowledge independent of the senses. Immanuel Kant gave this point of view its canonical expression: that the noumenal world may exist. Still, it is completely unknowable through human sensation. In Kantian philosophy, the unknowable noumenon is often linked to the unknowable "thing-in-itself," although defining the relationship's nature is a question yet open to some controversy. – Wikipedia

TAROT FUNDAMENTALS

Chapter 5

SELF-CONSCIOUSNESS

Begin this chapter by examining carefully, as a whole and in detail. Key 1, The Magician, Review the meanings of the number 1.

1. BEGINNING – Self-consciousness. First in the numeral series, because 0 stands for that which precedes manifestation, and is therefore not included in any sequence; inception; initiation; the *Primal Will*; selection; unity; singleness; individuality; attention; one-pointedness; concentration; the definite or manifest, as contrasted with the indefinable Source.

Everything represented in the symbolism of the Key is a development of ideas associated with the number 1. The Magician typifies the beginning or inception of the process whereby the life-power limitless possibilities are brought into expression as manifested actualities. The Key represents the *initiation* of the creative process on all planes.

In human personality, the creative process starts with the self-consciousness or objective mind. Self-awareness is distinctively a human aspect of mental activity. The objective mind is what you use to read these words.

Self-consciousness initiates the creative process by formulating premises or seed-ideas. Subconsciousness accepts these as *suggestions*, which it elaborates by the process of deduction. It carries out modifications of mental and emotional attitudes and definite changes in bodily function and structure.

The statements above outline an important process. You use it continually, whether or not you know you do, because it is the basis of your intellectual knowledge and determines the state of your physical health. Your physical and mental states are the results of your mental imagery. Any mental image tends to materialize itself as an actual condition or event, especially the images that are dwelled upon.

Number 1

Geometrically the number 1 is a point, particularly the CENTRAL POINT. In *The Pattern on the Trestleboard*, the statement attributed to 1 is:

"I am a center of expression for the Primal Will-to-good, which eternally creates and sustains the universe."

The beginning of the creative process is the concentration and expression of the Life-power at a center. The sun of our solar system is such a center. It transmits the Life-power as radiant energy, which humanity utilizes in many ways.

The number 1 is single and, therefore, isolation. It also stands for privacy, concealment, and hidden knowledge. Magic is the art of transformation, and it is closely related to alchemy.

However, from another perspective, one (1) is the beginning of the numeral series. It is a symbol of one thing standing relating to other things (the self and not-self). "What stands relating to other things is connected with them by various links or bonds. Magic is the science of hidden relationships. The practice of magic is based on the law of correspondence expressed in the Hermetic axiom:

That which is above is as that which is below, and that which is below is as that which is above, for the performance of the miracle of the one thing.

The bond between things is fundamentally their coexistence as manifestations of the one Life-power. All things are of one substance. All things are governed by one great Law. All things are masks of appearance for a single Reality. All things are parts of a great Whole from which nothing can be detached. *Whatever done to a part affects the whole.*

46

OBTW.

This idea, *the part that encodes the whole*, is unique to a hologram[1] or a holographic universe.

But what need is there, Arjuna, for all this detailed knowledge? With a single fragment of Myself I pervade and support this entire universe." – Bhagavad Gita 10.42

The Hebrew Letter Beth (ב)

The letter-name Beth (בית) means "house." It refers to a dwelling-place for Spirit. From one perspective, this is the human personality.

Personality is a center through which the Spirit or real Self expresses itself. This is not an abstraction. Think of *your* personality as a center of expression for your inner Self. Try to realize that this means what Jesus meant when he said, "The Father Who dwells in me. He does the works."

The title of this Key, The Magician, identifies the picture with Hermes or Mercury, who presided over magic. You will remember that Mercury is the messenger of the gods served to *transmit* or *express* their wisdom and power.

12th Path of Beth ב

The 12th *Path* is the Glowing Consciousness (Sekhel Bahir). It is the essence of the Great Wheel. It is called the Visualizer (Chaz.chaz.it). It is the source of vision of the prophets and those who see apparitions.

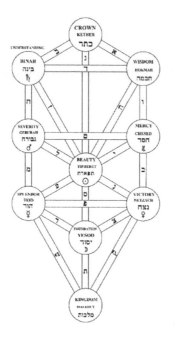

The path of Beth connects Kether to Binah. One of the titles of Kether is the Beginning of the Whirling's, and this is the Great Wheel. With the influx of energy from the 12th Path, Binah is *Ama* (אמא), the dark and sterile mother. Binah is in a state of rest. When activated with the 14th Path of Daleth (ד), Binah becomes the bright fertile mother, Aima (אימא), the Great Sea, the Mother of All Living.

Selfconsciousness – Concentration

In human personality, self-consciousness is the transformer. Only the human personality can set in motion forces that bring about change. The fundamental magical practice is concentration— one-pointed attention to some selected area of one's environment.

The practice of concentration enables one to perceive the inner nature of the object of their attention. This leads to the discovery of natural principles. By applying these laws, one can change their conditions. Hence concentration helps us solve our problems. Thus the alchemists write, "Our Mercury enables us to prepare the universal solvent."

The higher phases of the art begin with concentration. From one perspective, your reason for existence is to develop these powers. It is your birthright and responsibility to develop powers of concentration. You can begin your practice by looking at Key 1, The Magician, for five minutes a day.

Learn the following definition:

Concentration is the collection, at a center or focus of units of force.

They are units of Life-power because every unit of force in the universe, regardless of form, is a manifestation of that One Force.

Understand that you do not concentrate attention. Attention is the means that enables you to focus units of mental force. Your attention intensifies energy so that you may direct it usefully.

When you intensify the rays of the sun using a convex lens, they can burn. If you place your hand in the sunshine passing through a pane of the window, the result is a sensation of warmth. Never forget that when you practice concentration, you are working with a real force.

Note the posture of the Magician. This picture clearly shows the magical process involved in an understanding of the correct practice of concentration. With his right hand, he draws down power from above. With his left hand, he makes a gesture of concentration. He is directing energy drawn from higher levels to planes below that of his self-conscious existence.

The plane below the Magician is represented as a garden, which is a symbol of subconsciousness. When you concentrate, you seek to impress a specific image on subconsciousness. This will bring a particular modification of subconscious activity.

One crucial point to observe is that the Magician himself is not active. He stands perfectly still. He is a channel for power that comes from above his level, and after passing through him, that power sets up a reaction at a level lower than The Magician. The convex lens is the agency that intensifies the rays of the sun. However, it does nothing of itself, so self-consciousness in concentration is not itself active.

Magic is the art that produces effects by mastery of the secret forces of nature. It is the science of initiation. A real initiator is one who has mastered this hidden science of causes. They know how to direct the universal creative force to bring about the full realization and physical embodiment of their mental imagery's aims and purposes.

A perfected magician uses his objective mind, or self-consciousness, in the manner depicted by this Tarot Key. Endeavor, therefore, as you work with the coloring of the picture, to impress all its details on your memory. In the next chapter, you will find their significance explained. This week, concern yourself with only coloring and *looking* at the picture, as a whole, and in detail, into your mind.

Read this chapter once daily during your practice period. Be sure to look at the Key for five minutes. In this chapter, there is much material for careful study. Do not slight the chapter because you think you understand it after one or two readings.

DIRECTIONS FOR COLORING KEY 1

YELLOW: Background; spearhead on the table; lily stamens.

GREEN: Foliage.

BLUE-GREEN: The serpent girdle.

BROWN: Table.

WHITE: Inner garment; headband; spear shaft; uplifted wand; lily flowers.

GOLD: Pentacle or coin on the table; sword hilt; circle at the end of the spear shaft.

SILVER: Cup.

STEEL: Sword blade. (Mix a little blue with gray.)

RED: Outer garment; roses.

[1] Hologram.

I found the best definition of a hologram in a US Army Intelligence and Security Command memo with the subject: *Analysis and Assessment of Gateway Process*. The classified document was written in June of 1983 and declassified in September of 2003.

On page 7:

12. Holograms. Energy creates, stores and retrieves meaning in the universe by projecting or expanding at certain frequencies in a three-dimensional mode that creates a living pattern called a hologram.

A hologram can be understood by using an example cited by Bentov. He asks the reader to visualize a bowl full of water into which three pebbles are dropped as the ripples created by the three pebbles' simultaneous entry radiate outward towards the rim of the bowl. Bentov further asks the reader to visualize that the water's surface is suddenly flash frozen so that the ripple pattern is preserved instantly. The ice is removed, leaving the three pebbles still laying at the bottom of the bowl. The ice is exposed to a powerful, coherent source of light, such as a laser. The result will be a three-dimensional model or representation of the position of the three pebbles suspended in midair.

Holograms are capable of encoding great detail. For example, it is possible to take a holographic projection of a glass of swamp water and view it under magnification to see a small organism not visible to the naked eye when the glass of water itself is examined..."

Therefore a hologram is a derivative. That is *something that is **based on another source**.*

"There's a billion to one chance we're living in **base** reality." - Elon Musk

Therefore, a holographic universe is a cosmos that is based on something else. What this some else is the speculation of philosophers and writers of fantasy.

TAROT FUNDAMENTALS

Chapter 6 – THE MAGICIAN

The Letter Beth - ב

As a hieroglyph, Beth is a house or tent. A tent divides or partitions space into an inside and outside. Thus Beth suggests division and discrimination.

Nobody ever becomes a real magician, a wielder of nature's subtle forces, which permits themselves to be preoccupied with personal, subjective reactions to events. The first requisite is sharp, clear-cut, objective awareness of what goes on in one's environment.

The letter Beth's sound, like English "B," is a concentrated projection of breath. Hold the palm of your hand near your lips as you say, "B," and feel the air strike your hand, like an arrow shot from a bow.

Contrast this with the free, unmodified breathing expressed by the sound of Aleph (א), an almost soundless vibration of air, made with lips open and relaxed. The sound of Aleph is free, indefinite.

The contrast between the two sounds is just one instance of a principle that holds throughout Hebrew letters. In some manner, every Hebrew letter the antithesis of the letter, which immediately precedes it in the series.

Beth is a centralized expulsion of breath through lips almost closed. It points, like the Magician's finger. Thus we find that Beth agrees with its sound. A force intensified by concentration and projected toward a specific mark.

By determining what you want to be and do, you set energy in motion. Realize that the energy so aimed is derived from the super-conscious Life-power, pictured as the Fool. In so doing, you will have placed yourself mentally in the position the Magician symbolizes.

Raised Right Hand

The Magician lifts his right hand toward the sky. Usually, the right hand is dominant and symbolizes the act of establishing contact with super-consciousness. It is the highest and most potent use of self-conscious awareness.

First, we observe what goes on. Then we use inductive reasoning, which is observed effects to underlying principles, to reveal what lies hidden behind the veil of appearance. This leads to the discovery that our personal experience's succession of events is under the direction of a supervising Intelligence, which is higher than our objective mind.

Just what this supervising Intelligence maybe, we don't know. We may be sure it is not the sort of God, made in man's image, whose nature and intentions are outlined in religious dogmas. A Magician readily agrees when an atheist says, "There is no God," because every occultist knows there was never such a God as the atheist denies.

However, the wise know, "The fool hath said in his heart. There is no God." For any Magician worthy of the name knows that the supervising Intelligence IS. It is a **real presence** at every point in space.

The White Wand

The raised white wand is a phallic symbol. It represents the concentrated, purified nerve force used in magic — the ignorant waste of this force in uncontrolled sex-desire gratification. Their lack of control is due to their want of knowledge. To master the sex drive requires knowledge combined with technical training, which develops skill in the direction of desire-force.

Methods for effecting such control vary, according to the temperament of the person who employs them. What would be rigid and irksome asceticism for one person may be relatively easy for another. Extreme abstinence is avoided by persons who have learned this fundamental principle:

The practice of mental creation and constructive thinking automatically transmutes the sex drive from physical forms of expression to mental forms. This relieves physical and psychical pressures that accumulate when the sexual energy is not given a constructive channel.

It is the root of the matter. The force is generated automatically. It is both physical and mental. Physical austerity makes it accumulate more slowly and may even help to dissipate it. You lose what ought to be used. A real magician links himself to what is higher than man by making the right use of the very power which debases his ignorant brother.

The Infinity Symbol - ∞

The horizontal figure 8 (∞) over the Magician's head is a reminder that 8 is the number associated with Hermes or Mercury (Hod, the 8th Sephiroth is assigned to Mercury). It also represents education and culture, traditionally under the patronage of Hermes. Again, 8 is the numeral symbol of the control of natural forces by applying rhythmic vibration laws.

Such control is an essential feature in all works of practical magic. Moreover, a horizontal 8 is the mathematical symbol for infinity, so that it may be taken as an emblem of the limitless Life-power. Finally, it represents the law that **identical causes produce opposite effects**.

The same laws which make iron sink are what ship-builders apply to float iron vessels. The laws which make a kite fall to earth keep airplanes aloft. The laws which result in misery, failure, disease, and death are the same laws that intelligent adaptation employs to secure comfort, success, health, and long life.

By changing the method whereby you exercise your subconscious powers, you may produce effects directly opposed to whatever negative experiences you may have suffered in the past.

You do not have to acquire new powers. You change your life-expression by applying capabilities that are already yours. You learn to use your forces differently.

The Magician's Left-hand

The Magician's left-hand points to the ground. His gesture is one of concentration. It is made with the left, or secondary, hand because success in concentration depends on our conscious recognition that the force we concentrate comes down to us from super-conscious levels. The left hand is also a symbol of the habit-mind. Thus the pointing finger of this hand represents habitual concentration, resulting from prolonged, persistent practice.

The Magician's Black Hair

The Magician's black hair is a contrast to the Fool's yellow locks. Black stands for darkness, inertia, ignorance. The band surrounding this black hair is white, typifying purity, light, wisdom.

Self-consciousness is always an awareness of ignorance. The more you know, the more do we perceive the immensity of the expanse of what we do not know. However, we limit our ignorance by our enlightenment.

Red Mantle

The red mantle typifies action and desire. Its red color is associated with the planet Mars. In astrology, Mars is attributed to action, motivation, and the sex drive.

This mantle has no fastening. It is removed at will. This means that self-consciousness may or may not be involved in physical activity, according to our decision in a given circumstance. However, the Magician is not fully clothed without his mantle. The perfected self-consciousness controls the various physical manifestations of the Life-power in our bodies and the world outside.

On the other hand, self-consciousness may refrain from action and devote itself to contemplating the inner mental states symbolized by the white undergarment. The white color refers to truth and wisdom.

The Girdle

The girdle is a blue-green serpent, which symbolizes eternity because it swallows its tail. The significance of blue-green will be explained in a later chapter. Observe that the idea of eternity symbolized by the Magician's girdle contrasts with the concept of time symbolized by the Fool's girdle.

Table

Before the Magician is a table that symbolizes what psychology calls the "field of attention." The table is made of wood grown in the garden.

On top, the legs are by Ionic capitals used in architecture. An art presided over by Hermes. Beth (ב) means house and is related to architecture.

The capitals shown were used in the Ephesian temple of Diana, a Moon goddess. The Moon is associated with subconsciousness. It suggests that the materials utilized by self-consciousness are derived from below or from sub-human levels of the Life-Power's activity. The power which self-consciousness uses in controlling and arranging these materials is brought dorm from super-consciousness.

The implements on the table are those employed in ceremonial magic. The wand with a spear-like head is a symbol of WILL and the element of Fire.

The cup is made of silver, the metal of the Moon. The Moon is a symbol of memory and IMAGINATION and the element of Water.

The sword is made of steel, the metal of Mars. It stands for ACTION and the element of Air.

The coin or pentacle is associated with Saturn. It represents FORM and the element of Earth.

Every magical transformation results from human self-consciousness's ability to produce varying manifestations of will, imagination, action, and physical embodiment.

These four implements also represent what is known in hermetic wisdom as the *Power of the Word*. Words embody a subtle force not recognized by the uninitiated. Furthermore, certain words, unique combinations of *Sounds* and *Ideas*, whereby extraordinary results are produced when the words are correctly pronounced or intoned.

IHVH - יהוה

Because Hebrew ideas influence the Tarot, the four magical implements are shown as IHVH (יהוה), this is the four-lettered name of God, or *Tetragrammaton*, which is "Jehovah" in English.

This is not the correct pronunciation. Neither is "Yahweh" or "Yahveh." The pronunciations are guesses. Tradition says the true pronunciation is lost since the Temple's destruction at Jerusalem, where the High Priest of Israel uttered this IHVH in the Holy of Holies once a year, during a solemn festival. It should be read letter by letter: Yod, Heh, Vav, Heh.

English	Hebrew	Element	Correspondence
I	י	Fire	Wand
H	ה	Water	Cup
V	ו	Air	Sword
H	ה	Earth	Coin

Yod (י) is the wand, Heh (ה) the cup, Vav (ו) the sword, and final Heh (ה) the coin or pentacle. These letters are dimly shown in the folds of the Fool's white garment at the neck. This Hebrew name for God is used thousands of times in the Old Testament, and means *That which was, is and will be*. In connection with the Magician, it signifies that

58

self-consciousness utilizes the four aspects of a *single* reality in adapting to its needs the forms and conditions of human experience.

The Garden

Over the head of the Magician is an arbor of roses. An arbor is the simplest kind of shelter, a house made of growing plants. Thus the arbor corresponds to the meaning of the letter-name Beth (בית) – house.

The garden represents the field cultivated by the objective consciousness. This field is subconsciousness. The whole series of events, and all the forms of circumstance, of which we become aware through sensory channels, are events and forms of the activity of subconsciousness.

All that surrounds us is the manifestation of subconscious forces. Because the objective mind can control subconscious forces directly and modify and adapt the rhythms of vibration operate at subconscious levels, a trained magician can exert by mental means a degree of control over their environment, which amazes contemporaries who do not share their knowledge and skill.

Red roses are emblems of desire. They symbolize the creative and constructive work of self-consciousness is always motivated by a desire for protection against adverse conditions.

The 5 Roses

The roses and lilies symbolize two principal forms of subconscious activity in the garden. They represent desire and knowledge.

The roses are red to indicate active desire. Five are shown because every desire is rooted in one of the five senses. Every rose also represents the number 5 because all roses have five, or some multiple of five, petals.

Five (5) is the number of adaptation and adjustment, and self-consciousness, the unique human expression of the Life acts by adaptation. Thus 5 is the number of humanity who embodies the personal factor that carries natural forces' development beyond the averages characteristic of the sub-human and subconscious levels. Thus it is written: "Nature unaided always fails," because this personal factor is required to bring about the perfection of the powers which are only partially expressed in the kingdoms of nature below man.

The 4 Lilies

The lilies are white to represent abstract perceptions of truth, or knowledge of principles and laws, apart from desire considerations. They also represent the number 6 because they have six petals.

In its symbolic meaning, 6 represents universal energies like light, heat, electricity and magnetism, chemical forces, etc. Using concentration, we may perceive the true nature and laws of these forces.

There are four lilies because pure science comprises knowledge of the ancients termed Fire, Water, Air, and Earth. In modern parlance, these are radiant energy, fluids, gases, and solids. They are the forms taken by the WORD typified by the Magician's four implements.

Summary

Self-consciousness is the primary human expression of Life-power. It constitutes your awareness of your environment. This is awareness of mental impressions you receive from the world around you through the channels of sensation. The activities of your environment are manifestations of various powers of subconsciousness.

Self-consciousness is the consciousness of being ONE, relating to others. "I am I, and that is not I." At a higher level of unfoldment, what is usually called "myself," that is, the physical body is included among the things which are "not – I." Beyond this is a state wherein the personal consciousness is like the physical body, an instrument for expressing the real Self's super-conscious power.

In partly developed persons, the objective mind creates the illusion that the Real Self is a particular personality. That is, the personal "self" separate from others. Concentration and meditation lead to freedom from this illusion by enabling us to see that it is an illusion.

When you come to this recognition, you will no longer think and act as if you were a separate being. Then you will know that your personality is an instrument through which the One Force typified by the Fool finds expression.

Remember, Life-power works through your self-consciousness. Your will is not a delusive shadow but a specialization of the universal WILL. To know this is to be sure that your true will is irresistible. This establishes confidence in the happy outcome of all your undertakings.

It is the only knowledge that can make you genuinely Self-reliant, free from the least trace of worry or anxiety, and therefore able to give undivided attention to the experience of the moment. This consciousness enables you to live in the NOW. In truth, it is always NOW. This consciousness permits you to live in eternity instead of being time-bound to the past or the future.

Every bit of practical training explained in our curriculum aims to aid you in unfolding this consciousness. Until you read the next chapter, review this one carefully. Make sure you understand every detail of the symbolism of the Magician.

This Key is designed to awaken the power of attention. Attention is truly magical. By acts of attention, the etheric vibrations of external objects are concentrated on a brain center. These vibrations tend to organize that center per the intrinsic nature of the thing attended to. Thus the brain center is attuned to the idea, which is the inner reality of the thing under observation. This attunement is expressed as the conscious perception of that inner reality.

Then one sees *through* the form of the thing into its essential nature.

Be alert to the life around you. Use every instrument of sensation to gather accurate information. Resolve to see into life, instead of merely looking at it. You will find the world transforming itself before your eyes. This is one of the great, fundamental secrets of magic.

Use Tarot Key 1 daily to sharpen your powers of observation and attention. Be sure to record your impressions, *day by day*, in your diary.

Chapter 7

SUBCONSCIOUSNESS

Before you read this chapter, study the symbolism of Key 2, the High Priestess. Tarot uses pictorial symbolism's universal language, with which the deeper part of your mind is familiar. One purpose of the Tarot is to evoke thought, and by looking at a Key before you begin to read our explanations, you bring the knowledge already present in the depths of your subconsciousness closer to the surface. This will make it easier for you to grasp the significant text. Devote at least five minutes to looking at Key 2, The High Priestess, before reading this chapter.

Among the meanings of the number 2 is subordination. This word gives a clue to the relationship between subconsciousness, represented by Key 2, and objective mind or self-consciousness, represented by the Magician.

The symbolism of Key 1 shows the magician controlling the powers of subconsciousness, which are always amenable to his suggestive influence. This is why you can employ these Keys to bring into vigorous manifestation your inner life's latent forces. The principle involved is explained in Lesson 2 and 3 of *Seven Steps*.

Subconsciousness – Deductive Reasoning

The psychological law stated in *Seven Steps* is subconsciousness is amenable to control by suggestion. Therefore, you must consider carefully is how you use your self-conscious mind. For it determines what you plant in subconsciousness.

The garden represents subconsciousness in Key 1. The fertile soil of this garden will grow *any* seed planted by the Magician. Suppose he plants casual observations and incorrect reasoning, the weeds and tares of conscious thought. In that case, subconsciousness will develop these seeds of error a thousand-fold, with all sorts of uncomfortable consequences; however, if you learn to concentrate and make your mental imagery clear and definite. If you make accurate observations, then your reasoning is accurate. The seeds you plant in your subconscious garden will bear fruit in the renewal, revivification, and regeneration of your personality.

The ability of subconsciousness to develop seed ideas in this manner may be formulated thus:

Subconsciousness possesses perfect powers of deductive reasoning.

In *deductive reasoning*, conclusions are drawn from a data set. For example:

All men (A) are mortal (B).	1st premise
Socrates (C) is a man (A).	2nd premise
Therefore, Socrates (C) is mortal (B).	Conclusion

Or,

If $A = B$	1st premise
If $C = A$	2nd premise
Therefore, $C = B$	Conclusion

Inductive reasoning makes broad generalizations from specific observations. For example, you have a bag of coins. The first three coins you pull out are pennies. Therefore you conclude that all coins in the bag are pennies. Of course, the premise is that all coins in the bag are pennies, which may or may not be true.

When you study, always have a good dictionary at hand, for you will need it frequently in this instruction. You will find that the practice of making sure of the meaning and use of words will be of invaluable benefit to you in the orderly organization of your mental processes.

Number 2 and Duplication

Geometrically the number 2 is the *line*, the extension of the *point* (number 1). This is related to the subconscious power of deductive reasoning, where the consequences of conscious thought and observation (the premise) are developed (the conclusion).

Note that extending the central point of a circle into a diameter (an extension in two opposite directions) divides the circle into two parts, each the other's exact duplicate. This power of *duplication may be perceived as the basic function of subconsciousness, memory.*

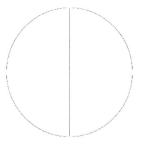

Memory

This brings us to a third psychological principle: *Subconsciousness keeps a perfect record of all experience and has a perfect memory.*

Not only does it retain every experience of a single personality, but it also holds a summary of the race experience, and this is the source of the greater part of our intuitions and our scientific discoveries.

The 13th Path of Gimel ג

The 13th *Path* is the Unity (אחדות) Directing Consciousness (*Sekhel Man.hig Ha.Achdut*). It (*Hu*) is the essence of Glory and the reward of the spiritual ones (אחדים).

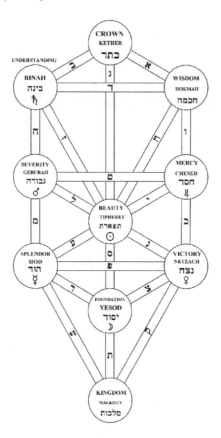

This is a difficult Path to translate. Notice the word unity is אחדות. It is from the root, *a.chad* (אחד), meaning one (1), single, someone; to unite, combine, and join. The last two letters are Vav (ו) and Tav (ת). Together they form a feminine plural end to the word. Therefore most authors translate *unity* or *unities*.

The same word is used to mean Spiritual (רוחניים) Ones (אחדים). Notice that *a.chad* (אחד) now has a masculine plural ending (ים).

Why I don't know, I took a six months Hebrew class to learn the basics of grammar. But that didn't stop me from doing a translation of the 32 Paths of Wisdom. You can find my work in the Appendix.

My best guess is the Spiritual Ones is the choir of angles associated with Tiphareth. They are the *Melekim* (מלכים); it means, Kings. Notice the masculine plural ending (ים).

Also, note that spirit is from the root Ruach (רוח). Ruach means breath, wind, and the human soul associated with Tiphareth.

OBTW.

In the Kabala, they are five souls, Nephesh, *Ruach*, Neshamah, Chia, and Yechidah. This is not the place to pursue the five souls. I mention it in passing to give you a hint of the complexly of unpacking the *32 Paths of Wisdom*.

Gimel - ג

As a hieroglyph, Gimel (ג) is a lower part of the leg with a foot. It means to walk, gather, and carry. It also suggests the gathering of people or things.

Therefore Gimel (ג) is in contrast to Beth (ב). Beth, the house is indoors while Gimel walks outdoors. Inside the house, we plan and think. Then, our feet put our plans literally and figuratively in motion.

Similarly, the subconsciousness represented by Gimel carries your conscious directives to successful conclusions. Self-consciousness makes your decisions. Subconsciousness *carries them out* – both literally and figuratively.

Note that the characteristics of subconsciousness are feminine, while self-consciousness is masculine.

Gimel (גמל), means camel. The camel is the ship of the desert that carries the load. Other implications of *Gimel* are transportation; motion from place to place; movement to and fro, as of the regular journeys of caravans over trade routes; hence, commerce, exchange, reciprocity, interchange, alternation, correlation, correspondence and communication, dissemination of information, consequently, education and science. Study all these words with the aid of a dictionary. They describe *your* subconsciousness and its powers.

Also, the Hebrew verb *gawmal*, spelled with the same letters, means,

1. To ripen as fruits, mature.

2. Requital - something given in return, compensation, or retaliation – for good or evil.

Gimel includes the ideas of reward and punishment. All these meanings are connected with the action of subconsciousness.

One familiar action of subconsciousness is "mind-wandering." When we fall into a state of reverie, this enables us to pass from one thought to another until we have traversed a vast field of ideas. Until we learn to control this power of associating an image with an image, it interferes with concentration. It is like a camel running wild. When we learn to drive it, this same power of association will take us quickly to any chosen goal.

As the seat of memory, subconsciousness "carries the load" of our personal experience. Also, the subconsciousness activity that is part or partition of the universal Life-power. The personal subconsciousness is merely a particular manifestation, through a single organism, of this great and all-inclusive universal subconsciousness. That is to say, *the part encodes the whole,* which is consistent with a holographic universe.

When we learn how we gain access to the records of *all* experience by tapping the cosmic subconscious memories, by this means, it is possible to arrive at accurate reconstructions of the past. Sometimes only the general principles are recovered. Occasionally, some ancient eras' particular details are recovered, and occult literature contains many examples of this type of recovery.

The Moon

Gimel corresponds to the Moon, a "ship of the skies," just as a camel is a "ship of the desert." The Moon center in the human brain is the pituitary body, which acts as a transmitting station. The mental states of self-consciousness are relayed to the nervous system centers, located in the physical body below the brain.

The ideas suggested by the Moon are reflection; periodicity (because it waxes and wanes); association, accompaniment, correlation (because the Moon is a satellite, consort or follower of the earth), and in like manner, subconsciousness follows the lead of self-consciousness.

As a crescent, the Moon suggests a bow and Gimel (ג). Thus it is connected with the goddess Diana (Roman) and Artemis (Greek). Diana is a *huntress*, and to hunt is to follow, to inquire, to pursue. While we sleep, it reviews all our experiences, ruminating (like a camel chewing its cud) over what we have sensed, felt, and reasoned. During sleep, this nocturnal mental luminary carries on the mental processes which lead to the consequences of what we have observed, felt, and consciously reasoned out during the day.

Diana or Artemis was closely related to Hekate. For the ancient Greeks, Hekate combined the moon's characteristics and earth goddess with the queen of the underworld, the abode of the dead. Hekate had a share in the rulership of earth and sea; gave aid in war, in athletic contests, and hunting; protected herds and children, but she was mainly the goddess of magic, mystery and occult powers generally. She also presided over the meeting-place at which roads cross. Indeed, it is principally from the attributes of Hekate that the symbolism of the second Tarot Key is derived.

All the powers attributed to these Moon Goddesses are actual, living powers of your subconsciousness.

One keyword for Gimel and the Moon is *association*. Not only the ordinary association of ideas within the limits of your mind. A broader kind of association, symbolized by the camel because the journeys of caravans connect distant places.

Subconsciousness has a perfect connection with all points in space.

This law is the basis of the phenomenon of telepathy. It is also the law that will put you in touch with your teacher when you reached a point where you are ready for higher instruction. This same law has many other applications in practical occultism.

During your practice period this week, color Key 2, per the following directions.

YELLOW: Left foreground, small space at right foreground.

GREEN: Palms on the curtain behind High Priestess (not centers).

BLUE: Background, from yellow foreground up. Her robe. The robe should have white in it also, where it shimmers down in front and out of the picture. It represents flowing water.

GRAY: Throne; veil background (veil need not be painted unless desired.)

WHITE: Inner garment; cross on breast; head drapery; right pillar; centers of palms.

Chapter 8

THE HIGH PRIESTESS

The title of this Key means *the chief feminine elder*. It applies to Hekate[1] and Isis of Egypt, and the Hindu Maya or Prakriti. Under these goddesses, the ancients concealed their knowledge of the powers of subconsciousness.

Remember that subconscious powers are universal as well as personal. Subconscious activity is the real substance of all things we call "physical objects." What appears to us like wood, stone, minerals, the bodies of plants and animals, as the *matter* (mind-stuff) entering into the forms around us, is the subconscious level of the manifestation of the One Force pictured in Tarot as the Fool.

The physical plane's actual substance, from which all forms perceptible to the human senses are built, is mental energy, working at the subconscious level.

Hence Key 2 pictures this *primary material or mind-stuff* is named *the chief feminine elder* because it symbolizes the original receptive, reproductive, and form-building power in the universe. You have access to the mind-stuff through your subconsciousness, like a bay opening into the ocean of universal subconscious mental energy.

Blue is the predominant color of Key 2, and in the Tarot color scale (there are many), blue is attributed to the letter Gimel (ג), the Moon, the element of Water and subconsciousness.

The Scroll - Memory

Much of the symbolism of the High Priestess is connected with memory. Her scroll contains the complete record of experience, but two things are necessary if you read it.

First, you must practice concentration. By careful observation and vivid awareness of what goes on around you, you focus your mental camera, and the resulting images are sharp and clear. Secondly, you must understand and apply the laws of recall, as outlined in this key's symbols.

The pillars represent two of these laws by their form and color, and another law by its position. You easily recall ideas or things *like* each other, ideas or things in sharp *contrast* to each other, ideas or things *near* each other in space or time. In memorization, these three principles are utilized. Use these identification tags when you file your experiences. Thus you make a mental index that enables you to recall whatever you wish. Link what you want to remember with something *similar* to it. *Contrast* it with something markedly different. Notice what things are *near* it in time or space. Do this when you meet a new acquaintance, and hear their name, and you will find that you have no difficulty whatever in recalling the name the next time you see them.

The scroll represents memory, the record of experience, and the basis of history. The word TORA (תעורא) signifies *law* and is a rearrangement of the letters of ROTA, Latin for a *wheel*. This is a reference to the Law of Cycles, or Rotation, and Key 10. The Law of Cycles is connected with the Law of Spiral Activity represented by the rolled-up scroll form. Both laws are aspects of the Law of Rhythm.

The veil behind the High Priestess is pomegranates (red) and palms (green), symbolizing opposite forces and the law of contrast. Thus both repetition and contrast are shown by design on the veil.

The many repetitions of these design units refer to the fourth law of recall, which is *frequency*. We recall easily what we repeat often. Along with frequency goes *recency*, since we tend to recall recent experiences more readily than those which occurred some time ago. This law of recency is represented in Key 2 by the writing on the scroll.

The High Priestess Hands

The High Priestess's right hand is hidden because the more powerful subconsciousness activities elude our attempts to analyze them. Therefore, her left hand is the only one visible, to intimate that we perceive only the results or manifestations of the hidden forces she represents.

The Blue Robe

The last chapter covers the law of association. On a personal level, this is the linking of one thought which leads to another. In a broader sense, this is the linking of the mind-stuff. In a holographic universe, everything is entangled.

> Quantum entanglement is a physical phenomenon that occurs when pairs or groups of particles are generated, interact, or share spatial proximity in ways such that the quantum state of each particle cannot be described independently of the state of the others, even when a large distance separates the particles. – Wikipedia

Einstein called quantum entanglement "spooky action at a distance."

The personal subconsciousness is a manifestation, through a single organism, of the great and all-inclusive universal subconsciousness. This is the robe of the High-Priestess; it's her *outer* garment.

This robe symbolizes Water, a symbol of *root matter*, or Prakriti, of the Hindus. The wavy lines of the robe represent **vibration**. This is one of the most important occultism concepts (and sadly abused by ignorant dabblers and mystery-mongers). We live in a vibratory universe, and *it is a vibration in the root matter which puts us in touch with other points of the universe*. These points are themselves centers of the conscious energy of the One Life-power.

The robe is a symbol of flowing and fluidity. Thus it typifies the ever-changing forms of life. It is drawn to seem to flow out of the picture.

This robe is the source of all streams and pools among the Keys' symbols, from Key 3 to Key 21.

The same vibration law, at work on the physical plane, brings us the sun's radiant energy and other forms of energy converging upon this planet from every point in space.

The Element Water

The root matter is identical with subconsciousness, of which the element Water is a symbol. Water was the first mirror, and because mirroring is duplication and reflection, the symbolism of Water is directly related to the number 2. The conscious energy of the One Force, acting upon itself in its subconscious aspect of root-matter, brings into being all physical structures, including the cells of your body. The function of every cell is the result of the Life-power flowing *through* that cell.

The Veil

The veil behind the throne of the High Priestess is a symbol of virginity. The design refers to the associative powers of subconsciousness. The designs are palm leaves and pomegranates, which are, respectively, masculine and feminine symbols.

The pomegranates are red, the color of Mars. The palms are green, representing the feminine Venus vibration. This is only one of many places in Key 2, where *the union of opposite forces* is symbolized. The veil itself, because it joins the two pillars, is another representation of this union.

The Pillars

The pillars, alike in form but opposite in color, symbolize all pairs of opposites, such as light and darkness, attraction and repulsion, affirmation and negation, active and passive, manifest and unmanifested. In each of these pairs, the first is represented by the white pillar, and the second by the black. On the white pillar is *Yod* (ʼ), the initial letter of *Jachin*. That on the black pillar is Beth (ב), the initial of *Boaz*. Thus the pillars of the High Priestess are identified with those at the porch of Solomon's temple.

Jachin (יכין) - He (it) will establish.

Boaz (בעז) – In him (it) is strength.

The lotus buds at the top of the pillars refer to the subconscious activity, which is the cause of growth and development in organic life. They are buds because this Key represents potencies or possibilities of subconsciousness.

The Stone Cube

The High Priestess sits on a cubic stone to show that subconsciousness functions are related to laws of space. It is a symbol of salt, a preservative because salt crystallizes into cubes. The cube is also a symbol of the element of Earth and the physical plane. Again, it stands for truth and order because all its faces are equal, and so are its boundary lines.

This cube is of *stone*, which signifies life, wisdom, and union. Briefly, the cubic stone means that every operation of subconsciousness is based on immutable principles of truth and order, operative throughout the physical plane and higher fields of activity.

The Crown

The High Priestess' crown is of silver, the metal of the Moon. Its form is waxing and waning lunar crescents, with the full moon between them. They suggest periodicity and alternation, as well as the reflecting and reproductive power associated with the Moon.

The Equal Armed Cross

The cross on the woman's breast is white to represent light. It is also the primitive form of Tav (ת), the last letter of the Hebrew alphabet, corresponding to Key 21. This cross has many meanings. Its four equal arms serve to remind us of the four implements on the Magician's table and their combined activity. Hekate, the Moon goddess, presided over where two roads meet, or crossroads.

The 7 Hermetic Laws

Finally, this Key symbolizes seven great Hermetic Laws or Principles given in the book, *The Kybalion*. They are:

1. THE LAW OF MENTALISM. The law that the totality of the universe is fundamentally mental. By details of symbolism, it suggests that subconsciousness is the matter or substance of all things.

2. THE LAW OF CORRESPONDENCE. Gimel is one of many expressions of this law represented by the symbols and occult attributions of Key 2.

3. THE LAW OF VIBRATION, represented by two (2) and the wavy folds of the woman's blue robe.

4. THE LAW OF POLARITY, of which the pillars are among the principal symbols.

5. THE LAW OF RHYTHM, symbolized by the crown, since rhythm is periodic action, like the waxing and waning of the Moon.

Notice that this is the *crowning* symbol, intimating that rhythm is the dominant law in subconscious mental activities. *Every utilization of occult powers in magic demands the establishment of some chosen rhythm.*

6. THE LAW OF CAUSE AND EFFECT, symbolized by the scroll and by the word TORA. This law is revealed by, and in turn makes intelligible, the record of human experience.

7. THE LAW OF GENDER, represented by the palms and pomegranates on the veil and many other symbolic details.

Summary

The main idea from Key 2 is that *your personal field of subconsciousness is materially connected with the most distant stars.* Your subconsciousness is a temporarily restricted portion of the potential mode of universal matter.

Mind-stuff is the original material from which everything is made. All primarily mental, the mind-stuff changes form through various processes, making it *appear* as physical objects.

These are actual objects. The mental quality is not a denial of their reality as things in our environment. But it is essential to know that their original and actual material is shaped by conscious control of human mental imagery. Your subconsciousness has access to an inexhaustible supply of the physical universe's original material. When you learn how to use powers already yours, *you may shape this material AS YOU WILL.*

Watch your daily experience closely. As you become familiar with these principles, you will put them more and more into conscious operation. Thus you will gain greater control over the forces of your personality. Persistent practice in directing your energies leads eventually to the attainment of extraordinary control over physical conditions, and this control is exerted by mental means.

[1] Hekate rides in Ra's barge as he journeys through the underworld. She was adopted by the Greeks, along with Medusa (Algol).

Algol is a binary star system that decreases in brightness every 2.86 days during an eclipse. The Egyptians kept star tables and considered bright Algol good luck. One culture's good luck charm is another's demon. It reminded me of the original Star Trek episode, *Is There in Truth No Beauty?*

Chapter 9

CREATIVE IMAGINATION

This week look at Key 3, The Empress, for five minutes before reading this chapter. Tarot Keys are a symbolic picture of some aspect of your consciousness. They are portraits of yourself. Tarot speaks by evoking thought— not merely an intellectual activity, but *all* the various mind-power expressions that externalize themselves in a human's life and consciousness.

Looking at Key 3 is the method for bringing closer to the surface, the deeper potencies of your inner life. When you study the chapters, always have nearby the Key to which the text relates, and often glance at the picture.

Number 3

MULTIPLICATION is a key-word attributed to the number 3. To multiply is to cause to increase in number, to make *more* by natural generation. Multiplication is the act or operation of increasing by multiplying.

CREATIVE IMAGINATION is the way the principle of multiplication manifests itself in your mental life. The secret of the process is in the definition of number 3. It is *the response of subconsciousness to self-consciousness in the generation of mental images*.

The combination of 1 and 2 produces 3, so is the Empress, a symbolic combination of ideas pictured by the Magician and the High Priestess. The activity resulting from the harmonious union of the forces symbolized by these two is shown by Key 3.

As the sum of 1 and 2, the number 3 is the union of the ideas of individuality (1) and repetition (2). The repetition of the unit through

80

the agency of the duad is a reproduction. Reproduction is manifested as renewal, generation, growth, fertility, development, and fecundity. Hence 3 is the number of production, formation, organization, propagation, elaboration. Representing organization, it suggests arrangement and the right adaptation of parts to a whole. This implies anticipation, expectation, purpose, plan, contrivance, invention. These meanings of 3 are shown in the Empress's symbolism because this Key typifies the working of your subconsciousness in the activities indicated by the words corresponding to the number.

Daleth - ד

Daleth (ד) means *door*. Not that opening, but the door itself. Hence it suggests the power to admit or bar, to retain and to let in or out.

The door has always been a feminine symbol, representing birth, reproduction, and life's entry into manifestation. Therefore Daleth represents the womb, the door of personal life, opening to receiving the seed, closing to retain the germ of life during the period of gestation, and opening again to send the newborn creature into the world. Similar activities, on planes above the physical, are represented by the same symbol.

Subconsciousness receives the seed impulse of observations made during periods of concentrated attention. Then follows a cycle of development within the field of subconsciousness.

When this cycle is completed, a new idea, or some new plan, comes forth through the door of subconsciousness into the field of self-conscious awareness. This finished result of creative imagination may be completely different from the form taken by the original seed-thought. But the *life in that form* is continuous with the life in the seed-thought, just as the life in a human body is continuous with the life in the spermatozoon and ovum from which that body was developed.

In this operation of subconsciousness, there is an apparent accretion of materials around a vital center. This is true in mental and physical creation. In this connection, remember that the Greek noun *delta*,

81

derived from *Daleth*, represents both the female organ of generation and the accretion of alluvial soil at the mouth of a river or river delta. And Delta (Δ) is the fourth letter's name in Greek, corresponding to Daleth (ד).

Daleth's original hieroglyphic represented the radiance of sunrise, the entrance of light into the world through the East's gateway. This may account for the attribution of the direction East to Daleth and this letter's aspect of consciousness *The 32 Paths of Wisdom* names the Luminous Intelligence.

OBTW.

You will find many translations of the 32 Paths of Wisdom. They lack one thing, the accompanying Hebrew text. The one exception is *Oedipus Aegyptiacus* by Athanasius Kircher. However, his translation is in Latin. But his Hebrew penmanship is excellent and easy to read.

The 14th Path is Illuminating Consciousness. It is the essence of electricity (Chashmal). It teaches the fundamentals of the secret mysteries of the Holy Sanctuary and its plan.

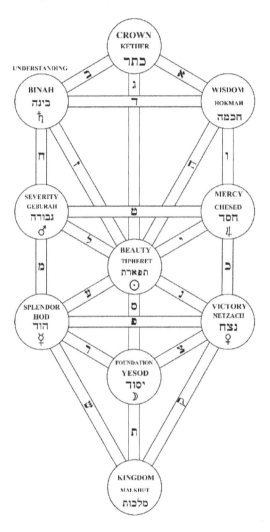

The essence of electricity, Chashmal (חשמל) flows into Binah through the Path of Daleth. Then the Dark Sterile Mother *Ama* (אמא), becomes the Bright fertile mother *Aima* (אימא).

Radiance is Vibration

Radiance is vibration produced by solar force. Sunshine is not the sun. The brightness and splendor are effects caused by the luminary. The rays make the sun visible. The beams are the Sun's power. Therefore, because the Sun is one of the Supreme Spirit's principal emblems, *sunshine represents the mysterious power of the cosmic Life-Breath –* the manifesting agency Hindus call Prakriti.

Radiation of solar energy, being the basis of all vegetable and animal life, brings about the gradual unfoldment of consciousness. It is also the cause of those physiological changes whereby a human personality manifests higher orders of consciousness. Also, this radiant energy is the physical force that assumes forms by your acts of creative imagination.

Keep this in mind. This will intensify your feeling that you are using *real powers* in your work. In their essence, these are spiritual powers. They who say there is no such thing as a separate entity called "matter" are entirely correct.

On the other hand, these relative states and conditions of spiritual energy manifestation are entirely *real*. Please understand that the life-power physical manifestations are NOT separate from the finer and subtler manifestations that are termed psychic, astral, and so on.

According to the Ageless Wisdom, all forms of manifestation are expressions of single energy that enjoy unbroken and unbreakable continuity. This energy is real, and its reality extends "downward" into the physical plane just as truly as it extends "upward" into realms of finer and more intense vibration.

"That which is above is as that which is below, and that which is below is as that which is above."

Thought Forms

Mental images are patterns or matrices for physical conditions. Mental objects, in their plane, are real and valid physical objects. Creative imagination forms mental images. *The Empress governs internal development and arrangement, which produces the external manifestation of physical conditions.* Under normal circumstances, the mental pictures gradually precipitate into physical expression through a series of subtle and complex transformations. Adepts and masters can speed up this series of changes so that their mental images are almost instantaneously manifested. This is the secret of instantaneous healing or the miracle of the loaves and fishes.

These extraordinary manifestations are no exceptions to the general rule. For the merest tyro and the adept, mental imagery is based on your physical and environmental conditions. The states of body and environment which you are now experiencing are the fruition of your mental images. If you want different external conditions, you must change the images. This is one secret of dominion.

Thus it is valuable to utilize every legitimate device to realize that our mental imagery manifests the real power of physical potency and metaphysical reality.

Our present political and economic systems' chaotic conditions are direct results of disorderly images held in millions of human beings' minds. To change external affairs, your mental images must be changed, which requires that each person undertake the cultivation of their mental garden. We must understand external circumstances are the physical embodiments of pre-existent mental patterns. Before we can change our present situation, we must take reasonability for it. Remember the 5th saying on the Trestleboard – I recognize the manifestation of the undeviating justice in all circumstances of my life.

Think about what circumstance you want to change. And remember, you can only change yourself, not other people. And if you're in an abusive relationship, you can change the situation immediately by walking away.

The Empress is a symbol of the attainment of the harmonious and constructive direction of mental imagery. This will be more apparent next week after considering the meaning of the various details of the symbolism.

In your study period, ponder this: *The point where the working power of subconsciousness may be controlled is the point where thoughts take definite form as mental images.*

A statement like "all is good" is not a specific mental image. Statements of truth do not work unless they are linked to specific imagery. The images must be concrete. They must prepare the *mind* and *body* for action.

This is not a denial of the value of general statements of principle as it helps us understand. The point is that intellectual statements of truth must be supplemented by detailed imagery before the mighty forces of the inner life can be made to emerge as actual forms and conditions of the physical plane.

This week, concern yourself with impressing these details on your mind as you color the Key 3. Plan your work to complete the coloring on the last day of your week's study. Such visual education is more valuable than any verbal interpretation since it calls into operation the symbols' powers. It also stirs the associative power of subconsciousness, whereby your mental image of the Key attunes you to wise who know every detail of the meaning.

DIRECTIONS FOR COLORING KEY 3

YELLOW: Background, shoes, staff of the scepter.

GREEN: Foliage, grass, wreath. Robe (except cuffs, girdle, collar edging and panel). Ball on the scepter.

BLUE: Stream and waterfall.

BROWN: Tree trunks beside a waterfall.

GRAY: Stone bench.

SILVER: Crescent.

GOLD: Stars, collar edging, girdle, cross, and bar on the scepter.

COPPER: Shield (except dove). Mix red and brown to secure copper color.

BLONDE: Hair, wheatears.

WHITE: Pearls, the panel in dress, cuffs of dress, dove, highlights in the waterfall.

RED: Roses, triangle on the breast.

Chapter 10

THE EMPRESS

By contrast with the High Priestess, a cold, virgin figure corresponding to the Moon, the Empress is warm and maternal. She is the Great Mother, pregnant with the world of form. In this figure, all the ancient world's mother goddesses are synthesized, but she is particularly Aphrodite or Venus.

The Planet Venus

According to Blavatsky's *Secret Doctrine*, the human race owes much to the earlier development of consciousness connected with the planet Venus. In the Rosicrucian *Fama Fraternitatis*, the entrance to the mysterious vault which contained all the secrets of the order was discovered when one of the Brothers happened to remove a tablet of brass, a metal associated with the planet Venus.

Furthermore, the vault itself had seven sides, and this heptagonal construction is found in many alchemical diagrams typifying the perfection of the Great Work.

Such perfection is a victory over all obstacles, and this idea of mastery is linked with the number 7. Seven is associated with Venus because Netzach, the 7th Sephiroth, is called the Sphere of Venus. The mental activities personified by the various mother deities, of whom Venus is a type, lead to the Great Work's completion. Hence, in the *Book of Formation* (*Sepher Yetzirah*), we find the idea of Wisdom associated with Daleth.

The same book attributes Folly to this letter. This is because the same activities, when understood and applied correctly, lead to the discovery of the Great Secret and enable us to complete the Great Work. However, this power, when misused, leads millions into all sorts of foolish thoughts and actions.

Tarot shows the positive, constructive aspects of the activity symbolized by the Great Mother. The negative, destructive activities are not represented. To picture them would be to synthesize all the Furies into one horrible figure. It would be a symbol of the menace of perverted and distorted mental imagery.

The Power of Words

Remember, subconsciousness accepts all mental imagery as real and proceeds to develop by deduction, whatever suggestions are impressed on it by the habitual mental attitudes of self-consciousness. Subconsciousness is particularly susceptible to the power of words.

Especially the words we use as predicates after the initial statement, "I AM."

A *practical* occultist watches their words. They are careful to say nothing they do not want, manifesting in their external circumstances.

Not even in jest will the student say anything which belittles the "I AM." Early in their instruction, we learn that the "I AM" is magic "Word of Power." This is the "Lost Word" that so much has been written. It was lost because the profane world has forgotten its significance and its real power. However, in every generation of humanity, the Lost Word is found by those who ripen into understanding.

Mother Nature

The Empress is Mother Nature, personified as Venus. She clothes herself in the web of manifestation which entangles the minds of fools, but the wise see through appearances, and Nature unveils herself. The veil hiding the truth is human ignorance. It may be taken away by those who know how to choose their mental images.

Green is the color associated with Daleth. It predominates in Key 3, as it does in Nature. Note that green is produced by mixing yellow and blue, the colors associated with the Magician and the High Priestess.

The Empress is a womanly figure, and traditional interpretations tell us she is pregnant. This agrees because creative imagination results from the impregnation of subconsciousness by impulses originating in self-consciousness.

Her hair is yellow, like that of the Fool, to symbolize radiant energy. The wreath binding it is of myrtle, a plant sacred to Venus. Myrtle is an evergreen shrub. Like the acacia, it is a symbol of immortality.

The Empress Crown

The Empress wears a crown of twelve golden, six-pointed stars. This connects her with the Apocalypse woman, clothed with the sun and crowned with twelve stars.

The stars represent universal forces. Thus, the crown's symbolism refers to the twelve modes of cosmic activity associated with the twelve signs of the zodiac. One idea conveyed by the symbolism is that subconsciousness. However, it is influenced by suggestions originating in self-consciousness. It is open to an influx of power that descends from the celestial or super-conscious level of the Life-power's activity.

The Moon

Like the Apocalypse woman, the Empress has the moon under her feet to show that the basis of her activity is the power symbolized by the High Priestess. Activities with growth, reproduction, and imagination are those in which the principle of *rhythm* operates.

Clothes

The Empress' green robe is bound by a golden girdle, above which there is shown a red triangle. The triangle is a Greek letter Delta, corresponding to Daleth. It is red to show that the influence of the universal fiery energy operates through subconsciousness.

Scepter

The Empress' scepter is surmounted by a globe bearing a cross. This is a symbol of dominion. The globe and cross are a union of feminine and masculine, or positive and negative.

Shield

The shield is copper, the metal of Venus. The dove on its face is sacred to Venus and is a Christian symbol of the Holy Spirit. Hence the dove is connected with the meanings of the number 3.

In *The Harmonies of Being*, P. F. G. Lacuria writes:

"The number three reveals to us the harmony of the Holy Spirit. The number three is the return to unity, which seems to be broken by the number two. It is in uniting the Father and the Son that the Holy Spirit realizes itself, and on this account, it may be considered as the efflorescence of the unity."

Stone Bench

The stone seat is richly ornamented, in contrast to the simplicity of the High Priestess' cube. The ornate bench shows the operation of self-conscious observation and induction upon subconsciousness. It results in modifications and adaptations of Nature— the arts, beautiful and useful.

Ripened Wheat

The ripened wheat in the foreground represents the completion of a cycle of growth. It carries with it the same idea of multiplication indicated by number 3. The *seed forms* are multiplied. Every act of creative imagination elaborates conditions spontaneously provided by Nature into new forms, which gives rise to future growth.

The fifty (50) shafts of wheat that are full of seeds. Fifty is Nun (נ) and Key 13, Death. Nun means a *seed sprout*.

The Stream

The stream and pool in the background represent the stream of consciousness. It has its source in the robe of the High Priestess. The water falling into a pool suggests the Law of Gender, the reciprocal relationship between the male and female modes of conscious energy.

This stream is also a symbol of *libido*, the driving energy or conscious life. The stream is modified and directed by the self-conscious activities symbolized by the Magician. The pool stands for the accumulation of those influences at the subconscious level. Thus the stream waters the garden and makes it fertile.

Cypress Trees

The cypress trees in the background are ten in number, corresponding to the ten Sephiroth. The cypress is a tree sacred to Venus. Roses are also sacred to Venus. They have five petals representing the five senses and have the same meaning as the five roses in the Magician's garden.

Pearl Necklace

The necklace of pearls is another Venusian symbol. Seven pearls are visible, representing the seven planets known to the ancients and the seven interior stars, nerve centers in the human body, called *chakras* by Hindu yogis.

When these beads are strung on a necklace, they are related together and put in order. Furthermore, a necklace touches the throat at the level of the Venus center.

The suggestion is that the Venus center is the one through which the seven interior stars are to be brought into orderly correlation to control the forces playing through them. This correlation may be called the secret entrance into adeptship, and thus, the Venus center is the *door* to mastery.

Summary

Regular use of the Empress will enrich your power of creative imagination and stimulate your inventiveness. It will increase your ability to make new combinations of ideas.

We live in an age of cheap printing and videos, combined with the cut-and-dried life of cities, endanger our power of creative imagination. We take too much of our mental imagery second-hand, from the screen and the printed page.

Consequently, psychologists are asked to help solve personal problems that have arisen because many persons do not realize, let alone utilize, the tremendous power of imagination.

Key 3 will help you use your imagination positively and constructively. It tells your subconsciousness what powers it has and how they should be exercised. You may not grasp the symbolism's inner meaning at first, *but your subconsciousness will* because this picture is written in your subconscious mind's language.

Pictorial symbolism is the language of dream, reverie, fantasy, and imagination. *It is not an intellectual affair, though intellect may analyze it.* It goes far deeper. Use Key 3 whenever you find yourself sterile of ideas, and it will help to start an abundant flow of mental imagery.

Chapter 11

REASON

This week look at Key 4, the Emperor, for five-minute before reading this chapter. As you gaze at it, remember that the Emperor is the consort and complement of the Empress. Compare the two Keys, and discover for yourself the contrast between them.

The key-word of the number 4 is ORDER. Other meanings include system, regulation, management, and supervision. Thus the number 4 relates to the classifying self-consciousness activity, induced by the subconscious response to impressions originating at the self-conscious level. This classifying activity is REASON.

Mental imagery becomes useful after it has been categorized or put in order. Then it becomes valuable in our daily lives to regulate, supervise, and manage our affairs.

When mental imagery is not so structured, we are creatures of our emotions and desires - impractical dreamers, unable to meet the problems life presents to us. Note that the verb "presents." Life's challenges are not evils. They are *gifts*. When understood, every problem conceals a principle that may be applied to producing different, useful, and beautiful results. Reason helps us to discover the principles hidden in problems. It is what enables us to face life's experiences squarely and transform all seeming evil into good.

The authority of the Emperor is exercised over the offspring of the Express. She is his consort, subject to her husband. Her motherhood depends on him. On the other hand, The Emperor's sovereignty depends on her motherhood. Unless the universal subconscious activities bring forth a universe, the cosmic self-consciousness has nothing to govern. The Empress is the manifesting power that brings forms into being. Then, the Emperor has something to rule.

In the Microcosm or "universe in little," imagination is a subconscious response to acts of attention and observation. It originates at the level of self-consciousness (the Magician). However, the magician, who appears now as the Emperor, would have nothing to control or transform if not subconsciousness sends up from its depths a stream of images to be classified and arranged by the exercise of reason. Hence in Key 4, we find the Emperor seated on a height *overlooking* a stream in his domain. The same stream waters the Empress' garden and has its source in the shimmering robe of the High Priestess.

Number 4

In geometry, four is represented by the square, a symbol for the physical plane, and concrete things. Specific mental images, in a logical order, are the foundations of reason and good sense.

The number 4 is connected with the idea of measurement. With reason, we are enabled to take the measure of our experiences and interpret them correctly. Without such a rational measurement of experience, we continue to mistake the illusory for real. Thus we make (for we cannot help being creative) conditions in our world that have the appearance of misery, poverty, disease, and discontent.

Numerically, the Emperor is the union or sum of the Magician and the Empress. This is one reason for identifying the Emperor with the Magician. Another is that the theosophical extension of 4, or sum of 1 to 4, is 10 $(1 + 2 + 3 + 4 = 10)$.

Also, 10 reduces to 1 by addition $(1 + 0 = 1)$. Thus the Emperor is essentially 1 (The Magician), and the extension of his power is 10, or the Wheel of Fortune.

Four is also the sum of 2 and 2, and the multiplication of 2 by 2. Therefore, though masculine, the Emperor is an expression of the power of 2, the *root matter* symbolized by the High Priestess.

This reminds us that reason is an expression of memory. Beneath all forms of reasoning is the fundamental activity of *retention* and *recollection*, symbolized by Key 2. Develop those number hints in your notebook.

Letter Heh - ה

Heh (ה) is a definite article, like the English "the." Reason defines things by assigning names. In the Garden of Eden, it was Adam that gave living creatures their names.

The letter name Heh (הא) means, *look, behold, look here.* The hieroglyph for Heh is a man with his arms raised.

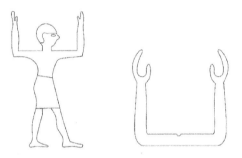

From right to left, these two symbols are A28 and D28 in the *Hieroglyphic Sign List.* The first glyph means high, joy, and mourn. The raised arms are *ka,* and mean, spirit, personality, mood, attribute, and fortune.

In its connection to the soul, the *Hebrew for Christians* website has this to say about the letter Hey:

"According to the Jewish mystics, Hey (ה) represents the divine breath, revelation, and light (the word 'light' is mentioned five times on the first day of creation (Genesis 1: 3-4), which is said to correspond to the letter Hey). Heh is five. This corresponds on a physical level to the five fingers, the five senses, and the five dimensions. On a spiritual level, it compares to the five levels of soul:

1. Nefesh – instincts
2. Ruach – emotions
3. Neshamah – mind
4. Chayah – bridge to transcendence
5. Yechidah – oneness

Last but not least, Heh is the name of one of the Ancient Egyptian Ogdoad or the
Eight Gods of Creation. They are:

Nu	Nut
Heh	Huhut
Kekui	Kekuit
Qerh	Qeret

The god Heh is the personification of eternity. His name means endlessness. His hieroglyph (C11) is a seated man with his arms held up. On top, his head is a palm branch, which is a symbol of time and record keeping (ordered memory).

The 15th Path is Stable Intelligence (Sekhel Ma'amid). From the pure darkness, it stabilizes the essence of Creation (Briah). The Masters say, "wrapped it in thick darkness." – Job 38:9.

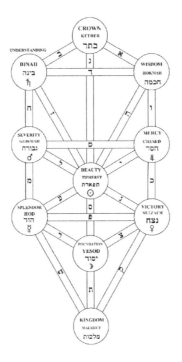

The 15th Path of Heh connects Hokmah to Tiphareth. The full passage from Job is,

"When I made the clouds its garment and wrapped it in thick darkness, when I fixed limits for it and set its doors and bars in place, when I said, 'This far you may come and no farther; here is where your proud waves halt'? Have you ever given orders to the morning or shown the dawn its place."

Notice God sets limits. The 15th Path is the aspect of God, and ourselves, that orders and arranges the universe.

The Power of Defining Things

Often one hears a colloquial used in connection with something unknown. "Name it, and it's yours." Whatever the origin of this bit of slanguage[1], it expresses an actual truth, which we see *as soon as we understand the real significance of naming anything.* Think it over.

Definition limits and sets boundaries, particularize, specialize, and enters into details. The activities enter into making a constitution for any social organization, from a high school club or a nation. Its constitution is, for any organization, the supreme authority.

All laws must agree with the constitution, and laws themselves are definitions. We call "laws of nature" are human definitions, and descriptions of the way events follow in some particular order.

Furthermore, our definitions (or naming) of the meanings of the events which constitute our life-experience have a significant *suggestive* influence on our subconsciousness. In one sense, every individual makes their law. We are the author of the constitution of our world. Our life-experience generally conforms to the constitution we make. We define our experiences.

However, at the same time, every human is living in the real world. And so, our happiness is based on our private world, conforming to the real world. And our misery if there is a discrepancy between our world and the real world.

Aries, the Ram, is the first zodiacal sign. It symbolizes the outgoing, ordered cyclic motion emanating from the Primal Will— the beginning of cosmic manifestation.

According to medical astrology, Aries rules the head and face, especially the eyes, and dominates the brain's higher functions.

Mars rules Aries. It is the planet of war and conflict and the protector of fields against the attacks of enemies. Mars stands for a force at work in the human body. It is active in the brain and gives energy to the entire muscular system. Thus it is the instrumentality of execution and realization. Through the Mars force, we deal with our environment's world and set that world in order.

The Sun is exalted (that is, finds its highest expression) in Aries. The highest manifestations of solar energy are expressed in the human functions governed by Aries (head and eyes) and symbolized by Key 4.

Every one of these functions and powers results from transformations of solar energy in the human brain cells. Of all mechanisms and organisms on earth, our brains are the most wonderful and the most powerful. They are run by solar force, as is every other organ in our bodies.

Strictly speaking, the brain does not transform solar energy into thoughts. It transforms solar energy into vibration rates that enable the personal consciousness to receive ideas eternally present in the Universal Mind and are being broadcast continually throughout space. The same principle applies to radio.

An antenna receives transmissions and conducts them to a crystal that turns the radio waves into an electric current. Then the speaker transforms the electric current into sound waves, which are heard by the ear and understood by the mind. As a project, you can purchase a *crystal radio kit* and assemble it.

The receiving set does not make the music. Neither does the brain make thought. What happens is that the brain provides the necessary conditions, as does a receiving set so that that thought may be *expressed*.

Summary

The Emperor is the Establisher, the Founder of all things, The Framer of the Universal Constitution. In the field of human personality, the universal constituting power is made manifest in our ability to see through outer appearances into the real nature of our environment. The power of vision embraces the whole complicated machinery, mental and physical, whereby the spirit within becomes aware of the universe.

As you color the Key this week, compare its symbolism with that of the Empress. Look for contrasts. Look for details that bring out what the Emperor represents complements the Empress pictures.

COLORING INSTRUCTIONS

YELLOW: T-cross and circle in right hand.

GREEN: Foreground.

BLUE: Stream at the base of the cliff.

GRAY: Stone cube, except ram's head.

VIOLET: Belt, flaps on the tunic (not borders nor medallion on left shoulder).

WHITE: Borders of tunic flaps, bolt, ram's head, medallion, beard and hair, border of inverted T on the globe in the left hand, sleeves.

GOLD: Inverted T, and cross on globe, framework, and points on the helmet.

BROWN: Slopes from height in the foreground to stream's edge.

ORANGE: Background, above mountains.

STEEL: Leg armor and breastplate.

RED: Globe in left hand (not inverted T or cross), helmet (except borders and points), mountains and cliffs.

---

[1] Frank Sinatra released a song called, *Name It and Its Yours* in 1961. These chapters were written circa 1936, so the expression must have been popular for a while.

Chapter 12

THE EMPEROR

In the last chapter, the general meaning of Key 4 is REASON. This has two aspects, as do all Tarot Keys. The universal aspect is the rational Cosmic Mind, which sets in order all manifestations of the Life-power. The personal element is the reflection, or specialization, of this universal rational quality in our action and experience. Thus Key 4 represents the Life-power as the Sovereign Reason, the Great Lord ruling all of manifestation. It is also a symbol of that in yourself, which enables you to control your environment's conditions.

The Cube

The seat of the Emperor and the High Priestess are a cube. A cube is one of the five Pythagorean solids (tetrahedron, cube, octahedron, dodecahedron, and icosahedron). The cube is a representation of the physical plane. It is also a symbol of order, regularity, and truth. It is composed of equal faces, has boundary lines of the same length, and has faces that are squares, corresponding geometrically to the number 4.

A cube is bounded by twelve lines, eight points, and six faces. The sum of these is 26, the numeral value of the Divine Name יהוה (IHVH, or the Tetragrammaton). This name means "That which was, that which is, that which will be." Without attempting to define, it declares that whatever is real now has been, and will be, eternally the same.

The cube is a symbol of the physical plane, order, and truth. It represents the One Reality, manifested as the universe, is the limitless Life-power's real presence, which is the universe's sovereign ruling principle.

In Solomon's temple, the Holy of Holies is a cubical room that contained the Ark of the Covenant. The ark's mercy-seat rested the Shekinah, or Divine Presence, located at the Holy of Holies' inner center. In Revelations, the heavenly city represents the completion and perfection of the Divine Order is a cube. The lamb's throne (a young ram) is said to be in its midst, or at the inner center, as a *light source* for the whole city.

White Hair

The white hair and beard of the Emperor is a symbol of the Ancient of Days, or Great Lord, designated by the word IHVH (יהוה). He is shown in profile so that only one eye is showing.

This is an ancient symbolism intimating that even our highest concept of Reality is necessarily one-sided and imperfect. Note also that this white-haired, white-bearded ancient is the figure described in the first chapter of the Apocalypse as he who is Alpha and Omega, the first and last, who is also the Lamb (Ram).

Alchemical Sulfur

The Emperors' head, chest and arms form a triangle while his legs form a cross. This is the symbol of Sulfur.

In Alchemy, Sulfur is the concord of elemental Air and Fire. Sulfur is the flame (Fire) of our self-consciousness (Air). It is hot and penetrating. The Soul is the Sulfur principle because it is a unique expression of the Life-power. In the plant kingdom, the essential oil is the Sulfur principle because it is unique to the plant.

Aries the Ram ♈

The ram's head on the side of the cube is the symbol of Aries. The medallion on his shoulder and at the top of his helmet is also Aries. The symbol of the ram is ancient. In India, it denotes Agni, the god of fire. As a noun, the Sanskrit word *Agni* is an alternative name for the element of fire, usually termed *Tejas*. In writings on Hindu occultism, the *Agni Tattva* is said to be the subtle principle of sight. This agrees with the attribution of sight to Heh (ה) and Key 4.

The Freemason white lambskin apron is a symbol of many of the ideas represented by Key 4. First of all, it is a square with a triangular flap. This combination of square and triangle is a symbol of Sulfur.

Furthermore, the lambskin refers directly to the sign Aries. Thus it represents the first stage of a time cycle. In Freemasonry, the lambskin apron is "the emblem of innocence" because innocent is spotless or without blemish. And this is the Life-power condition at the beginning of a self-expression cycle, pure, innocent, and holy.

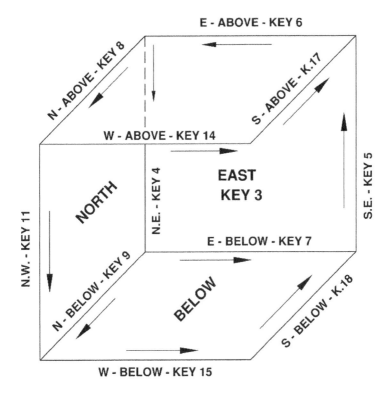

On the Cube of Space, Heh (ה) is assigned to the north-east. The West's combination is attributed to the letter Daleth (ד), and the north – Peh (פ) and Key 16, the Tower. The Empress is Venus. Key 16 is Mars, who is in Rulership in Aries.

Therefore, Key 4 represents a combination of the powers of Mars and Venus. This is the Emperor's meaning; consort of the Empress would have no subjects to govern unless his mate had borne him children.

The combination of the number 3, suggested by the triangle in which are the Emperor's head and arms, with the number 4, indicated by the cross formed by his legs, is another intimation of the same combination of feminine and masculine powers.

The Helmet

The helmet, surmounted by Aries' symbol, is also ornamented with twelve triangular points, of which six are visible. These are equivalent to the stars on the Empress' crown and the jewels on the Fool's girdle. The colors on the helmet are gold (Sun) and red (Mars). In Aries, Mars is in Rulership, and the Sun is in Exaltation.

The Globe

The globe and cross in the Emperor's left hand are symbols of dominion. They are similar in form to the ornament at the top of the Empress' scepter, but her globe is green, and the Emperor's is red. These are complementary colors, the green corresponding to Daleth (ד) and Venus, the red to Heh (ה) and Mars. The little cross at the top of the globe comprises five equal squares: Heh's number.

Mountains

The mountains in the background are volcanic rock, colored red to emphasize Aries' fiery quality. These barren rocks are in sharp contrast to the fertility and productiveness of the Empress' garden. They represent the sterility of intellect for its own sake, without any practical life application.

The mountains suggest the fruitlessness of mere regulation and arrangement unless something is warm and vital to set in order. However, *disintegrated rock* is the principal component of the soil that supports vegetation. Thus the bleak cliffs behind the Emperor are based on all the lush growth in the Empress's garden. So is pure reason, properly broken down into its elements, and mixed with the emotional qualities predominating in subconsciousness, based on all the creative works of human imagination.

The inverted T on the globe represents Tav (ת), the last letter of the Hebrew alphabet. In the Tarot system, Tav is attributed to the planet Saturn.

In Aries, Saturn is in Fall, which is opposite of Exaltation.

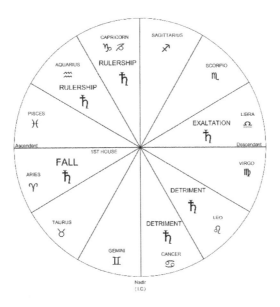

Also, Saturn is dignified by Triplicity and Term for the last four degrees of Aires. In the weighted system of essential dignities, Saturn is +1.

Planet	Sign	Fall	Fire Triplicity	Term 26 - 29.59°	Total
Saturn	Aries	-4	+3	+2	+1

Not bad for a planet in its Fall. But what does it mean?

Saturn is the astrological symbol of restriction. Hence the inverted Tav on the globe of dominion intimates that the Emperor's rulership and authority are expressed in his ability to reverse Saturn. That is, to reverse the action of Saturn's aspect of the Life-power's self-expression, which seems to limit our freedom. Such reversal of apparently restrictive conditions is what you may accomplish by the right use of the Constituting Intelligence symbolized by Key 4.

This right use consists of a higher vision of reality – a higher view based on accurate observation of the physical plane's actual situation. Real occult science does not attempt to deny the fact or minimize the importance of the physical world. What we reject is the opinion materialists hold as to the nature of the physical world. There is no need to deny the reality of material things to combat the errors of materialism. Nor is it necessary to explain away, using high-sounding verbal trickery, the actualities of time and space.

The higher vision includes insight into human's powers and accurate observation of the physical conditions surrounding them. Insight allows us to watch a train of events as it occurs in nature, apart from introducing the human personal factor. Our patient observations are rewarded by the conscious perception of the law or principle at work in the train of events we have observed. The reason, the eye of the mind, sees this law or principle, and sooner or later, it stirs up the inventive power of subconsciousness. Then, through the combination of the invention (creative imagination) and reason, the human personal factor enters the situation.

With this personal factor, new trains of events are set in motion; new forms are produced, new conditions are made manifest. Thus engineers apply the law that makes a piece of iron sink to float great steel ships. By obeying the laws which make a stone thrown into the air fall to the ground, humans make all-metal airplanes, which have added another dimension to our journeys.

By seeing things as they *are*, instead of as they merely *look*, the Sovereign Reason, manifested through the human brain, reverses, one by one, all semblances of bondage that afflict humanity. For the Spirit of freedom is the perfect liberty of rational order, operative in everything, everywhere.

Scepter

From one perspective, the Emperor's scepter is a modified form of the symbol of Venus. The bottom vertical line is extended.

♀

It means that the Emperor's active power of regulation has to do with mental imagery control.

The scepter is also a Sun symbol ($\odot$) sitting on top of a "T" with a long handle, a symbol of Saturn ($\hbar$).

The Sun is Exalted in Aries. Exalted means "to raise," and Sun is sitting on top of the scepter.

Also, the Sun is sitting on top of a Saturn symbol. It reminds me of a Bible verse.

> "Rejoice greatly… See, your **King** comes to you, righteous and victorious, lowly and **riding on a donkey**, on a colt, the foal of a donkey." – Zechariah 9:9

The King is the Sun, and the donkey is a symbol of Saturn. Therefore the scepter is also a reference to Sovereign Reason (The Sun) overcomes restrictions (Saturn).

The skirt of the armor and the flaps which cover the Emperor's arms are violet. In the Tarot color scale, violet is attributed to Jupiter (Key 10).

In astrology, Jupiter represents expansion, the reversal of contraction or constriction. Jupiter is associated with law, scientific research, philosophy, and religion.

Also, in connection with law and scientific research, the Emperor's armor or protection is the *truth*. There is a saying, "You can't cheat an honest man." This implies that cheaters rely on the dishonesty of other people. And an honest person cannot be exploited in this manner.

Also, Key 10 represents the scientific vision of the universe's mechanism as seen by the wise. Hence the violet flaps of the Emperor's dress mean:

Reason clothes itself in the Vision of Reality.

Vision is a revelation of truth concerning humanity and the universe. It is connected through the color violet to Key 17, a symbol of that unveiling.

Key 17 is associated with the sign Aquarius. The woman in this figure is nude. Nudity in the tarot is a symbol that nothing is hidden. The truth is in plain sight.

Reason and insight are always contrary to mass-opinion. Hence they always stir up conflict. Knowing this, and foreseeing the immediate consequences of his ministry, Jesus said: "I came not to send peace, but a sword." Peace comes later, with fulfillment, not in the initial stages of the work.

Thus the Emperor is shown as a man of war, in contrast to the peaceful scene shown in Key 3. Every step forward in man's dominion over the conditions of his environment has been contested bitterly by those who prefer to adhere to the "good old ways."

The mass mind resents innovations, clings to comfortable errors, scoffs at seers, and stones prophets. The Sovereign Reason is protected by the armor of truth, pictured in Key 4 as made of steel, a metal attributed to Mars. The final test of our vision is to carry it into action, and since Mars rules actions, the symbols here tell us that the mass mind will surrender its follies when confronted by the beneficent results of real vision expressed in action.

Many people who cross the continent by airplane today would have ridiculed the notion in 1900. The Wright brothers made their first flight in 1903, but as late as the spring of 1908, a magazine rejected an article by Byron Kewton, who had witnessed their achievements.

The editor's comment was, "While your manuscript has been read with much interest, it does not seem to qualify either as fact or fiction." Remember this when you encounter skepticism concerning the value of your occult studies. Long ago, the wise learned the futility of trying to convert the world by words. Even deeds sometimes fail to convince those who are blinded by prejudice.

Summary

Key 4 is intended to impress upon you a clear pattern of the ruling power of consciousness. Whenever you express right reason, interpret experiences correctly, and frame a satisfactory definition, you employ the power which defined the universe in the beginning. Working through you, this power is the maker and framer of worlds, including yours.

*It rules everything **now**, at this moment, and always. It has absolute command over every circumstance and condition.*

Chapter 13

INTUITION

For every Key, there are two chapters. The first chapter includes meanings of the number, title, and letter explained with the emphasis being placed on the key's general sense.

During the week, study this chapter, color the Key to fix its details in memory. It prepares you for the more extensive analysis of the symbolism given in the second chapter. Every day begin your study period by meditating for five minutes on the Tarot Key. Then study the chapter, reflect as you read, and write your observations in your diary.

This week is Key 5, The Hierophant. After looking at it for five minutes, review the meanings of the number 5.

Number 5

5. MEDIATION (an idea suggested because 5 is the middle term in the series from 1 to 9); adaptation; intervention; adjustment; hence *Justice*; accommodation; reconciliation; the result of the classifying activities symbolized by 4.

Five is the subconscious elaboration of classifications and the formulation of deductions. These conclusions are projected back into the self-conscious level and result in the mental state called *intuitions*.

Our cyclic mental process gives rise to perceptions. Every idea projected intuitively from subconsciousness into self-consciousness becomes another suggestion to subconsciousness and is the beginning of yet another series of deductions.

The working out of this process may be instantaneous. This is what happens when we "think fast." On the other hand, it may be a matter of days or longer. A typical example is what occurs in reading some difficult passages. At first, it may seem to be very obscure. However, the next time one sees it, the meaning is clear, even though no conscious thought is given to the text in the interval.

Intuition means, literally, *interior teaching*. It is defined as,

The direct perception of eternal principles may be applied to our problems' solution and perfect our control over the environment.

This direct perception results from the union of personal consciousness with the super-conscious I AM, the Central Self. Such perception makes a human being *immediately aware* of eternal principles. Included in this awareness is a perception whereby the laws are applied to the solution of particular problems.

Intuitions of this kind differ significantly from those whose roots go no deeper than the upper layer of subconsciousness, which is merely a record of personal experience. The deeper strata of subconsciousness record the race experience and correspond to what Carl Jung names "the collective unconscious." Intuitions coming from the upper, personal level of subconsciousness are what we commonly call hunches.

Intuitions originating in super-consciousness clothe themselves in the symbolic imagery of the race experience, stored in the collective subconsciousness. These may be correctly termed *spiritual* intuitions.

The word *union* is the key to the reception of spiritual Intuitions. One does not contact the higher plane where eternal principles are perceived unless there is a union between the personality and the Central Self. Key 5 symbolizes this union in many ways.

The 16th Path is the Eternal Intelligence (Sekhel Nitz.chi). It is the pleasure (Eden) of the Glory. There is no Glory like it (beneath it). It is called the Garden of Eden prepared for the Merciful Ones (Saints).

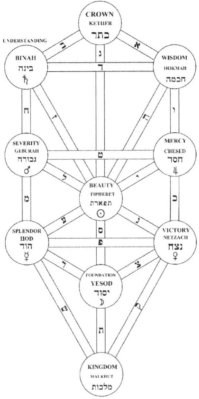

The Path of Vav connects Hokmah with Chesed (חסד). The Merciful Ones are the Chasadim (חסדים). It means "Saints." Notice that the Merciful Ones is the plural form of the Chesed or Hesed (חסד).

In Hebrew, the masculine plural ending to a word is Yod and Mem (ים). The feminine plural is Vav and Tav (ות).

117

Vav - ו

The letter name Vav (וו) means *nail, hook,* or *peg.* It represents union since nails and hooks join objects together.

The idea of *sustenance* is connected with the nail or hook since it is by nails that the house is sustained, and a hook is that from which something depends. When the Central Self is consciously linked with the personality, one gains first-hand knowledge that all things are sustained and depend on that One Self.

Key 5 and Vav are assigned the function of hearing. This means both the interior or spiritual hearing, as well as regular physical hearing. Knowledge of the higher aspects of reality comes to us through the "soundless sound" of an Inner Voice.

When they reach a stage of finer development, the hearing centers in the brain are stimulated by higher vibration rates, which serve as a means of communication with the Central Self. The same receptivity of the hearing centers put us in contact with advanced humans who are the Inner School members.

The Voice vs. voices

A word of warning is necessary. The awakening of the interior hearing centers may put us in communication with intelligences, neither wise nor good. Do not let this frighten you. There is a way to distinguish between the "voices" and the VOICE.

Often the little voices flatter. They promise great things – wealth, knowledge, prominence, and power. Sometimes they appeal to spiritual pride by announcing that the person who hears them is destined to save humanity from some terrible catastrophe. Always they demand complete obedience. If they give what they claim to be secret instruction, they require its recipients to follow the teaching without criticism and often insist that all other instructions be abandoned.

The true VOICE *never* flatters. Often it gently, but firmly points out our shortcomings. Seldom does it promise anything. Never does it coerce. Invariably it points out some universal and eternal principle that applies to an actual problem confronting the person who hears the instruction. The VOICE does not say: "Do thus and so." It instructs us concerning some law of nature involved in our problem to see for ourselves what we should do.

Hence this mode of consciousness associated with Vav and Key 5 is called "The Eternal Intelligence." Because the inner Voice shows us an eternal principle that will work out in a successful course of action, the Voice reveals a law of nature that applies to our problem.

Throughout the ages, wise men and women have taught and practiced union with the Central Self. When we recognize this power, which is eternally present in human life, it releases us from limitation. This power sets us free when we know it and act in obedience to its law.

OBTW.

The lesson of the inner voice does not have to be "profound." For example, I have a sensitive stomach. I can't eat spices and drink alcohol. When my stomach is acting up, I go into atrial fibrillation.

Once, I was sitting in meditation, searching deeply for an answer. I could see that a group of nerves behind my stomach was the cause of my problem. I spoke to my inner teacher. "Do you see that spot? What is that? Using my finger, I pointed to the place and asked. How do I fix that?

The Voice answered, "Wade, if you stopped poking at it, it wouldn't hurt as much."

I laughed. It's good advice. And the impression that I received is my sensitivity comes with a price.

And so it goes.

Number 5 and the Pentagon

Geometrically, five corresponds to the pentagon, or figure of five equal sides, and the pentagram, the five-pointed star, developed from the pentagon.

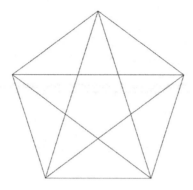

The pentagram is one of the most important occult symbols. Each of its five lines is divided in exact proportion (the famous Golden Section or Divine Proportion).

Golden Mean or Phi Ratio

The Divine Proportion is also called the Golden Mean, Golden Cut Divine Proportion, or Phi (ϕ) ratio.

One unique point exists that divides a line into two unequal segments so that the whole is to the greater as the greater is to the lesser.

Consider the line segment A + B. If we divide it in the right spot, we find that the length of the entire segment (A + B) is to the length of segment A as the length of segment A is to the length of segment B. If we calculate these ratios, we see that we get an approximation of the Golden Ratio.

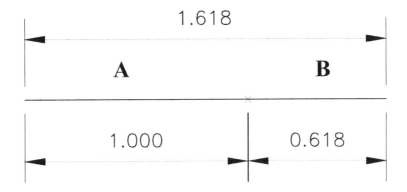

Please note that 1.618 is only an approximation of the golden ratio. The Golden Ratio is an irrational number. An irrational number has no exact decimal equivalent, although 1.618 is a good approximation.

In a pentagram, the Phi ratio looks like this.

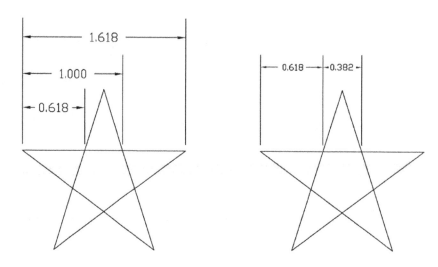

Notice the ratios all based on Phi or 1.618.

	Divide by		Equals	
1.618		1		1.618
1	÷	0.618	=	1.618
0.618		0.382		1.618

Therefore the pentagram is a symbol of the *Part is Encoded in the Whole*. That is, the *All is in THE ALL*. Thus, the pentagram is a symbol of the *holographic universe*.

With a single point uppermost, it suggests the head and four extremities of the human body. Therefore, the pentagram is a symbol of humanity and the microcosm.

Also, 5 is the number of mediation because it is the middle term between 1 and 9. So is man, whose number is 5, the mediator between God and nature. Here is a clue to many mysteries of practical occultism.

Taurus, the Bull, is attributed to Vav (ו) and Key 5. Taurus is an Earth sign, yet the bull's symbol is related to an ox, represented by the letter Aleph (א). Aleph is a symbol for the Life-Breath, Spirit, super-consciousness. However, Taurus is a symbol that is practically the same as Aleph, attributed to Earth and the physical plane.

What seems at first to be a contradiction is a clear suggestion that the spiritual and the material are essentially the same. The Divine Force, which is health to the soul, medicine to the body, and the source of all real wealth, is *omnipresent*.

The average person thinks of the Divine Force as far away and makes a sharp distinction between Spirit and Matter. The wise who know that there is no separation from the One-Self. For knowers of Reality, the *substance* of anything whatever is the actual *presence* of the One Spirit.

Venus rules Taurus, and wherein the Moon is exalted. Intuitions are the offspring of the Empress (Venus). And the Empress is the High Priestess (Moon) in her highest expression of active creation in Taurus. Therefore, Key 5 is a picture that tells us that *super-consciousness is to be reached through the functions of subconsciousness*.

Hearing

In the older Tarot decks, Key 5 was named The Pope. This refers to the attribution of hearing to this Key. For tradition, the first pope was the Apostle Simon, nicknamed Peter, Greek for Rock.

Simon (Σιμων) is derived from the Hebrew name Shim'on (שועמון) meaning, "he has heard." Read the passage in St. Matthew 16: 13 to 19, which is the basis of the papal tradition. There you will find a clear intimation that Simon's answer, for which Jesus blessed him, was the result of the interior hearing.

13 When Jesus came to the region of Caesarea Philippi, he asked his disciples, "Who do people say the Son of Man is?"

14 They replied, "Some say John the Baptist; others say Elijah; and still others, Jeremiah or one of the prophets."

15 "But what about you?" he asked. "Who do you say I am?"

16 Simon (Listening) Peter (Stone) answered, "You are the Messiah, the Son of the living God."

17 Jesus replied, "Blessed are you, Simon son of Jonah, for this was not revealed to you by flesh and blood, but by my Father in heaven.

18 And I tell you that you are Peter, and on this rock, I will build my church, and the gates of Hades will not overcome it.

19 I will give you the keys of the kingdom of heaven; whatever you bind on earth will be bound in heaven, and whatever you loose on earth will be loosed in heaven."

The Hierophant means "revealer of Mysteries," or "he who shows that which is sacred." In the Greek Mysteries, the hierophant explained the meanings of the sacred symbols. Thus the Inner Voice pictured by Key 5 will reveal to you the mysteries of Tarot and the inner, sacred meanings of its symbols. When this occurs, you have a true understanding of the meaning of life and its expression. Thus you will enjoy practical working knowledge, enabling you to employ all your powers to the best advantage.

Summary

Finally, Key 5 follows the Emperor, who represents Reason, to show:

(1) The individual who wants instruction from the Inner Voice must first train their mental vision, to see their situation clearly, even though that situation presents a problem;

(2) Even though Intuition goes beyond Reason, it is not a substitute for reasoning.

Be sure you get this last point clear. Some lazy-minded persons think their "hunches" (echoes from the personal level of subconsciousness) and the messages from flattering "voices" free them from the need for reasoning. Their sad failures should teach them better.

Read this chapter carefully with your diary at hand. Remember that Key 5 has the power to arouse your intuitive ability because the symbols act as forceful suggestions to your subconsciousness, which is the channel of intuition.

The force of these suggestions is intensified as the symbolism's details are impressed on subconsciousness while you color Key 5.

COLORING INSTRUCTIONS

YELLOW: Crown (not trefoils, crossbars or circle at top), yoke behind ears (except fringe), staff in the left hand, orphreys (Y's) on priests' vestments.

GREEN: Garments of figures in the foreground (except collars, sleeve edges, flowers, and orphreys.)

VIOLET: Fringe of the yoke.

GREY: Background (light), pillars, and throne (darker shade for the throne).

GOLD: Crown ornaments, the key with the handle pointing to a priest whose garment is embroidered with roses (except dots in a circle.)

SILVER: Crescent at the throat, the key with the handle pointing to the priest where the garment is embroidered with lilies (except dots in a circle).

BLUE: Undergarment showing at the bottom. The scarf or border of the outer robe should be blue-green.

WHITE: Undergarment at throat, navel, and sleeves. Shoes, collar, and sleeve edging of the chasuble, dots in the key circles. Lilies in a chasuble at right.

RED-ORANGE: Outer garment (not scarf or border). Dias. (Mix equal parts of red and orange).

RED: Roses on chasuble at left.

Chapter 14

THE HIEROPHANT

In the Sepher Yetzirah, Chapter 5:7, Taurus is assigned to Vav (ו). Kabbalist attribute Vav with the aspect of the Life-power called Lesser Countenance, or Son and the 6th Sphere of the Tree of Life, Tiphareth (Beauty). Recall the Trestleboard – *In all things great and small and see the Beauty in the divine perfection.* This sixth aspect is understood to be the particular manifestation of the universal Life-force as the human Ego.

In the last chapter, you learned that Key 5 is called The Pope in some Tarot versions. The traditional first pope is Simon (hearing) Bar-Jonah, or Simon, son of Jonah. Jonah (יונה) means dove. Therefore Simon Bar-Jonah means, "hearing, son of the dove." The dove on the Empress' shield is a Christian symbol for the Holy Spirit and the bird sacred to Venus, ruler of Taurus.

The first pope's name is Simon Peter. In Greek, Peter is *Petros* (Πετρος) and means stone. Its meaning is similar to *ehben* (אבן), stone.

The first two letters spell Ab (אב), meaning "father," and the last two spell Ben (בן), meaning son, and offspring. Thus *ehben* (אבן) signifies the union of the Father (God) and the Son (humanity).

From the perspective of the Tree of Life, it is the union of Chokmah (Wisdom) and Tiphareth (Beauty). Note that the path of Heh (ה) connects these two Sephiroth. Metaphorically speaking, when we see the world as it is and understand our place in the Universe (Heh, ה), then the star (Sphere of the Zodiac, Chokmah) is released from the stone (אבן) and is Beauty (Tiphareth) incarnate.

Therefore, wherever stone is shown in Tarot, it refers to some phase of the Divine Life-force union with the human Ego.

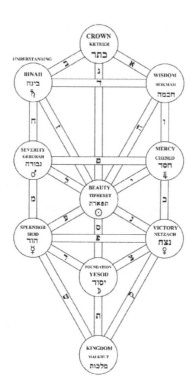

The Egyptian Text of the Bronzebook has this to say about the stone,

"Is a stone a thing unchanging, or is a star always a star? Who among you, people of ignorance, can see the bond between star and stone? Yet, there is a kinship in all things. The stars hanging above are not wholly apart from the heart of man." – Manuscripts 11:9.

And also,

"Unlock the secrets of a stone, and perchance you will find a star; open the body of water, and you may discover a heart of fire." – Morals and Precepts 34:4

Enough about the stone for now.

In Key 5, the principle of antithesis, which runs throughout the Tarot. It is shown by the contrast between the shaped stone and the jagged rock in the background of Key 4.

The emblem of the Emperor are those of *earthly rulership*; those of the Hierophant represent *spiritual dominion*.

The Hierophant sits between two carved stone pillars, on a stone throne, in a stone temple. In Key 4, the Emperor sits out-of-doors because the activity he symbolizes is concerned with the ordering and arrangement of external conditions. Like the High Priestess, the Hierophant sits within a building because the mental activity he pictures has to do, mainly, with the inner significance of the conditions that the Emperor rules.

The Hierophant and the Emperor are not two, but one. The old title shows this. The Pope means "The Father." It refers to the conditions of early social organization, in which the head of the family was also the foremost authority in religious matters.

When the Magician has brought into existence a family over which he rules as father and king, he assumes the responsibility of transmitting his wisdom to his children. Thus he becomes the Revealer or Hierophant.

The Father is Chokmah, Wisdom. This is the Wisdom mentioned in *The Pattern on the Trestleboard*, in the statement numbered 2. *Through me, its unfailing Wisdom takes form in thought and word.* Your observations of Key 5 will show that it pictures the transmission of wisdom from the Parent Source.

The Emperor wears armor, but the Hierophant wears the vestments of the peaceful priestly office. These are adaptations of feminine garments to indicate that Intuition is an extension and development of Reason. This happens when an external situation's conditions are linked with the inner, subconscious memory of universal principles. The scroll of the High Priestess pictures memory.

129

Hierophant's Garments

The Hierophant's outer robe is red-orange, assigned to Taurus (♉). It is trimmed with blue-green edging the color complement to red-orange and refers to Scorpio (♏). His undergarment is blue like the robe of the High Priestess and has the same meaning. Over it is a white robe, which symbolizes enlightenment.

The outer garment is fastened at the throat by a silver crescent. In medical astrology, the neck, throat, ears, and jaw are under the dominion of Taurus. The silver crescent refers to the Moon (☽), which is exalted in Taurus.

The Crown

The crown is similar to the triple crown of the Roman Papacy. It is egg-shaped, denotes the One Force (that is, the reality represented by the Cosmic Egg symbol) bestows spiritual sovereignty on man, whose life includes *all the universe's potencies.*

Hanging from the crown, behind the Hierophant's ears, is an ornament in the form of a yoke. It falls behind the Hierophant's ears to call attention to the ears. Observe that only one ear of the Hierophant is visible, just as only one eye of the Emperor is visible. What the inner ear hears is the revelation of a single truth that has many applications. What the Eye of Reason sees is a single Reality having countless aspects.

The Staff

The golden staff represents the life powers dominion through the planes of nature, represented by the knob and three cross-bars. These bars are similar in meaning to the three crowns.

The lowest bar and crown represent the Earth element and the physical plane. Magician's coin or pentacle is also a symbol of Earth. The next bar and crown, counting upward, symbolize Air and the formative world or astral plane, corresponding to the sword in Key 1. The top bar and crown stand for the element Water, end for the creative world or mental plane, represented by the Magician's cup. The knobs at the tops of staff and crown are Fire, and Atziluth or the Archetypal World, corresponding to the wand on the Magician's table.

Crossed Keys

The crossed keys at the Hierophant's feet represent the Sun (gold) and Moon (silver). They suggest that an understanding of the power of light (gold) and its reflection (silver) unlocks the mysteries of life. The keys' wards show a bell and clapper design, intended to indicate the importance of sound vibration and hearing function.

These are the traditional keys to heaven and hell. The key to heaven is gold, where the Sun ($\odot$) rules. The silver key is associated with hell because of the relation between the Moon and Hekate. Thus the silver key is the powers of subconsciousness, and the golden key represents the powers of super-consciousness.

From another perspective, the gold key is Astrology, and the silver key is the Tarot.

The Throne

The stone throne is ornamented and, therefore, a product of human adaptation. Wherever one finds a throne in the Western Tradition's symbolism, it refers to ehben (אבן). Stone is a symbol of union because its first two letters spell Ab (אב), meaning "father," and the last two spell Ben (בן), meaning son.

Place in a row the three Tarot Keys corresponding to the letters א, ב, and ג (ן). These are Keys 0, 1, and 13, and you will *see* something that will give you a better understanding of the word's inner significance.

Pillars

The pillars, like those of the High Priestess, represent the Law of Polarity. Each capital part of the design resembles the letter "U," one English equivalent for Vav (ו). The rest of the pillars' ornamentation represents the union of masculine and feminine potencies and thus relates to the Law of Gender.

The Two Priests

The priests who kneel before the Hierophant wear robes embroidered with flowers in the Magician's garden. Thus the two ministers stand for desire and knowledge. The orphreys or Y's on their garments are variants of the yoke symbol. They are yellow, the color associated with Mercury and the Magician, to show that both desire and knowledge are under the yoke (direction) of self-consciousness.

The Grey Background

The background is gray, a color associated with Hokmah (Chokmah) Wisdom, which the Hierophant symbolizes. Gray is a balanced mixture of white and black. It's another suggestion of the union of the known and the unknown or the blending of spirit and matter. Gray is also the result of the mixture of any pair of complementary colors. Thus it is a symbol of the mixing and balance of the influence of all pairs of opposites.

Checkered Carpet

The alternating squares of white and black represent order and reason. By their alternating colors, it suggests the alternation of day and night. Thus they refer to the Law of Rhythm and periodicity.

Ten crosses of equal arms appear on this Keys, one on each hand of the Hierophant, four (enclosed in circles) on the carpet, and two in the keys' handles. They represent the ten Sephiroth.

They also represent the mystical number, 4,000. This is because each cross is a letter Tav (ת) in ancient Hebrew. The value of Tav is 400. Therefore ten Tavs represent 4,000. This number 4,000 is one of several numbers used to describe perfection. It is a symbol for the ALL.

Summary

Key 5 shows the One Life-power as being the Teacher of humanity. Its correspondences and associations instruct us that our contact with the Inner Teacher is using mental hearing.

The Inner Teacher is the Guru so often mentioned in writings on Hindu occultism. In those books, we find many counsels who may be summed up in the admonition: "Revere your Guru." Exoteric Hinduism corrupts this into the most slavish obedience to a personal teacher, but the real meaning is different.

To receive instruction from the Inner Teacher, we must first recognize His presence in our lives. Having known Him, we must submit to His authority. This chapter and the Key it explains are intended to help you gain this recognition. They will enable you to arrive at the degree of understanding and discrimination which will permit you to distinguish the Inner Voice of Intuition from telepathic invasions from other personalities, incarnate or discarnate, human or non-human.

To avail yourself of guidance and instruction from the One Teacher, study this chapter carefully. The steps to be taken are:

1. Acknowledgment of the actual presence of the Teacher;

2. Daily acts of attentive *listening* for His instruction;

3. A careful study of the content of all messages received through interior hearing. True Intuition unfolds principles. It does not counsel what is merely convenient. It is always concise, clear, and its meaning is unmistakable. It never flatters: more likely. It will reprove. It never misleads and can stand the severest spiritual, moral, and intellectual tests. As Lao-tzu says: "Its counsel is always in season."

4. Obedience to the instruction. When you distinguish a genuine intuition, take steps to carry it out in action. You will never be pressured or intimated, yet you MUST obey because implicit obedience will be understood as the only way to solve whatever problem you have to master.

Chapter 15

DISCRIMINATION

As a pictograph, the letter Zain (ז) is a handheld weapon, like a sword. Thus it suggests active instruments employed in overcoming hostile forces or entities.

A sword is an instrument of *cleavage*, something capable of making sharp divisions. This refers to a mental faculty the Hindus call Buddhi. It is the *determinative* or *discriminative* faculty, the power to perceive *differences*. This power is at the root of self-consciousness because it is the self-consciousness that things are regarded as many separate parts rather than a single unity.

Note carefully that the *Many* are only *apparently* unrelated. Buddhi is the power that makes things and conditions *seem to be real in and by themselves*. These seeming realities are but reflections of the One Reality, mirrored in the universal subconsciousness.

All such reflections, that is, everything which changes and is impermanent, are phases of illusion. Therefore, in the absolute sense, unreal since it is the attention of self-consciousness to certain ideas that act upon subconsciousness to bring your thoughts into active expression. This power of perceiving differences, that is, *to create illusions*, is a fundamental necessity to manifest individual self-consciousness.

Recall that manifestation is the way the One Identity appears to *Itself*. The instrument of its self-perception is self-conscious awareness. *The Book of Tokens* says, "For the sake of creation, the One Life that I am seemeth to divide Itself, becoming Two."

The two units from this semblance of division are termed, respectively, the *superior* and *inferior* natures. Though distinguished as superior and inferior, one just as important as the other. The superior nature is self-consciousness and represented The Magician (Key 1). The inferior nature is the universal subconscious matrix, which reacts to the superior nature's direction and is the High Priestess (Key 2).

Discrimination becomes most valuable when we use it to perceive the difference between the real and the unreal. While appearances enslave us, we mistake the unreal for real. When we wake from our dream to our true nature, we begin to understand reality.

Tarot pictures reality in terms that subconsciousness understands. It tells the truth about appearances. The intelligent study and contemplation of its symbols constitute a phase of right discrimination. This is a practical method whereby you may turn from the unreal to the real.

Number 6

Recall the keywords for number 6 from Chapter two.

6. RECIPROCATION; interchange; correlation; response; coordination; cooperation; correspondence; harmony; concord; equilibration; symmetry; *Beauty*.

The number 6 means reciprocation, the act of giving and receiving mutually. This is a relationship between distinct and seemingly separate entities or a relationship between parts of an organism or mechanism.

Reciprocation is the relationship between self-conscious and subconscious phases of mental activity. Self-consciousness *gives* suggestions to subconsciousness. The latter *receives* the suggestions, works them out, and *gives back* the results to self-consciousness.

In Key 6, the relationship is reciprocation between super-consciousness and human personality, when the latter is considered a combination of self-consciousness and subconsciousness. Recall that subconsciousness means the totality of the Life-power's activity below the level of self-consciousness.

Also, *self-consciousness* is not the SELF. The true SELF is identical to super-consciousness. Self-consciousness is that phase of the Life-power's activity, which manifests an *awareness* of the SELF, but the SELF, which is the subject of this awareness, is superconscious.

The 17ᵗʰ Path is the Perceptive Intelligence (Sekhel Ha.Her.gesh). It is prepared for the Faithful Ones (Saints), so they are clothed with the Holy Spirit. It is called the Foundation (Yesod) of Beauty (Tiphareth) and is placed among the Supernals (upper realms).

Perceptive Intelligence suggests ideas of the arrangement, to classify, and to set in order. Primarily, it means *to separate*. This indicates activity characterized by duality, contrast, and a tendency to divide things and conditions to distinguish one from another.

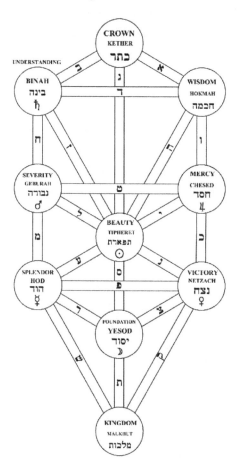

The 17th Path connects Binah to Tiphareth. Notice that the Path of Zain is the Foundation of Beauty. That is because the Tree of Life has its roots in Heaven, and the fruit is Malkuth.

"There is an eternal tree called the Ashvattha, which has its roots above and its branches below."

"Its roots above, its branches below, this is the eternal banyan tree (ashvattha). That alone is the brightness of Brahman! That alone is called the Immortal! On it, all the worlds rest!" – Katha Upanishad 6:1.

Love and Hate

Reciprocity between opposites, when it is harmonious, expresses itself in emotions as *Love*. An inharmonious relationship is akin to *Hate*, the inversion of Love. Love and hate are human emotions. Also, they are *spiritual* emotions because love and hate are root-emotions. All other emotions and desires take on the character of either one or the other. The Bible says God is Love, but it also speaks God's wrath. Jacob Boehme says the wrath, or fire-spirit, is the root of nature.

Through love, we approach the inner, superconscious life of God. Hate takes us into the Divine wrath field, and we become identified with the cycles of necessity and pain that characterize nature in its apparent separation from the Divine.

If both Love and Hate are spiritual, they must be eternal. When cosmic manifestation takes place, the process of involution becomes operative. This process is the separation of the One Thing into the appearances of parts. Jacob Boehme described this as the "fiery anguish" of the turning wheel whereby all things come into separate manifestation. As humans, we are on the Path of Return, which is the process of evolution. We are headed back toward Unity.

To keep going in the right direction, we must employ the synthesizing, attractive force of love, and our desires and emotions must be rooted in that. Love is always a uniting power.

This is related to discrimination because we employ the separative faculty to determine our emotional life's true color.

Key 6, The Lovers, brings out the idea that pairs of opposites, however antagonistic they may seem to be, are complements. The Lovers are not merely the man and woman in this Key. These symbols stand for all opposites, including the opposition of self-consciousness and subconsciousness. The main lesson in this Key is the universe is an expression of the power of love, producing harmonious balance in the operation of the various pairs of opposites that enter into the manifestation pattern.

Gemini - ♊

Key 6 is attributed to Gemini, the Twins. This is another expression of discrimination and separation. The symbol for Gemini is ♊. By its shape, it shows that opposites are different aspects of the One Thing. For example, heat and cold are the two extremes of temperature, and past and future extremes of time.

Mercury (☿) rules Gemini and is symbolized by the Magician. Self-consciousness is the phase of mental activity that controls the faculty of discrimination and utilizes it for acquiring knowledge concerning the true meaning of man's environment.

No planet is exalted in Gemini. Right discrimination balances all our internal forces' activity without exalting any one of them above the others. Remember, the inner powers of humanity are the inner planets or chakras. Because the universe is ONE, and all things in it are related, there is a correspondence between the stars outside man's body and those interior centers of force or chakras. The stars, the wise rule, are the *interior* stars, not the celestial bodies in outer space.

Mercury, or self-consciousness, is the maker of interpretations and has rulership over subconsciousness through the law of suggestion. Unskillful use of this power leads to misinterpretation experience. The result is confusion in mind, which uncertainty is reflected in our external lives as misery of various kinds.

Discrimination

As we become better trained, our interpretations become more accurate, and order takes the place of chaos in our mental life and external circumstances.

Discrimination begins with accurate classification of differences. From this knowledge is passed to a yet higher perception, wherein it finds that every pair of opposites is a dual manifestation of a single activity.

Through discrimination, we discover that these reconciling unities are themselves under the law of polarity. When we succeed in discovering the unity, which is a reconciler between two opposites, we have found something neither positive nor negative.

The process of right discrimination leads, at last, to mental recognition of a Unity that transcends all pairs of opposites. A Unity we cannot define, a *Unity* for which *silence* and *darkness* are symbols.

This Unity is not an intellectual abstraction. It may be directly known and perceived, even though words can describe it. Such direct perception is the outcome of right discrimination, resulting from our learning to unify the pairs of opposites and rise above their influence.

Smell

The function assigned to Zain (ז) and Key 6 is the sense of smell. Smell is associated with discrimination. Our English noun "scent" is from a French verb meaning "to discern by the senses." Odors are among the most powerful and subtle means of stimulating the associative functions of the mind. Hence the Egyptian god Thoth, corresponding to Hermes and Mercury, was sometimes represented as having a jackal's head because of that animal's keen sense of smell.

Summary

Keep close watch this week upon your desires and impulses. Check on your tendency to obey impulses without first submitting them to the light of reason. Discriminate between helpful actions and unimportant ones, between those which are purely selfish, and those that reflect the influence of the unifying force of love.

Be careful to discriminate intelligently. There is a false notion that it must be wholly unconcerned with personal happiness or pleasure for an impulse to be good or useful. This is a big mistake, for love expresses itself in happiness, joy, and well-being.

Poor discrimination makes people believe that happiness and well-being are selfish. Anyone developing awareness between their own mental and physical states and other people suffers from no such delusion.

Keep up this practice from now on. Unselfishness and consideration for others are marks of the true master of occultism.

YELLOW: In every case, except the sun, the yellow in this card is beside red, or red and green. The five fruits on the tree behind the woman are yellow, with red checkers. The flames behind the man are yellow, with red at the base, after the blue and yellow manner in a flame from an old-fashioned gas-jet. The angel's hair is yellow, red, and green. The angel's flesh is yellow but diluted somewhat to give the appearance of flesh.

BLUE: Background, but not above the angel's head.

GREEN: Foreground and foliage, the serpent on the tree, angel's hair (with yellow & red)

VIOLET: Angel's garment; mountain (dilute.)

GOLD: Sun and background above angel (if not gold, use yellow).

WHITE: Clouds.

BLONDE: Woman's hair.

BROWN: Tree trunk behind the woman.

RED: Angel's wings. See also note under YELLOW.

Chapter 16

THE LOVERS

The sun in Key 6 is golden. It is a symbol of that which is the goal of work, namely, enlightenment or illumination. It also represents the One Force, which is differentiated into the various pairs of opposites.

Raphael - רפאל

The angel is Raphael, archangel of Air (△), an angel of the planet Mercury (☿), which rules Gemini (♊). By its form, his hair suggests flames. The yellow represents the influence of Mercury. The red stands for Mars (♂), and action and passion. The green is the color of Venus and symbolizes the power of imagination. Thus, the planets' colors that rule Aries, Taurus, and Gemini are blended in the angel's hair. The suggestion is that in discrimination, we make use of reason (red, Aries, Emperor), and imagination and intuition (green, Venus, Empress, and Hierophant) to make correct classifications (yellow, Gemini, Lovers).

The angel's skin is yellow for the element of Air and the Life-Breath. In the Tarot color scale, yellow is Key 1, the Magician and Mercury. Also, yellow is assigned to Gemini, a Mutable Air sign Ruled by Mercury.

His wings are red to show that right discrimination includes right desire and finds expression in right action.

The angel's robe is violet, blending the red of action with the blue of mental substance. Violet is also the color of royalty and dominion, showing that right discrimination leads to control of conditions. Recall from Chapter 12 that violet is the color of Jupiter and the Wheel of Fortune. It represents that *reason clothes itself in the vision of reality.*

The angel is superconsciousness. He rests on a cloud symbolizing superconsciousness's powers and activities are partly hidden from us because we have not yet developed, as yet, the organic centers in our brains through which superconsciousness is realized.

The angel's name, Raphael (רפאל), means "God is the healer." In Alcalay's dictionary, רפ means, to cure, heal. The last two letters,אל , are the name of God associated with Chesed.

This agrees with the Egyptians that say Thoth (Mercury) is the god of medicine. It also suggests that right discrimination leads to the recognition of Unity, which is the ALL. The real healing is the attainment of inner and outer *wholeness*.

The Mountains

The mountain in the background is a symbol of attainment and realization. It is the height whereon stands the Fool and the Hermit in Key 9. In Key 6, the mountain is in the background symbolize the truth that we can discriminate because there is that in us which has already reached the loftiest pinnacles of understanding.

The mountains and Raphael's tunic are Purple, the color of Jupiter. In the Mixed Triplicity system, Jupiter is dignified by day and night in Air signs.

That Man and the Zodiac Tree of Life

The man corresponds to the Magician, the Emperor, and the minister in Key 5, whose dress is decorated with lilies. He is also Adam in the Bible allegory of Genesis. In Tarot, he is self-consciousness.

Behind him is a tree, whose leaves or fruit are triple flames. They represent the twelve signs of the zodiac, subdivided into three decans (divisions of ten degrees) for each sign. Hence they represent the twelve basic types and the thirty-six subtypes of human personality.

145

The Woman and the Tree of Knowledge

The woman corresponds to the High Priestess and the Empress, and the minister is wearing roses in Key 5. She is also Eve, the mother of all. Thus she stands for subconsciousness.

Behind her is the Tree of the Knowledge of Good and Evil, in contrast to the Tree of Life behind the man. It bears five fruits representing the five senses and the five subtle principles of sensation known to occultists as the five elements: Ether (Quintessence), Fire, Water, Air, and Earth.

Nachash – נחש – The Serpent

The coiled serpent around the tree is the serpent-power, kundalini. It is also the serpent of temptation. In Alcalay's Dictionary, Nachash נחש means serpent, snake, sorcery, magic, and *coppersmith*. That is someone that works with copper or desire. Nachash is numerically 358, which is also Messiah, משיח, the Anointed. Messiah is translated Christos in Greek and Christ in English.

It means the serpent-power of vibration is the force that at first leads us into temptation through delusions and then delivers us from evil when we know how to apply it to overcome our errors.

The man looks at the woman, but the woman looks upward toward the angel. Whatever self-consciousness observes is some activity of subconsciousness. However, *subconsciousness, brought under the influence of right discrimination, may reflect the activity superconsciousness.*

The right exercise of self-conscious powers brings this about. All our miseries and limitations result from subconscious developments of erroneous interpretations of our experience. Self-consciousness makes these wrong interpretations, and Self-consciousness must correct them. Subconsciousness has the power of independent inductive reasoning. The premises determine its production of mental imagery, *or mental seeds*, planted by self-conscious thinking.

The first step in taking advantage of this law is to learn it, as you have just done. It follows that if you plant correct premises, then subconsciousness will work out the corresponding consequences. Subconsciousness is the body-builder and ruler of the electrochemical and other phenomena of the organism. Therefore, if you interpret your place in the universe correctly, an inevitable consequence will be that subconsciousness makes adjustments to your body to express this accurate interpretation.

In Key 6, the man and woman are nude because self-consciousness conceals nothing of its nature in right discrimination. Either member of the mental pair assumes no disguise. They have nothing to be ashamed of, nothing to hide. Their relation is that of lovers, not that of opponents. Thus we know that this Key is a symbol of mental health and the right adjustment of the relationship between the two fundamental modes of human consciousness. There is no confusion here. The two stand apart, each in the right place. The practical application is this:

Practical Exercise

Subconsciousness is amenable to suggestion. It is the High Priestess, and through its connection with Gimel, it is associated with the 3rd Path of the Uniting Intelligence.

"The 13th *Path* is the Unity Directing Consciousness (*Sekhel Man.hig Ha.Achdut*). It is the essence of Glory and the reward of the spiritual ones.

Meditate upon the idea of the power and knowledge of the superconscious plane. From one perspective, the *Tree of Life the connecting Paths map and describe the powers and consciousness available to humanity.* They are literally and figuratively our constitution. From another perspective, the Tree of Life is God's covenant with humanity. It is the Laws that govern the Universe.

The Unity Directing Consciousness is accessible to you through your subconsciousness. The highest function of subconsciousness is to act as an agency of the Uniting Intelligence.

Consider a suggestion that releases subconsciousness from bondage to your former misunderstandings. Speak directly to subconsciousness, as if to another person, and say:

Henceforth, you are free from the influence of any misinterpretations of experience resulting from errors in my self-consciousness. You will refuse to accept, or act upon, such misinterpretations of experience. Instead, you will be guided by the influx of superconscious life and wisdom.

Under this influence, you will set my body in perfect order. Through this wisdom, you guide me alright in all my affairs. By reflecting on this boundless power, you will give me the ability and strength to accomplish all I have to do.

This is a magical formula. Use it as given here. Elaborate it to fit your unique aims. It will work marvels of transmutation in your life.

Look at Key 6 five minutes every day before reading the chapter.

At least once a day, pause long enough to call up mental images of the Keys you have now studied, from Key 0 to Key 6. Remember that they are portraits of certain aspects of your real self. As you complete this brief mental review, try to realize that what the Keys picture is operative throughout your life.

Whatever you do, at work or play, is an expression of powers pictured by these Keys.

If you think of this, you will transfer the Tarot's printed designs into your brain, where they will become incarnate centers of power within you.

Chapter 17

RECEPTIVITY-Will

From Chapter 2, we learned the meanings of the number 7.

EQUILIBRIUM (the application of the laws of symmetry and reciprocation); *mastery*; poise; rest; conquest; peace; safety; security; art; *victory*.

Number 7

In Hebrew, seven is שבע, *sheh.vah*. Spelling the same letters with a different pronunciation is the word meaning: full, satisfied, and abundance. Also, these letters from a verb meaning to swear, to vow, to confirm by oath.

Among the meanings of 7 are mastery, conquest, peace, safety, security. These words are related to the root verb, meaning to be filled, satisfied. We associate peace and safety with abundance and plenty. Conquest, another meaning of 7, is the result of carrying definite purpose into action. Peace follows conquest, and conquest itself leads to the establishment of equilibrium between contending forces. Seven suggests two contending forces and one reconciler between them. Therefore Key 7 symbolizes a power that can establish harmony and brings order out of chaos. It is a power of adaptation and adjustment.

Willpower

Seven is power and WILL, but the esoteric concept of Will is not a *personal* facility. Will is not something strong-minded people possess, while the timid are devoid of it. Will is the living, motivating power behind the entire universe.

Every person and thing in creation has an equal share in it. Remember the Pattern words: "All the power that ever was or will be is HERE, NOW."

We all have access to an unlimited supply where we differ in the degree of our ability to express this power through our personalities.

Will-power is cosmic energy, not a personal force. So long as men suffer from the delusion that they possess wills of their own, they remain in bondage. To think of Willpower as one's personal property or attribute is absurd. One might as well claim to own the air one breathes.

In all the universe, there is only One Willpower. It is the power expressed through all the laws of life. Through want of right discrimination, an individual may presume to have "will." They may go so far in their delusion as to think they can pit that imaginary will stand against the laws of life. Men and women who discriminate are not so deluded.

Hence, Key 7, The Chariot, pictures the true willpower and humanity's relation to it. Notice how this Key follows the one which represents discrimination. Key 6 shows the power-source behind and above self-consciousness, and subconsciousness (the two aspects of personal life) is a superconscious reality. It is superior to every personal limitation. Therefore, it is a logical consequence that willpower must be super-personal.

Invariably people whose achievements express mastery deny that they have any will of their own. Jesus said, "I have *no will* save to do the will of him that sent me." The counsel of masters to seekers is to follow in their footsteps: Above all else, rid yourself of the delusion of self-will. Learn to be receptive to the inner guidance of the only Willpower there is. Obey the true Will which is above you and behind you. Remember always that the true Will is *never* your own.

The pictograph for the Cheth is a *wall of a tent* or *fence*. This implies an *enclosure* or *field under cultivation*. Primarily, the field intended is the universe, including all manifested objects and energies. In man, the field is the personality, and the master of the personality is the true I AM or Inner Self.

A fence implies a field that has been set aside for a particular purpose. And like a field, the personality may be cultivated. That is, the potencies of willpower may be brought into active manifestation through a personal vehicle that has been adequately prepared.

Willpower may be likened to the seed from which all possibilities are developed and brought from latency into active manifestation. Give this idea of attentive consideration. It will shed light on the correct function and purpose of personality. You will begin to understand the actual value of personality as an instrument whereby you may make progress.

Personality is an instrument. It must never be mistaken for the workman who employs it. It is always the field, never the cultivator. You are not your body. You are not your emotions. You are not your mind. If you were, you could not apply the possessive case to them. You do not possess what you are.

The 18th Path is called the Intelligence of the House of Influx (עפש). From investigations, a secret is transmitted/attracted to all who dwell/cleave to its shadow. Those who walk the 18th Path bind themselves to investigate the substance (reality) transmitted (emanating) from the Cause of Causes.

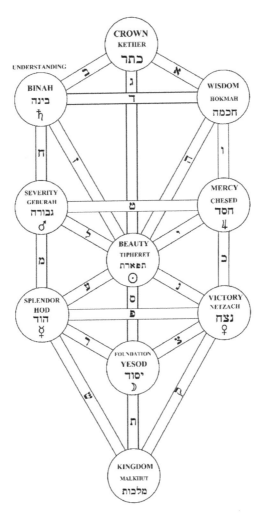

The noun *she.fah* (עפש), meaning influence, suggests water. The Hebrew *she.fah* occurs once in the Old Testament.

They will summon peoples to the mountain and there offer the sacrifices of the righteous; they will feast on the abundance (שֶׁפַע) of the seas, on the treasures hidden in the sand (חוֹל)." – Deuteronomy 33:19

The mental state which permits the greatest possible expression of willpower, and the highest degree of control of circumstance, is one that grasps the truth that human personality is the abode or dwelling of a power which flows into the conscious and subconscious levels of personality from a plane above. This descending influence is the only true Willpower. It is free from every restriction whatever; it is the only free Will.

OBTW.

Notice that the same letters that spell sand (חוֹל) form a verb meaning, twist, turn around, and dance in a circle. Numerically this word is 44, which is also the value of blood (דם) and magic or flame (לדט). And so the secret treasure hidden in the blood is your source of magic. I add this note to show you just how much mining it takes to extract the meaning from The 32 Paths of Wisdom and the Bible.

A field is a specific, limited area. *A word is a definite idea linked to a form* that makes it intelligible; a word endows an idea with a specific meaning. All definite words are words of power. That's why speech is assigned to Cheth. Speech, we mean both spoken words and the silent language of thought.

Our habits of speech reveal the degree of Will development. Words we use continually, every day, and the meanings we attach to them, are the patterns of our life expression. This does not mean that persons who use big words express life more completely than those whose speech is simple — quite the contrary. A magician uses care in selecting their words so that they accurately express their thoughts. In your selection, choose positive, strong, courageous words. These words are essential requirements for the unfoldment of willpower.

Words and thoughts that express positive ways of overcoming problems build positive mental, emotional, and physical states. Complaining while doing nothing leads to confused thinking, chaotic feelings, physical disease, and a chaotic environment.

Certain words have specific vibratory power when spoken or sung. Words like *Om*, various divine and angelic names as well as certain artificial sound combinations have power. The use of such unique words is a difficult art. Hindus call it Mantra Yoga. [*Mantra Yoga and Primal Sound* by Dr. David Frawley is a concise book on the subject.]

Mantas are real power. Of the power of sound, Madame Blavatsky says in *The Secret Doctrine* that it is "a tremendous force, of which the electricity generated by a million Niagara could never counteract the smallest potentiality when directed by occult knowledge." Not a plaything for the idly curious, who merely "want to see what will happen."

Cancer - ♋

In the *Sepher Yetzirah,* Cancer, the Crab, is attributed to Cheth and Key 7. The crab is a shelled animal and related to the meaning of Cheth, the fence which suggests ideas of safety and security.

In medical astrology, Cancer rules the chest. It is the fence of bones that protects the heart and lungs.

The Moon rules Cancer, and the planet Jupiter is exalted. Our habitual subconscious mental states (the Moon, Key 2) have rulership over our expression of Willpower. And Willpower expresses itself in cyclic activity as Key 10, the Wheel of Fortune and Jupiter.

The Chariot

The Chariot is a movable fence that protects its rider. Also, the Chariot is a *vehicle.* The Bhagavad-Gita 6.34 reads:

> The chariot of the body. The five horses represent the five senses (tongue, eyes, ears, nose, and skin). The reins, the driving instrument, symbolize the mind, the driver is the intelligence, and the passenger is the spirit soul.

This is what is meant by "Intelligence of the House of Influx." Right discrimination shows that personality has no power of its own. Personality is a vehicle of power, an instrument through which power is made manifest. The place of personality in the cosmic order is an intermediate agency that the one Willpower is brought to bear upon the states and conditions which constitute our environment.

Once you comprehend this, you see just how powerful you are. Understand the awesome responsibility placed upon humanity to shape our thoughts, words, and deeds in agreement with the *House of Influx Consciousness.*

Summary

This week, look at Key 7 while you color. Bring repeatedly to mind that your personality is an instrument or vehicle for the expression of the limitless Willpower which manifests itself throughout the universe. It is the power that formed our personalities into specific fields of expression for the One Life.

Dedicate yourself to an ever-increasing measure or receptivity to the influence flowing into your field of personal consciousness from the superconscious plane above. Frame this vow of dedication in a sentence that expresses the idea briefly and clearly.

WATCH YOUR HABITS OF SPEECH AND THOUGHT so that you may make them harmonize with your vow of dedication.

COLORING INSTRUCTIONS

YELLOW: Background, chariot wheels.

GREEN: Trees and grass, wreath under the rider's crown.

BLUE: Stream, and faces in crescents on shoulders. Deeper shade on the canopy. The panel behind the charioteer and wings in front of the chariot (not the disk between them) should also be of this darker shade.

GRAY: Chariot and chariot pillars, wall before the city (on both sides of the chariot).

GOLD: Crown, belt (not figures), collar edging, ornament in the square on the breastplate, disk between wings, scepter in right hand (except the crescent at the top of scepter).

SILVER: Crescents on shoulders, and crescent on scepter: stars on canopy and back panel.

WHITE: Cuffs, castles in the city (not rooftops), shield on the chariot, white sphinx, stripes on headdresses of both sphinxes. The design on the skirt of the rider is also white but difficult to paint. It is advisable to leave it as is.

STEEL: Armor on arms of rider.

BRASS: Breastplate (this is a greenish-yellow, to simulate brass).

BLONDE: Hair.

RED: Roof-tops. The symbol on the shield in front of the chariot.

Chapter 18

THE CHARIOT

The title of this Key is related to the number 7 because the Pythagoreans called seven the *vehiculum* of man's life. Key 7 symbolism is an adaptation from the Pythagorean description of the Spirit as the rider in the chariot of personality. The *Kathopanishad* says:

"The Self is the rider in the chariot of the body, guided by the intellect as charioteer, drawn by the senses as powerful horses, controlled by way of the mind serving for the reins. Thus runs the vehicle throughout experience. The Self, conditioned by the senses and the mind, is called the Enjoyer by those who know. He who is forsaken by the charioteer (intelligent discrimination) and has no idea of guiding the reins his mind, in the proper manner, has no control over the senses and is like a driver of restive horses. He who has the intellect for his driver and the mind for proper reins can reach the other end of the course, the highest essence of the All-pervading THAT ever concealed in all is never manifest. Still, it is grasped by the sharp intellect of those who are trained to minute observation."

This quotation emphasizes the Magician's (Mercury and intellect) importance and Beth (ב), the House. A city is shown in the background of Key 7. It suggests the discriminative power of self-consciousness is behind all that is shown in the foreground.

Walled City

The buildings behind the city's wall have towers surmounted by triangles or pyramids. These are red, and the towers themselves are masculine phallic symbols. The correct development of Willpower symbolized by Key 7 has behind it the constructive function of self-consciousness. Our exercise of this function brings about a lifting-up or sublimation of the physical body's reproductive forces. This is accomplished by a release of the subconscious force psychology calls *libido*.

The wall is a stone fence. In front of it is a wind-break of trees like those growing in the Empress' garden – a living wall. Then comes the river, a wall of water. The foreground is the chariot, a portable fence, carrying a rider wearing armor, another kind of barrier. Thus Key 7 contains repeated references to the letter Cheth (ח).

Ehben (אבן), Stone

The body of the chariot is a cube. Recall that the cube is a symbol of the element of Earth and the physical plane. Also, it stands for truth and order because all its faces are equal, and so are its boundary lines.

The first stone cube in the Tarot is found on the High Priestess. The cube of stone is her throne and seat of power. Therefore, every operation of subconsciousness is based on immutable principles of truth and order, operative throughout the physical plane and higher fields of activity.

The first two letters of *ehben*, Ab (אב), meaning "father," and the last two spell Ben (בן), meaning "son." Thus *ehben* (אבן) signifies the union of the Father (God) and the Son (humanity).

The noun *Ab* (אב), Father is a name associated with Chokmah, Wisdom, and the 2nd Sephiroth on the Tree of Life. Chokmah's attributes are:

1. The forces of the zodiac;

2. The life-force expressed in the perfect order manifested by astronomical phenomena.

From the same source comes our life-force, which is derived from the heavenly bodies' radiant energy.

The cycles of the transformation of this radiant energy within our bodies and our environment's physical things cause all phenomena. The chariot's wheels represent these cycles. And the wheel refers to the symbolism of Key 10, associated with the planet Jupiter (♃) that is exalted in Cancer.

Cheth and Key 7 are assigned the direction East-Below. This is a combination of the directions Below (Gimel - the High Priestess) and East (Daleth - the Empress).

Cheth and Key 7 connects the lower end of the north-east vertical line (Key 4 - the Emperor) and the south-east vertical line (Key 5 - the Hierophant).

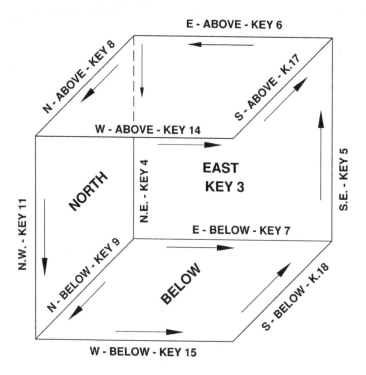

East-Above is the line at the junction of the upper face (Key 1 – the Magician) and the east face (Key 3 - the Express). This line of East-Above is the one assigned to the Lovers. Note that it connects the *upper* ends of the Emperor's lines or (North-East) and the Hierophant (South-East), just as the line East-Below, assigned to the Chariot, connects the lower ends of the same two vertical lines.

This suggests that the mental activities represented by Key 6 link together reason and intuition (Emperor and Hierophant) at the level of *self-conscious* mental activity described by the Magician.

The functions described by Key 7 unite the powers of the Emperor and the Hierophant at the level of *subconscious* activity represented by the High Priestess.

Key 7 refers to operations of the Life-power at subconscious levels. They are combinations of creative imagination (East - Empress) and memory (Below - High Priestess). These activities link together the subconscious consequences of reason (North-East - Emperor) and intuition (South-East - Hierophant). These operations are related to Cancer, which governs nutrition and digestion. Subconsciousness is the ruling power in those functions (Moon Rules Cancer). Also, the highest functions of Jupiter, working through the solar plexus, or abdominal brain, are brought into play (Jupiter is Exalted in Cancer).

The Chariot

Key 7 shows the vehicle of personality, built by subconsciousness. The emphasis in this Key is on the *vehicle*, considered the portable "House of Influx." Hence, the chariot's body is a cube, to indicate that the personal vehicle is no more than a particular shaping of the same materials that constitute its environment.

These materials flow into the personal vehicle's enclosure, as the river in the picture's background flows into the scene. Like the river, the various cosmic forces flow out of the personal vehicle after forming our activities. None of these activities originates in the vehicle. None remains within it.

Four pillars rising from the body of the chariot support a canopy. Four (4) is the number of order and measurement. It also refers to the four elements: Fire, Water, Air, and Earth. Each pillar is divided into two equal parts, reminding us of the Hermetic axiom: "That which is above is as that which is below."

A ring surrounds the center of each pillar. This is a symbol of Spirit, for the rings are circles or zero-signs. The idea symbolized is that each of the four elements is encircled by the One Spirit.

The starry canopy represents the celestial forces whose descent into the physical plane through the four elements' activity is the cause of all external manifestation. This canopy represents the forces surrounding the earth and seems to be above us in the sky. It also describes the subtle metaphysical forces which are above the level of personality. It is, therefore, a symbol of what Eliphas Levi called "Astral Light."

A shield on the face of the car is protection. It has the same meaning as Cheth (ח), the wall, and wind-break of trees, the river, and the chariot itself. The symbol on the shield is the Hindu lingam-yoni, typifying the union of positive and negative forces.

Above the shield is a variation of the winged disk or globe of Egypt. It is yellow to represent the power of the solar rays, and the wings are blue to symbolize the moisture of the atmosphere, which brings these rays to the earth. It is a symbol of royalty and divinity.

The crown of the charioteer is ornamented with three golden pentagrams (See Chapter 13). Three are shown because the mental dominion we exert through the right use of the power of speech extends over three planes or worlds.

The rider's fair hair is bound by a green wreath, like that on the Fool's head, and symbolizes victory and the plant kingdom. The Charioteer is clad in armor, like the Emperor. The crescents on his shoulders refer to the Moon's rulership in Cancer and symbolize the two aspects of the Life-power Mercy (Chesed) and Severity (Geburah). There is a smiling face in the half-moon on Mercy's side, and in the crescent on the side of Severity is a frowning.

The charioteer's breastplate is greenish-yellow to simulate brass, the metal of Venus. It signifies the protection by using the Empress's power, who carries a shield as a symbol of her protective function. The square on the breastplate represents order and purity, while the three T's of which it is made up refer to Saturn's limiting power, attributed to the letter T, or Tav (ת). The skirt below the armor is divided into eight parts. The designs are geomantic symbols used in making magical talismans. The belt of the charioteer suggests the zodiac. Close examination reveals the symbol for Cancer in one of its panels and a crescent moon in another.

The charioteer's scepter is surmounted by a figure 8, combined with a crescent. This is a combination of the symbol over the Magician's head with the lunar crown of the High Priestess. Thus the charioteer's ensign of authority shows his dominion is the result of a blending of the powers of self-consciousness and subconsciousness.

The Tarot Table

Key 7 is the end of the first row of Keys in your tableau and is a synthesis of them all. It tells you that the chain of events leading to your ability to express willpower starts with the Magician.

Acts of attention (Key 1) set in motion the associative function of subconsciousness (Key 2), which results in the creation of mental images that externalize as our environmental (Key 3). The observation and orderly correlation of the images present themselves to us as facts and circumstances, which we call reason (Key 4). This enables us to test our intuitions (Key 5) to discriminate between the real and the unreal. Thus we become aware of the differences between self-consciousness and subconsciousness and perceive their relation to super-consciousness (Key 5). This discrimination (Key 6), worked out by subconscious processes of deduction and imagination, affects the body-building activities which give us our physical vehicles. Thus, we become aware of Will-power's true nature and perceive that the Universal Self is the rider in every chariot of personality (Key 7).

By the invisible reins of the mind, we *let* the Self-guide the vehicle of personality. The result is that the motive-power of sensation is brought to rest, as are the sphinxes in Key 7.

The Sphinxes

The sphinxes put forward of riddles, and so do the senses. By sensation, we experience all the pairs of opposites — what we like and what we dislike; what seems favorable to our aims, and what seems adverse.

But when the One Self, through the intellect, guides the vehicle of personality, it controls the senses, and the result is security, safety, and peace – as represented by the number 7.

Summary

This week spend some time to realize that your inner Self is above and beyond your personality. Try to understand that this Self is the true Actor in all that you do. Think of your personality as a vehicle, having no power of its own. The power comes flowing from the One Will and taking form as Astral Light and the Sun's rays. By repetition, this concept will become so habitual and natural that everything you think, say and do will be influenced by it. Thus you will be cultivating your field of personality.

Above all, watch your words. Say what you mean, and mean what you say. Get the dictionary habit, and begin enriching your vocabulary with strong, positive, cheerful, hopeful words that express the highest truth you can think.

Use your Thesaurus and dictionary daily. With their aid, you take long strides toward learning the art of genuine magical speech.

Figure 1 represents the Cube of Space viewed from the west, showing the top, west, and south faces. The boundary lines are named, and arrows indicate the direction of the current flowing in each line.

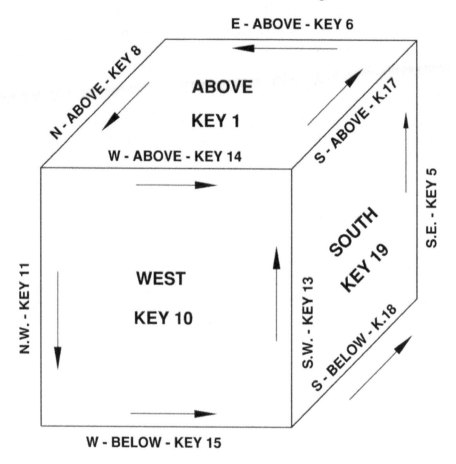

Figure 1

Figure 2 shows the top, bottom, north, and east faces.

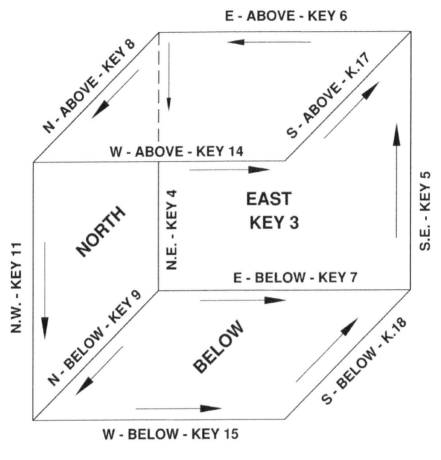

Figure 2

The 12 edges of the cube are assigned to the simple Hebrew letters that are Astrological Signs.

The seven double letters are planets and are assigned to the cube faces with Saturn in the center.

169

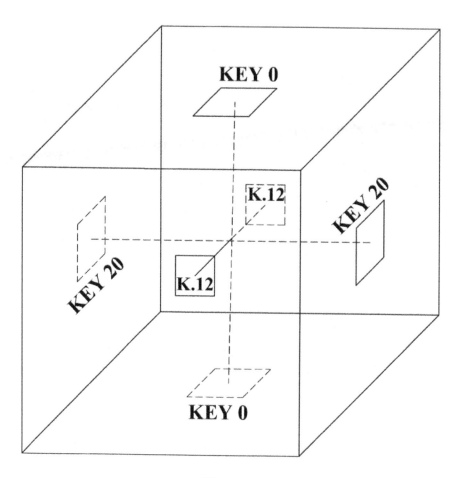

Figure 3

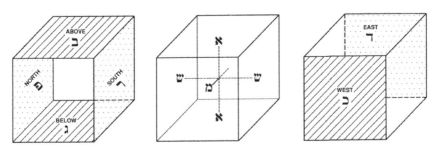

Figure 4

The 3 Mother Letters interior lines connect the faces of the cube.

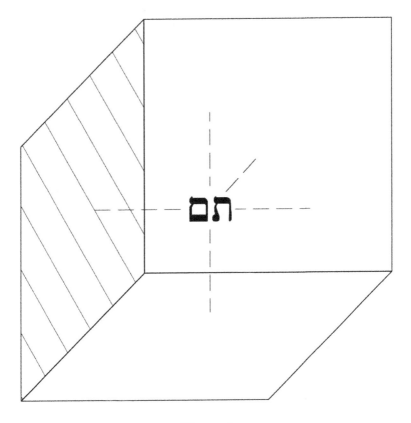

Figure 5

Tav (ת) and final Mem (ם) are in the center.

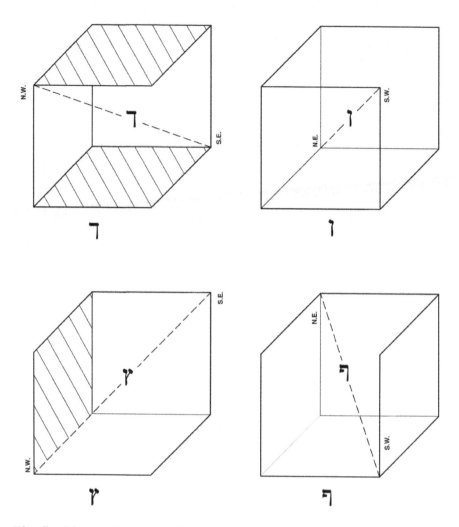

The final letters Kaph (ך), Nun (ן), Peh (ף), and Tzaddi (ץ) are the diagonals.

Key	Hebrew				Direction
0	Aleph	א	F	Mother of Air	Above – Below
1	Beth	ב	I N		Above
2	Gimel	ג	A	double	Below
3	Daleth	ד	L		East
4	Heh	ה	S		North East
5	Vav	ו			South East
6	Zain	ז		simple	East Above
7	Cheth	ח			East Below
8	Teth	ט			North Above
9	Yod	י			North Below
10	Kaph	כ	ך	double	West
11	Lamed	ל		simple	North West
12	Mem	מ	ם	Mother of Water	East-West
13	Nun	נ	ן	simple	South West
14	Samekh	ס			West Above
15	Ayin	ע		simple	West Below
16	Peh	פ	ף	double	North
17	Tzaddi	צ	ץ	simple	South Above
18	Qoph	ק			South Below
19	Resh	ר		double	South
20	Shin	ש		Mother of Fire	North-South
21	Tau	ת		double	Center

173

Chapter 19

THE SERPENT POWER

The Hebrew letter Teth (ט) looks like a coiled serpent, a Great Magical Agent symbol.

The Great Magical Agent

The Great Magical Agent is a force, like gravity and electromagnetism. It is employed every day by everyone. It is cosmic electricity, the universal life-principle, the *conscious* energy which takes form as all existing things and builds them from within. In humans, it manifests as a subtle nerve-force called *Kundalini*, which means "coiled one" in Sanskrit.

Learning to control the Magical Agent is part of the daily work of every student of Ageless Wisdom. One step toward control is establishing a clear perception that the various forms of physical existence are merely transformations of this *one* energy. The world is full of many things. All are disguises for the ONE THING. The essential nature of the One Thing is SPIRIT.

19th Path of Teth - ט

The 19th Path is the Intelligence of the Secret All Spiritual Activities (Sekhel Sod HaPaulot Haruchniot Kulam). It is the influx that permeates from the Supreme Blessing and the Glory of the Highest.

The secret of the right work is to make sure that whatever one does will bring about the intended result. What is the essence of that secret?

The working power is the inexhaustible energy of the One Spirit.

> Don't you believe that I am in the Father and that the Father is in me? The words I say to you, *I do not speak on my authority. Rather, it is the Father, living in me, who is doing his work.* – John 14:10.

That is the secret. Compare it with the word ABN (אבן), *ehben*, in the last chapter. To be sure of success, we must identify the working power as being the One Spirit. By so doing, *we rid ourselves of concern as to the outcome of our works.*

This unconcern about results is by no means indifference. Neither is it a vague, dreamy feeling that "all will be well." One must be specific, knowing what is intended, and fully resolved to bring about positive results. *The thing to avoid is anxiety.*

The *Bhagavad-Gita* says the secret of right work is to have no attachment to results. Many have misunderstood this teaching, especially by those who have twisted it into an excuse for mental laziness.

To be *anxious* about the future, to be *concerned* about results is to make mental images of failure. Anxiety is concentrating on a mental pattern of *what we do not want.* Often, fear is a subconscious determination to fail. Their *will to fail* is based on a *subconscious fear that they lack the power* to carry their projects through completion.

Therefore to remove fear is essential. This is easily affected by understanding that every one of us has at our disposal a power adequate to accomplish whatever we intend to do and whatever we can imagine clearly and definitely.

When we grasp this truth, subconscious fears are dissipated, and with them goes the hidden will to fail.

Begin now to thinking of everything as being a manifestation of Spirit. Think of everything as a direct expression of one radiant *mental* energy. Only those who fail to understand its nature do the Great Magical Agent seem to be a blind, mechanical force.

Learn to think of the *Great Magical Agent as conscious, intelligent energy. Practice* thinking this. Repeatedly, as you contact the various objects in your environment, remind yourself of their real nature. Try to see, hear, smell, taste, and touch the One Spirit everywhere. No matter if this idea is familiar. Get it to permeate your whole organism. Knowing it in your brain is not enough. *Make it second nature by repetition.*

Kundalini

Kundalini is the particular form of the Great Magical Agent utilized for "works of power." Fortunately, it is dormant in most persons. We say, fortunately, because it is a force potent for destruction and debasement as well as for integration and illumination. The Great Magical Agent is not to be trifled with. Do not attempt to awaken it until you understand our instructions and take all the precautions we recommend. You will know what to do, and why, if you study these chapters carefully, for they explain the real secret.

We appeal here to your good sense and your prudence, not to base fears. The ability to control this force may be developed quickly once its nature is understood. The conditions under which it may be brought into activity safely include purity of mind and desire, high aspirations and ideals; it is complete unselfishness in action.

Every attempt to express these states of consciousness through right action makes an actual change in your body. When the sum of a great number of small changes affects a sufficient total alteration, you will find yourself ready to awaken the serpent power, and you will know what to do.

Why is this force called the serpent power? Many persons suppose the snake to be a symbol of evil. These ideas are based on a literal reading of the allegory of the Fall. In the third chapter of Genesis, the serpent more *subtle* than any other beast of the field. (This is the same field represented by the Cheth and Key 7.)

The subtle (ערום) is from a root (ערם) *ah.ram*. It also means *shrewd, astute,* and *crafty.* The same word with different vowel-points *ah.room*, means *naked, bare* and *uncovered.* Here is a marked characteristic of the Great Magical Agent. **It conceals the true nature of things by seeming to expose them uncovered**.

The Great Magical Agent is the indefinable *something* that presents itself to us in various appearances. Under every guise, it seems to show itself openly, without the least concealment. It has taken millenniums for man to learn that every visible form is a veil of concealment for a hidden truth.

They who call themselves "realists" are often farthest from having any idea of the actual Reality. For them, appearances constitute the only truth worth a moment's consideration.

A true "realist" is one not taken in by externals. They understand the subtlety of the serpent's power and turns it to good use. Remember, Genesis, which tells us the serpent was among the creatures of whom it was said: "And God saw that it was good." When reading Scripture, we must take its *whole* teaching into account. The Bible is explicit that the law of the Lord is perfect, and all his works part of a successful process. Throughout the history of humanity, initiates have called themselves and their pupils "good serpents." The Christian warning, "Be wise as serpents," echoes this ancient custom.

The motion of the Magical Agent is serpentine because it is wavy, undulating, and spiral. This coiling, spiral, vibratory movement of the serpent power is one reason for associating it with the number 8, for 8 is a numeral symbol of rhythmic vibration.

To write 8, one begins at the top and describes a letter S, serpentine in form. And the sound of an S is hiss. Writing an 8, one forms curves *reciprocal* to each other. In writing figure 8, we make the same curved lines as Hermes' caduceus by the two intertwining snakes. These are also the lines of movement traced by the serpent power as it moves within the human body. Thus 8 is a diagram representing the serpent power path when it moves through humans' nervous system.

Except 0, figure 8 is the only one that can be written repeatedly, without lifting the pen from the paper. Thus it is a sign of endless activity. This relates 8 to the serpent because snakes shed their skins. The ancients thought snakes renewed their whole bodies. So from time immemorial, the serpent has been a symbol of immortality and eternity.

In Christian occultism, eight is sometimes said to be the Dominical Number because Jesus in Greek is Ιησους, which adds to 888.

Eight is also a symbol for the Holy Spirit, sometimes described as feminine. Thus Key 1, the Magician and Strength have a horizontal (feminine) 8 over their heads.

Again, 8 symbolizes the ancient doctrine that all opposites affect a single cause and that balanced, reciprocal action and reaction between opposites results in harmony.

Leo - ♌

In the *Sepher Yetzirah*, Teth (ט) is assigned to Leo, ruled by the Sun. Leo governs the heart, back, spine, and spinal cord. Note that the spinal cord is the primary channel for the physical manifestations of the serpent power. Among Israel's tribes, Leo is represented by the Tribe of Judah, whose standard bore a lion.

The Hebrew name for Leo is ARIH (אריה), *Arieh*. The letters of this word may be rearranged to spell RAIH (ראיה), *reaiyah*, sight. Sight is attributed to Heh (ה) and Aries (♈).

The numeral value of these two words, 216, is the same as that of the noun RVGZ (רוגז), *rogaz*, meaning "trembling, vibration." This word is connected with Samekh (ס), Sagittarius (♐), and Key 14. Also, 216 is the number of the word GBVRH (גבורה), Geburah, Strength, or Severity. Geburah, Strength is the title of Key 8 and the fifth. This is the Sphere of Mars, or field in which the power of that planet is active.

These correspondences indicate that strength, or working power, is to be sought in the form of vibration, which is fiery in quality. It is active in the sense of sight and connected with the functions of the heart and spine.

This power is the *light power,* which makes vision possible. It is also the *life power* centered in the heart and coursing through the "main cable" of the spinal cord, where the nerves distribute it to every part of the physical organism.

Summary

Pay particular attention to this chapter and the next. They deal with the force you are using for the regeneration of your personality. Use it, and you will attain the heights. Abuse it, and it will destroy you. It is the *cosmic electricity* mentioned by Madame Blavatsky in *The Secret Doctrine*:

"Mighty word, and still mightier symbol: Sacred regenerator of a no less sacred progeny; of fire – the creator, the preserver, and the destroyer; of light – the essence of our divine ancestors; of flame – the Soul of things."

Practical Instruction

Concerning the Kundalini energy Paul Case says above:

The ability to control this force may be developed quickly once its nature is understood. The conditions under which it may be brought into activity safely include purity of mind and desire, high aspirations and ideals; it is complete unselfishness in action.

Every attempt to express these states of consciousness through right action makes an actual change in your body. When the sum of a great number of small changes affects a sufficient total alteration, you will find yourself ready to awaken the serpent power, and you will know what to do.

This instruction above offers no practical exercise other than complete unselfish action and high aspirations.

Okay, I get, I'm not good enough. I've never found a competent teacher, but I found a few techniques on my own.

Consider your aura as an egg filled with fields and forces. Then visualize your egg is a black stone that you want to extract the ore, that requires heat. But you don't want to raise the temperature too fast.

Once, I was melting 8 ounces of silver and put my carbon rod stirrer into the molten metal. There was a tiny drop of moisture on the top of the rod, and when I put it into the 1800+ sterling silver, the water turned to steam and exploded. A half-ounce of silver splattered onto my face shield. That's what happens when you don't preheat your equipment.

That's also what happens when you get a surge of Kundalini. It can turn all your watery emotions into steam.

To rouse the Kundalini, the first thing you do is preheat your aura by looking at Key 8. Then after a few years, you can crank up the heat to 350 degrees and burn off the volatiles. These are the misinterpretations of reality and the desires that form from illusions. The alchemist calls this "turning your copper (desire) white (pure)."

Then you crank the heat up to 1400+ degrees and burn out the carbon. These are all the old structures that stand between you and what you're seeking or wanting to achieve.

After the fire, what is left in the crucible is put in an acid bath. What doesn't dissolve in the acid is leftover Saturn particles and discarded. Then the gold is precipitated out of the solution, and gold particles' clumps sink to the bottom. Then you pour the solution through the filter, put it into a crucible and heat to 2000+ degrees — the particles of gold fuse together and from a drop.

For a drop of gold (wisdom), the process is an ordeal. But well worth the effort. To be an Alchemist or caster of metals, you have to like Fire.

Enough metaphorical information. For practical instruction on rousing the Kundalini, I recommend KUNDALINI EXPOSED by Santata Gamana.

COLOR DIRECTIONS FOR KEY 8

YELLOW: Background, lion's eye.

GREEN: Foliage, rose leaves, leaves in woman's hair, foreground (but do not extend in the right foreground, because the mountain range carries over to the right).

VIOLET: Mountain (both sides of background).

WHITE: Woman's dress, lion's teeth.

BLONDE: woman's hair.

RED: Roses, lion, flower in woman's hair.

Chapter 20

STRENGTH

In your tableau, Key 8 is the first of the second row of Keys. The second row represents the laws or agencies whereby the Keys' principles from 1 to 7 are carried into operation. Key 8 represents the law, which is the means for expressing the magician's principle of attention.

This law is a *suggestion.* It is explained in Chapter 5 of *Seven Steps.* Review this chapter. In brief, subconsciousness is amenable to control by suggestion. The best suggestions are clear and precise images.

Using a *suggestion,* the force concentrated by acts of attention is carried into manifestation to modify external conditions. Remember, the energy so concentrated is a perfect *Unity*, designated by the Hebrew noun AChD (אחד), *ah.chad or eh.chad.* It is also the Love-force because AChD (אחד), Unity, and AHBH (אהבה), *ah.h'vah*, love is numerically 13. Ponder this in meditation, and you will find another clue to the Secret of Works.

Note that 13 is the number of a Key 13, Death, which you will learn later is related to Unity and Love.

The Woman

The woman in Key 8 is the High Priestess, the Empress, and the Lady Eve of Key 6. She symbolizes the subconsciousness, controlling and directing the functions of our body's organs and directing the currents of Prana, the vital energy or Life. The changes to our personality direct changes to body structure and chemistry. These changes make possible the practical application of the potencies of superconscious life. This work is carried out by subconsciousness operating in conformity to the law of suggestion.

Like the Empress, the woman is fair-haired and crowned with flowers instead of stars. This tells that Key 8 is concerned with organic processes rather than with the inorganic cosmic forces symbolized by the hexagram on the Empress' crown.

Furthermore, flowers are the vegetable kingdom's reproductive organs, and a crown always stands for *will* because the name for the Primal Will is KThR (כתר), Kether, the Crown. Thus the crown of flowers means the human subconsciousness's sovereignty is over the various grades of beings below the human level. Its sovereignty has to do with intelligent control of the serpent power, the agency at work in vegetable, animal, and human reproduction.

Infinity sign - ∞

Like the Magician, over the woman's head is a horizontal 8 or infinity sign in math. She partakes of the Magician's influence and typifies subconscious reaction to the principle the Magician personifies. In one sense, everything symbolized by Key 8 is the development of the symbolism of the roses and lilies growing in the Magician's garden.

Sitting and Standing Symbolism

The Empress and High Priestess sit. This woman, like the one in Key 6, stands. The High Priestess is subconsciousness, conceived as the recorder and preserver of the various impressions originating at conscious and superconscious levels. The Empress typifies the *germination* of mental images through subconscious responses to conscious and super-conscious stimuli.

The standing woman in Key 6 shows a more *active* response of subconsciousness to superconscious potencies and guidance. In Key 8, the standing woman controls all the forces of nature below the human level.

The White Robe

The woman's robe is pure white, like the inner garments of the Fool and the Magician. The clothing represents the purified aspect of subconsciousness. This is accomplished by the intelligent application of the law that subconsciousness is amenable to control by suggestion. White symbolizes the Divine Unity and is an emblem of purity and innocence. This unity leads to regeneration, which results in our realization that the ALL is ONE.

Chain of Roses

The chain of roses which goes around the woman's waist and encircles the lion's neck is intended to represent a figure 8 but is not clearly shown in the picture. Roses symbolize desire. Hence the chain is a systematic series of desires woven together. Rightly cultivated and combined, desires are the most potent form of suggestion. By unique formulation of desire, in harmony with the real nature of things, we can dominate nature's mighty forces below the human activity level.

The Red Lion

The lion is the king of beasts and represents the highest development forms in the kingdoms of nature below the human's level. The lion is the ruling principle of the animal nature. He is also an alchemical symbol of the transmutation of natural humanity's gross forms into the Stone of the Wise, perfected man.

The Lions of Alchemy

In alchemical books, there is Green, Red, and the Old Lion. The Green Lion is the animal nature before it has been ripened and purified. The Red Lion is the animal nature brought under control of human's spiritual being's higher aspects. The Red Lion is in Key 8.

The Old Lion represents a unique state of consciousness that becomes manifest after purification has changed the Green Lion into the Red Lion. In the state of consciousness, which the Old Lion symbolizes, one senses the eternal radiant mental energy directly. Because the Great Magical Agent is before anything in manifestation, it is older than anything else.

Among the ideas suggested by the word *lion* are: rulership, courage, bravery, valor (also symbolized by the color red), tenacity, resolve, decision, and will. We say that a person having these qualities have "backbone." In medical astrology, Leo rules the back and spine.

North-Above is the direction attributed to the letter Teth (ט), and Key 8. The north face is assigned to the letter Peh (פ), Key 16, and Mars. The top face corresponds to the direction Above, assigned to Beth (ב), Key 1, and Mercury.

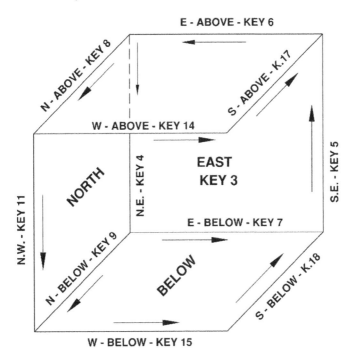

Thus in North-Above are joined the powers symbolized by Keys 1 and 16. Key 1 represents the self-conscious level of mental activity. Key 16 represents the fiery energies that are symbolized by the red outer mantle of the Magician.

Key 8 shows what happens when self-conscious acts of attention control the cosmic fire. Furthermore, since Key 8 is North-*Above*, we may understand that what is pictured in this Key is a direct consequence of the *intentional, conscious practice*. The situation represented by the symbols of this Key is not a spontaneous natural development. It is the result of deliberate intentions and purposes consciously formulated. It is the consequence of knowledge consciously acquired. The outcome of practice is deliberately undertaken.

The law of suggestion works whether we know anything about it or not. But it does not work this way unless we apply our knowledge. Key 8 shows the positive and constructive use of the law of suggestion in the work of personal regeneration. Thus it symbolizes a situation that never occurs without the introduction of an impulse proceeding from the Magician.

The Paradox of Ageless Wisdom

Here we approach one difficulty of Ageless Wisdom. To perform the Great Work, we must undertake the initial stages *as if* we were doing something of our own volition.

It seems that way because it involves a distinct sense of effort. There is a deliberate exercise of power. Ways and means are carefully selected. The initial steps in work require strict self-discipline. No person who does not determinedly "take himself in hand" ever performs the Great Work of regeneration.

The exercises feel like a personal effort in the early stages of the practice. However, this is an illusion. Our discipline consists of mental practice, which gradually realizes that personal effort does not accomplish the work.

By the prolonged practice, sometimes pursued for months and years without any visible result, subconsciousness changes the body. These changes are symbolized in Key 8, and produce the result shown in Key 16, the Tower.

More will be written when you study Key 16. Briefly, we can say the *overthrow of a false conception of personal activity by a lightning-like flash of true inspiration.*

Because few persons have courage and persistence to pursue the preliminary work, all vaporings to the contrary, the time will never come when these first steps will not be required. No suspension of the discipline, for any reason whatever, can be made for the adherents of any school or teacher. For the discipline is not imposed by men or higher beings. It is the consequence of natural laws of physical and mental growth. They can never be changed *because they are part of the essential nature of all living beings.*

Karma – Work – Action

The line of North-Above connects the top end of the North-East line (Heh - the Emperor) to the upper end of the North-West line (Lamed - Justice). Thus Key 8 symbolizes the conscious (Above – Magician) link between Keys 4 and 11.

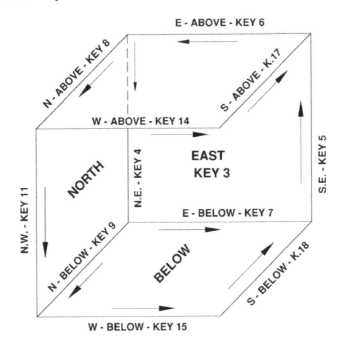

One of the meanings of Key 11 is *Work, Action, or Karma.* Therefore Key 8 is the connecting link that carries the power of Reason, the Constituting Intelligence (Key 4), into the field of activity which has to do with human action and its results (Key 11).

Key 8 is the agency whereby the power of control over our external environment's conditions, symbolized by Key 4, is brought to bear upon all the complex operations of natural law designated by the term *Karma* (Key 11).

This means that Karma *can be modified*. Action and reaction are equal, and today brings us into situations resulting from our past actions. We have to work with these situations as they arise. But it makes a great deal of difference whether we approach them ignorantly or intelligently.

If we know the law, we may produce results not provided by natural reactions to past stimuli. By taming the Red Lion the Cosmic Reason, it can be used to adjust Karmic reactions.

Strength the Link between Zain and Samekh

Also, Key 8 is the link between the Zain (Key 6, The Lovers) and Samekh (Key 14, Temperance). The north ends of these two lines are joined by Key 8. Therefore Strength is a link between that part of Key 6, which shows the woman, the Tree of the Knowledge of Good and Evil, and the serpent, and the part of Key 14, which shows a lion, a vase of water, and a range of mountains over which floats a crown. You have not yet studied Key 14, Temperance, so no explanation is given now. However, interiorly, you already know the meaning by bringing it to your attention now, the seed idea will grow in your subconscious. When you study Chapter 32, you will find that the explanations are easier to grasp.

Key 6	Key 14
Woman	Old (brown) Lion
Tree of Knowledge	Mountain Range & Crown
Green Serpent	Vase of Water

In most Tarot Keys, the picture on the observer's left corresponds to the north's direction. The right is south. The background is east. The foreground is west.

The exceptions are Keys 16, 17, 18, and 19.

We look at the Tarot Keys from the symbolic West, facing the East, so do we look at the Cube of Space from the east, which is an important clue to the meaning of Tarot.

The Outdoors

The scene in Key 8 is an open plain, in contrast to the walled city of Key 7. This symbolizes natural conditions and not artificial conditions of human-made civilization. The law of suggestion is a natural law that is always in operation. It is the *first* law of subconsciousness.

Every kingdom of nature is represented in this picture. The woman stands for the human kingdom. The lion is chief of the animal kingdom. Roses are the royal flowers, and the flowers, grass, and trees belong to the vegetable realm. They grow from the earth, which is disintegrated stone. The background, a mountain, like that in the background of Key 6, completes the mineral kingdom's representation.

This reminds us that all-natural forms and forces are expressions of the *One* and are all subject to the law pictured here. The animal nature is subordinate to the human, the vegetable to the animal, the mineral to the plant. This control does not need to be established. It is already in effect. Many humans experience are the consequences of their negative operation because they do not know to use its positive application.

The difference between a beginner in practical occultism and a great adept is this: The novice has little or no knowledge that subconsciousness at the human level *automatically* responds to the predominant suggestions which originate at the conscious level.

Ignorance sets up reactions that are negative and pain-bearing. Subconscious *control* of forces below their conscious level and molds them into a destructive reaction in their bodies and others. Furthermore, this harmful reaction extends into the realms of nature below the animal kingdom, and the result is that the person finds their control of subconsciousness working *in reverse*. Therefore it seems that everything and everybody *seems* to be against him.

An adept knows that the Great Magical Agent's subtle power conceals the true nature by seeming to expose them uncovered. The adept takes nothing at its face value. They look attentively at the world reported by their senses. Thus the adept detects hidden relationships that gradually become consciously and subconsciously under the One Self's guidance. The One Self is symbolized by the Hierophant, the angel in Key 6, and the charioteer in Key 7. Therefore the personal subconsciousness is purified and wears the white garment of wisdom like the woman in Strength. The result is the kingdoms below the human level become favorable to an adept.

There has been no change in the underlying law. The adept does not gain powers the beginner lacks. The adept uses the already existing law positively. The novice employs the same law *negatively*. The adept is wise, and the beginner is ignorant. That is all, but in that single difference is the difference between freedom and bondage, joy and misery, success and failure, health and disease.

Summary

Your practice this week is highly important. Spare no effort to carry it out. The most valuable chapter you can learn is *seeing through appearances* and discovering the One Reality veiled by them. When dealing with people, keep in mind that it is not the appearance or external details of personality that you speak or write to or that you are in any way concerned. Remember that their inner nature is *identical* to yours. Try to see, with the mind's eye, the real individual behind the mask of personality. Do this with your family members, friends, and business associates, even with the strangers you pass on the street.

At first, this may seem difficult, especially when dealing with those who, for any reason (or unreason), are unpleasant or repulsive to you. Attempt just the same. You will find greater practical values under such circumstances than in your dealings with persons you like.

Don't make the mistake of being sentimental or emotional about it. This is an exercise in mental suggestion. Look deliberately for the good and the beautiful in everyone. Don't just affirm it. Don't pretend it's there, LOOK. You'll find it when you develop eyes to see.

Watch your tongue. Don't gossip. Do not discuss the unlovable qualities of any other person. Make an effort to see the One Self of all men and women you meet as perfect. By telling yourself the truth about all humanity, the power of your thoughts will bless others.

This exercise has far-reaching consequences, which we purposely refrain from discussing now.

It will be better and more enjoyable for you to find out for yourself. This is one of the most valuable, though simple, means of developing a penetrative vision. The individual who has this insight possesses a key to limitless power.

OBTW.

PFC states the practice of looking for the Divinity is not sentimental or emotional. Also, it's not a license to act foolishly.

When I lived in a big city, and my meth neighbor shouts at his walls, I don't knock on his door and look for his divinity when he opens it. And those two people across the street warming themselves at a trashcan fire will kill you for a pack of cigarettes. So I'll practice looking for their divinity from inside my apartment.

Yes, the world is made of subconscious mind stuff. And yes, the Universe is mental, and energy follows thought. However, can you overcome the race mind of 7.5 billion people?

Some things I can affect change. However, many things are above my pay grade.

And so it goes.

TAROT FUNDAMENTALS

Chapter 21

RESPONSE

The law attributed to Key 9 is *Response*. This is:

*Every activity of the human personality is a response
to the initiative of the origination principle of the universe.*

No personal activity has its beginning, source, or origin within the limits of the personality. All *personal* action is derived, reflective, and responsive.

To every one of us, it seems that our states of mind and our actions express personal motives. This semblance of personal initiative affects the most illumined just as it does anyone else. A wise, however, *knows* better. They think differently from those who try to live on the assumption that personal thoughts, feelings, and actions are self-caused. Whenever they are recorded, their words are sure to include some reference because he does nothing of himself.

Personality is the mask of the true Identity. This Identity is superior to and is not limited by the conditions of personality. It is from this inner and superior Identity that all original impulse flows. All the personality activities — the instrument or vehicle— affect this outward and downward movement of the True Identity's energy, or working power, or I AM.

Ageless Wisdom declared there is One Identity in the universe. *This One Identity is the single source of all forms of existence here or anywhere.* Its presence is the substance of everything. The mental quality of the One Identity is what is manifested in any particular expression of consciousness. The energy of the One Identity is what is released in any specific form of activity.

Your personality is but one of its innumerable forms of expression. Your real nature is none other than that ONE. Hence, whatever laws

195

and forces condition your personality activity must be laws and forces proceeding from your *True Identity*.

Yod - י

"The letter *Yud*, a small suspended point, reveals the spark of essential good hidden with the letter Tet (ט). After the initial *tzimtzum*, the contraction of G-d's Infinite light to make a "place" for Creation, there remained within the empty void a single, potential point, or 'impression.' The secret of this point is the power of the Infinite to contain finite phenomena within Himself, and express them to apparent external reality. Finite manifestation begins from a zero-dimensional surface. This is alluded to in the full spelling of *Yud* (יוד): point (י), line (ו), surface (ד). The initial point, the essential power the *Yud*, is 'the little that holds much.'" – *The Hebrew Letters*, by Rabbi Yitzchak Ginsburgh.

Additionally, the letter name Yod (יוד) means hand. It is connected with the doctrine that *the universe's fundamental reality is identical with the power expressed by human beings' handiwork.*

Kabbala says the top point of Yod represents the Primal Will (Kether), while the rest of the letter corresponds to Chokmah (Wisdom, 2nd Sephiroth). This means that all mental activity is derived directly from the essential Will of the *One Identity*. This mental activity, or volition, takes form as Wisdom, based on the entire cosmic order. Thus, the Primal Will's mental activity, symbolized by the upper point of the Yod, expands into the life-force of all beings.

The 20th Path is the Intelligence of Will (Sekhel HaRatzon). It is the trait from which everything is formed. Through this consciousness, everyone can know the essence of Original Wisdom.

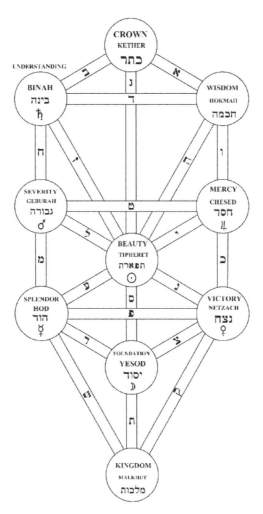

The Path of Yod connects Mercy to Tiphareth. In Alcalay's Dictionary, *Ratzon* (רצון) means *will, goodwill, wish, desire; acceptance; favor*, and *grace*. This state of consciousness reveals that God's Will is the Will to Good. By aligning with God's will, his abundance flows down from Chesed into the One Ego seated in our heart (Tiphareth). From one perspective, the Tree of Life is a symbolic representation of you. And by studying the Tree of Life and its meanings, you're building thought-forms in the Yetziratic Plane. And since these thought-forms are in alignment with the Universe, the mental images persist well beyond the span of human life. This mental is called the Solar, Immortal or Rainbow Body, depending on the author.

What is essential is mentally wrestling with these ideas. Even if you feel mentally overwhelmed, the subconsciousness understands what to do - build a vehicle to house an intelligence between lifetimes.

Astral/Etheric/Spiritual/Soul Body

I hesitate to use the words astral or etheric because many ideas are attached to these words — first, a review of the Four Worlds of the Qabalah.

Atziluth is beyond symbols, words, time, and space. And so there is no need to speculate about some beyond human thought. That leaves three other worlds.

Assiah is the world of the name and form. To understand the nature of your physical body, all you have to do is look in a mirror. Many good books are written on how to maintain a physical body.

That leaves the Briatic and Yetziratic World.

World	Element	Body
Atziluth	Fire	?
Briah	Water	Astral
Yetzirah	Air	Etheric
Assiah	Earth	Physical Body

The idea to keep in mind is the Tree of Life is a part of your occult constitution — the Tree of Life resonance through all worlds. By studying the Tree of Life and its connecting paths, you tell your subconscious that you want to know more about yourself. It's not so important how much you grasp the information intellectually; *what is important is your desire to seek the truth about the Self.*

Subtle Sense of Touch

The hand is the highly organized center of the sense of *touch*, which is assigned to Yod.

The hand is a symbol of how the human mind makes contact with the superconsciousness above it. Thus in Key 1 (Mercury – self-consciousness), the right hand of the Magician has a lifted wand to symbolize the mental activity necessary to contact the higher levels. Furthermore, the uplifted wand symbolizes the sublimation of the serpent-power or libido.

The most intense forms of ecstatic union with the Absolute are often described in imagery approaching the erotic. Why? Because the most intense feeling of pleasure is experienced through the sense of touch. The higher forms of interior union with the One Identity are bliss experiences so intense that those who attempt to describe such experiences usually turn to erotic imagery. Therefore, Key 9 represents attainment through union.

The end of the Path is reached when the personality meets the inner Self. A graphic symbol of this is the slow, steady growth, throughout the ages, of stalagmites and stalactites in a cave. In that growth, the stalactite that extends itself down from the cave's roof is the active agent. The stalagmite's upward growth from the floor of the cave responds to the steady downpour of drops of a limestone solution from the stalactite. The stalactite symbolizes the *One Identity*, ever-moving itself nearer to union with the ascending personality symbolized by the stalagmite.

When the stalactite and stalagmite reach the growth stage where contact is made, their united form is a pillar, approximately the letter I's shape, which is the English Latin and Greek equivalent for Yod.

Number 9

In writing figure 9, the first part of the character is like the zero sign, and from the point where the circle is closed, a straight line, or figure 1, descends. In writing the circular part, one's hand describes a complete circuit, suggesting the completion of a course of action. Then the straight line is drawn, a figure 1, symbol of beginning.

The end of one cycle is always the beginning of another. Attainment is never complete. After the union of the personality with the One Identity, there are greater heights to scale.

Virgo - ♍

In the Sepher Yetzirah, Chapter 5:8, Yod is assigned to Virgo.

He made the letter *Yud* (י) king over coition [sexual intercourse].
And He bound a crown to it
And He combined one with another
And with them, he formed
Virgo in the Universe
Elul in the Year
And the left hand in the Soul, male and female.

Mercury (The Magician) Rules and is Exalted in Virgo. Exaltation means the highest expression of what is pictured by the Magician.

Mercury represents the Life-power working at the self-conscious level and is associated with the brain's frontal lobe. This organ is involved in problem solving, spontaneity, memory, language, initiation, judgment, impulse control, and social and sexual behavior.

In medical astrology, Virgo controls the upper part of the small intestine, where food is assimilated. Therefore, one of the most important things we use our minds for is to regulate what we eat.

At one stage of digestion, food is transformed into an oily, milky substance named *chyle*, from which the lacteals absorb nourishment for the bloodstream.

Under proper self-conscious direction, the finer forces always present in the chyle are liberated into the bloodstream. These forces energize brain centers, which function in the experience termed illumination.

Pursue this thought as far as you can, beyond this brief explanation. Consider that in legends of World Saviors, the Great One is born of a virgin. Consider also that Jesus is born in Bethlehem (ביתלחם), which means, "The House (Beth, בית) of Bread (לחם)." When the shepherds came to adore Jesus, they found the babe lying in a *manger*. The liberating power is born or released in the dark cave of the House of Bread.

Among the highest expressions of human consciousness are those who control the intestinal tract's activities. This may seem strange, but it is true. We control the assimilative activity of the intestinal tract by choosing what we eat and utilizing the law of suggestion to affect the release of the subtle forces from chyle.

Summary

God chooses the weak things of the world to confound the wise. The fact is that illumination depends on the release into the bloodstream of a subtle force generated in the intestinal tract.

Ponder the ideas of this chapter during the coming week. Try to see in how many ways you can penetrate the veil of appearances. Try to see with the mind's eye that your activities are responses to the impact of the Universal Will. Imagine how, little by little, in the dark cave of the House of Bread, the Life-power is weaving the vesture of a finer vehicle, through which you will, eventually, become consciously aware of your union with the One Identity.

COLORING INSTRUCTIONS

YELLOW: Lantern rays, between black lines.

BLUE: Hermit's cap.

BROWN: Staff, shoe.

GRAY: Robe (not right sleeve of undergarment), foreground (not peaks)

WHITE: hair, beard, right sleeve, mountain peaks.

INDIGO or BLACK: Background. Indigo is deep blue, violet, and black. The scene is a night sky. Better use black, if you are now skilled with colors.

Chapter 22

THE HERMIT

Nine (9) is the number of adeptship and prophecy. The Hermit stands on a mountain peak. His staff is in his left hand to show he does not need it for climbing. He has reached the top and stands at the summit of the path of attainment.

A prophet is not the only one who makes predictions. If that were all, any fortune-teller, or any political campaign manager, might be called a prophet. A true prophet is one who knows their vision of the future is true because it is founded on an accurate understanding of principles.

By applying knowledge of principles to the study of nations and races, a true prophet can predict their future. Sometimes the writings of great prophets offer hope, "Change your ways, and the evil I see may be averted."

At other times, their prophetic knowledge shows that a person or a nation has gone too far in the wrong direction to avoid the consequences of evil behavior. Then the voice of prophecy is a voice of doom.

The Mountain Path

The Hermit stands looking down over the path he has ascended. Others are climbing the same way, and he watches their upward progress with benevolent interest.

The Hermit is familiar with every step. He knows all the by-paths. The Hermit has surmounted every danger. He feels for every climber and holds out his lantern as a beacon of encouragement.

We need to keep remembering this. For the Hermit is a symbol of the I AM, which is *above* and *within* us all. Key 9 tells us we are in continual contact with a Reality that knows every thought and deed. It knows every step of the path ahead of us.

This does not mean fate, as it is generally understood. It is a kind of predestination because we are all destined to reach the height where the Hermit stands. No "outside" force is driving us remorselessly onward. It is an *Indwelling Presence*, timeless and eternal. It knows every experience we must pass through in terms of time and space, to fulfill our destiny.

Sympathetic and loving, this Presence guides us. It sends the light of its omniscience into our consciousness to give us the courage to continue the journey.

The Ancient of Days

The Hermit is "He who stands alone." The title shows this is derived from a root meaning "solitary." Thus the name of this Key connects with the Hebrew noun IChIDH (יחידה), *Yekhidah*, meaning "the single, the indivisible." In Sanskrit, the name for the One Identity is *Atman*.

"There is a bridge between time and Eternity, and this bridge is Atman, the Spirit of man. Neither day nor night cross that bridge, nor old age, nor death nor sorrow.

Evil or sin cannot cross that bridge because the world of the Spirit is pure. This is why when this bridge has been crossed, the eyes of the blind can see, the wounds of the wounded are healed, and the sick man becomes whole from his sickness.

To one who goes over that bridge, the night becomes like unto day; because in the worlds of the Spirit there is an everlasting Light". – Upanishad 8:4

Yekhidah is seated in Kether, the highest sphere of being on the Tree of Life. The Crown is the Primal Will to which the upper point of the

204

letter Yod (ʼ) is assigned while the rest of the letter is assigned to Chokmah.

The Hermit represents the Ancient of Days, or the One Identity, as the Will Power in the universe. To this Power, all forms of its self-expression respond. It has no support other than itself.

"He who stands alone" also symbolizes adeptship. By consciously identifying with One Identity, this attitude sets the Hermit apart from all but others like himself because he cannot share his knowledge with those who do not comprehend it. The adepts' superior knowledge requires that they are hermits. However, the adept is not a proud egotist. When he was alive, Einstein had no more than twelve men in the world that understand his theory of relativity. The loneliness of a sage is not as the lonesomeness of the unenlightened. A sage has what the ignorant do not enjoy — continual companionship with the One Self, unbroken awareness of union with the One Reality, which is the sage's own Identity.

Key 8 vs. Key 9

The scene in Key 9 is an antithesis to Key 8. In Strength, we see a fertile valley warmed by the sun. Key 9 is an icy, wind-swept peak, wrapped in darkness.

The Icy Peak

The frozen peaks do not mean sterility but the icy perception of abstract truth. The Hermit himself is warmly clad. *He carries his light.* The cold and darkness are symbols of the *latency* of the One Force's fiery activity and contrast to the lion of Key 8. The heights of spiritual consciousness seem cold and dark to those who have not scaled them, but they who stand upon these lofty peaks endure no discomfort.

The ice at the Hermit's feet is the river's source in the Empress' garden, the same river that flows behind the Emperor and the Chariot. This ice is the substance of the High Priestess' robe, in another form.

205

Her robe symbolizes the *root matter,* which underlies all variations of form. In Key 9, the root matter's vibratory motion is being arrested and crystallized (ice). The symbolism of Key 9 refers to THAT, which does not enter into action, though it is the *source* of all activity throughout the universe.

The Ancient One

A bearded ancient is the "Most Holy Ancient One," the Primal Will. He is clad in grey, a mixture of black and white, the colors of the High Priestess' pillars, the wand and rose of the Fool, and the sphinxes which draw the Chariot. His garment represents the union and equilibration of all pairs of opposites.

His cap is shaped like a Yod (ʼ). It is blue, the High Priestess' robe's color to suggest that the One Identity always perfectly recollects its nature and powers.

The cap is a sort of crown, and therefore *The Crown is Yod.* No further comment is required. They who are ready to receive the instruction compressed into these four words will perceive the statement's tremendous import. It would be impossible to give any more light to the unprepared, though we devoted many pages to attempts at explanation.

Staff and Lantern

The Hermit has brought his lantern and staff from the valley below. The staff, a branch of a tree, is a product of the organic side of nature. It refers to the fiery activity of the serpent power of Key 8. The Hermit used this power to help him climb the mountain, and in some decks, the staff is drawn like a serpent. This is an unnecessary addition. The staff itself is a sufficient indication of the serpent power. The Hermit holds the staff in his left hand to show that he no longer needs climbing.

The staff grew, but the lantern was made. It is of glass and metal, derived from the inorganic side of nature. Our understanding of cosmic law is discoverable in the mineral kingdom's physical, chemical, and electrical activities. Our chief source of illumination (the lantern) is man's adaptation of these essential activities. We rely on the Life-power's expression through organic beings (the staff) to assist us in our efforts to rise above the limitations of self-consciousness to the heights of superconscious realization.

The light in the lantern is from a six-pointed star. The star is composed of two interlaced equilateral triangles that symbolize the union of opposites. Because it is a symbol of the number 6, the star has a particular reference to Key 6. It indicates that discrimination is the source of enlightenment. Astrologically, it refers to Virgo (♍), the sixth sign of the zodiac and Yod (ʼ).

Cube of Space – North-Below

Yod also is assigned the direction North-Below. North is Peh (Key 16); below is Gimel (Key 2). Yod unites these two faces from Below (subconsciousness). Even though the Hermit stands on a height, what is at work is at a subconscious level. Our contact with the One Identity is an *interior* contact, made in the *darkness* of the subconsciousness.

Subconsciousness is our instrument for communion with superconsciousness. Thus the Tarot tableau in Chapter 2 shows the number 9 *between* 2 and 16. Below the keys are shown laid out from right to left to save room.

Key 9 is the agency that carries the power of 2, the High Priestess, into the *field of expression* represented by Key 16. The power expressed by the Hermit is drawn from the High Priestess, and it is applied to the activity symbolized by Key 16. Through right recollection (Key 2), we come to know the One Identity (Key 9), and this knowledge overthrows all structures of separative delusion (Key 16). The lightning-flash in Key 16 is a ray from the Hermit's lantern.

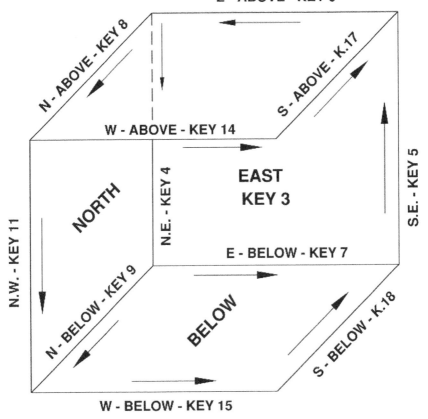

The line North-Below connects the lower end of the line North-East (Heh, Key 4) to the North-West (Lamed, Key 11). Key 9 represents cosmic forces working at subconscious levels to bear upon Karma (Key 11), the ordering and controlling power of the Constituting Intelligences (Key 4).

North-Below connects the northern end of the line East-Below (Cheth, Key 7), with West-Below (Ayin - Key 15). This relation must wait until Key 15 for an explanation. In the meantime, take careful note of all the symbols on the left-hand, or northern, side of Key 7. In these, you will find indications of the sources of power expressed through Key 9 and brought to bear through that agency on what is pictured by Key 15.

209

Every Key is in contrast to the Key which precedes it. In Key 8, the emphasis was on personal effort, *conscious* control of the animal and other subhuman forces. The chapter in Key 9 is that personal action is a response to superconscious influence. These transformations are unconscious. They occur below the threshold of conscious awareness in that region of our bodies governed by Virgo.

These transformations are direct consequences of the conscious effort pictured by Key 8. We become aware of the One Identity is the working power of the Magician through the agency of the woman in Key 8. The woman is the instrument through which the Magician works. It is *his* power that tames the lion, not hers.

Therefore Key 9 and Virgo represent the *rulership* AND *exaltation* of Mercury. This means that taking conscious command of the Virgo region processes in the human body enables us to set a subconsciousness pattern. This pattern is where the human body is transformed into a finer, regenerated vehicle for the *One-self*. Changes in the bloodstream make the building process. These changes are initiated in the Virgo region of the human body.

These changes are never begun until one understands, intellectually and rationally, the law which makes them possible.

1. Subconsciousness is amenable to suggestion.

2. Subconsciousness controls body functions and body structure.

3. The patterns impressed on subconsciousness from the self-conscious level will begin alterations in blood chemistry, cellular functions, and the structures of certain parts of the body.

4. The human body is built from materials taken into the bloodstream from the small intestine's chyle.

All this knowledge is a participation in the Constituting Intelligence symbolized by the Emperor. It is *abstract* knowledge, brought into our field of consciousness by the brain, ruled by Aries. It is a sharing of reality's vision, which is always present to the Universal Mind's all-seeing eye. Thus it corresponds to the Emperor and the direction North-East.

Through physical changes occurring in the Virgo region, this head knowledge is incorporated into the physical organism.

Summary

In conclusion, the Hermit tells us that above the personal level of our daily experience is real Presence, which now IS all that we aspire to be. That Presence, however far off it may seem, however inadequately we may understand it, yet shrouded in darkness and obscurity its real nature, is friendly and helpful.

Comprehend it we may not. Touch it we can, whenever we remember to do so. Only by an illusion are we separate from it. In truth, it enters into every detail of our lives. The One Identity is actively present in all we think, say, or do. The Ancient of the Ancient Ones is the fundamental and only Will, whence all manifestation proceeds.

Key 9 has a direct connection with each of the Keys preceding it. As the number 9, it is the end of a numerical cycle and includes each of the preceding numbers.

For instance, the Hermit is connected in many ways with the Fool. He is the Fool after the Hermit has ascended from the valley of manifestation. The Fool is Spirit in its aspect of Eternal Youth. The Hermit is the same Spirit, in its aspect of the all-embracing experience. Both are one, for youth and age are but appearances of the No-Thing, the youngest and the oldest reality in the universe.

This week try to establish a logical connection between Key 9 and the other Keys from 0 to 8 inclusive. You will find this exercise of great benefit in your Tarot work since you must learn to recognize the Keys' relationships. Skill in this comes from practice. At first, it may seem difficult, but it will be easier and easier if you persist. Be sure you attempt. Write about what you have discovered in your diary.

Chapter 23

ROTATION

The sum of the numbers from 1 to 4 is 10.

$$1 + 2 + 3 + 4 = 10$$

That is to say, the full expression of the number 4 can be found in 10.

Recall statement 4 on the Pattern of the Trestleboard:

4.   From the exhaustless riches of its limitless substance, I draw all things needful, both spiritual and material.

And the tenth statement:

10.   The Kingdom of spirit is embodied in my flesh.

Ponder these ideas in your study period this week.

Number 10

The number 10 is the combination of 0 and 1. Ten symbolizes the eternal creativeness of the Life-power, the ceaseless whirling forth of the Primal Will's self-expression, the ever-turning Wheel of Manifestation. This is Key 10, The Wheel of Fortune.

0 is a symbol of the One Force. One is the POINT wherein that Force concentrates. At the Central Point within itself, the One Force becomes active. This is the *point where the motion begins*.

What we are thinking now is before all physical manifestation. It precedes the manifestation of things. It is the concentration of energy in free space. The open space is *mental* space. There is nothing but the consciousness of itself at this POINT where the One Spirit wakens into activity.

At this first awakening of consciousness, the action is wholly self-sustained. Judge Troward says:

"The law of reciprocity, therefore, demands a similar self-sustained motion in the material correspondence, and mathematical considerations show that the only sort of movement which can sustain a self-supporting body *in vacuo* is a rotary motion- bringing the body itself into a spherical form.

Now, this is what we find at both extremes of the material world. The spheres of the planets rotating on their axes and revolving around the sun. Also, the atoms contain subatomic particles that rotate around a common center at distances that are astronomical compared with their mass. Thus the two ultimate physical manifestation units, the atom and the planet, both follow the same law of self-sustained motion that expresses the primary activity of Spirit. This rotary or *absolute* motion combines the two modes of *relative* motion, centrifugal and centripetal motion. In rotary or absolute motion, we find that both *polarities* of motion are included, thus repeating on the purely mechanical side the primordial principle of the Unity, including the Duality in itself."

This quotation from *The Creative Process in the Individual*, pages 29-30, deserves careful study. It is full of meat. Build up in your mind an image of the initial whirling motion in the vast expanse of the Limitless Light.

OBTW.

The Creative Process in the Individual was written in 1915, so I thought it was time for an update.

The following is from the declassified memo titled, Analysis and Assessment of Gateway Process, Paragraph 11 – Consciousness and Energy.

"It is essential to define the mechanism by which the human mind exercises the function known as consciousness and describes how consciousness operates to deduce meaning from the stimuli it receives. To do this, we will first consider the fundamental character of the material world. Our physical existence to accurately perceive the raw stuff with which our consciousness must work. The first point which needs to be made is that the two terms, matter and energy tend to be misleading if taken to indicate two distinctly different states of existence in the physical world that we know it. Indeed, if the term matter is taken to mean solid substance as opposed to energy, which is understood to mean a force of some sort, then the use of the former is entirely misleading. Science now knows that both the electrons that spin in the energy field located around the atom's nucleus and the nucleus itself are made up of nothing more than oscillating energy grids. Solid matter, in the strict construction of the term, does not exist. Rather, the atomic structure comprises oscillating energy grids surrounded by other oscillating energy grids that orbit at extraordinarily high speeds. In his book, *Stalking the Wild Pendulum*, Itzhak Bentov gives the following figures. The energy grid which composes the nucleus of the atom vibrates at approximately 20^{22} Hertz (which means 10 followed by 22 zeroes). At 70 degrees Fahrenheit, an atom oscillates at the rate of 10^{15} Hertz. An entire molecule, composed of several atoms bound together in a single energy field, vibrates around 10^9 Hertz. A live human cell vibrates at approximately 10^3 Hertz. The point to be made is that the entire human being, brain, consciousness, and all is, like the universe which surrounds him, nothing more or less than an extraordinarily complex system of energy fields. The so-called states of matter are variances in the state of energy, and human consciousness is a function of the interaction of energy in two opposite states (motion vs. rest)."

Troward describes the initial motion of the creative process as a *rotation*. In 1983 when the memo was written, motion is described as *oscillation* and *vibration*.

Back to the original text.

The doctrine of Rotation is one of the most important, for it is concerned with the principles of growth, involution, evolution, action and reaction, and the reciprocal relation between every pair of opposites throughout the manifest universe. Do not confuse absolute motion with the Absolute. Absolute motion is so-called because it is self-derived and self-sustained, without being dependent on, nor conditioned by, other modes of activity.

Recall from Chapter 19 that the Magical Agent's motion is serpentine because it is wavy, circular, undulating, and spiral. Thus, growth and evolution come into being. The motion appears to return to its starting point, but it begins at a higher level at each revolution.

Kaph or Kaf - כ

The ancient form of *Kaph* (כ) is an open palm of a hand. The letter name Kaph (כף) also means palm and is used as an image for clouds in Job 36:32, "With clouds, He covers light, and thereby commands with forcefulness."

As a verb, *Kaf* means to *subdue* or *coerce* and suggest power to suppress nature's forces, including our passions. Through toil and labor, and the application of the law of cycles, we express the power to rule and govern our environment. Thus, we are a positive force to subdue and control natural phenomena for the benefit of humanity.

Kaph as hand, suggests comprehension or grasp. The law of manifestation is within our mental grasp. It is a law operative throughout unimaginable immensities. It is finite, and we can comprehend it. The principle of rotation and cycles at work through the entire series of cosmic manifestations is intelligible. We can understand and apply it. Its symbol is the ever-turning wheel.

Jupiter - 24

Kaph and Key 10 are assigned to the planet Jupiter, which is associated with *Faith*. Rabbi Ginsburgh has this to say about the three lines that form Kaf (כ),

"Relate to the three properties of the superconscious: simple and absolute faith, sublime pleasure in the experience of unity with G-d, and superconscious desire to dedicate one's life to fulfilling G-d's Will. These properties are referred to as 'the three heads of the crown,' and in turn, relate to the three actual meanings of the word for crown, Keter. The highest of the heads, simple faith, corresponds to Keter meaning 'to wait,' as in כתר לי זעיר, 'wait for me a little.' This implies that faith entails the patience and confidence that G-d's ultimate good in His Divine intention for each soul, together with all the Creation will in time be fulfilled." – *The Hebrew Letters*, p. 171.

Additionally, Jupiter is exalted in Cancer (Key 7). The wheels of the Chariot in Key 7 represent the Law of Rotation.

Review Key 7, and you will see some of the practical applications of the Law of Rotation to your own life. Try to comprehend the idea that even the least of your activities is a particular expression of the same more extensive cosmic activity cycle. Then you will begin to understand that every detail of your life-expression is adjusted to the *Influx* of currents of universal energy.

Such comprehension enables us to free ourselves from every disease, misfortune, and semblance of bondage. The power of Jupiter, the sky-father, is *our* power.

It must be comprehended truly. The grasp of this truth is more than a mere intellectual understanding of words. We must *realize* whatever we do is part of the cosmic ebb and flow. The Tarot Keys may plant a seed- idea in subconsciousness, where it will grow, and bear fruit in the comprehension we seek.

Jupiter means sky-father and is the god of cloud, rain, lightning, and thunder. Everything physical is some unique form assumed by the electrical energy which permeates the atmosphere. The circulation of this energy produces everything. A physical form is a condensation of the electromagnetic "rain," which is the root-matter pervading all space and veiling the One Force's fiery energy. This root-matter, with its inner fire, is the "water" of the Alchemist.

The 21st Path of Kaph - כ

The 21st Path is the Seeking and Delightful Intelligence (Sekhel HaChafutz ha.M'vu.qash). It receives the Divine Influx (שפע) to bless all, everyone.

M'vu.qash is from a root word meaning "emptiness" and meaning *hunger* and *thirst*. Our quest for abundance is a response to the descending influence (שפע) of the Life-power. We seek because what we want is within us, and whatever we gain is a recollection of what the One Identity already has in store for us.

To comprehend the Law of Rotation is to secure the satisfaction of every desire. This comprehension comes to real *seekers* and nobody else. Lazy minds cannot grasp the truth. Without a definite idea of what you want, you cannot perceive the Law of Rotation's inner significance.

In some respects, this law is one of the most obvious. We see it in operation everywhere. Few persons understand even part of what it means.

One plain meaning is that what we send out comes back to us. The present state of the world is evidence that most persons do not see this truth. If humanity realized that its future depends entirely on its immediate actions, wars, strife, and selfishness would come to an end. The idea of separate existence, that is, *of good being obtained at others' expense*, is contrary to Law. Do all you can to perfect your grasp of this truth.

Practical Exercise

This week attempt to see the Law of Rotation in your daily life. Begin by calling to mind every instance of cyclic or spiral activity you can identify. Then examine yourself. Look back over your past, and see how your experiences have run in cycles.

Watch your moods, and you will find the same alternation of ebb and flow. Think of your present activities, and try to picture their logical results in future experience.

COLORING INSTRUCTIONS

YELLOW: Serpent, eagle's eye, lion's eyes.

BLUE: Background, Sphinx (not headdress).

ORANGE: Entire body of the wheel.

BROWN: Animals, Lion should be tawny, a mixture of brown and yellow.

GOLD: Sword hilt.

STEEL: Sword blade.

GRAY: Clouds, but they are gray and white storm clouds.

BLONDE: Man's hair, eagle's beak (upper and lower).

WHITE: In headdress of the Sphinx, clouds as stated above, bull's horns, the eye of Hermanubis, the rising figure.

RED: Hermanubis (jackal-headed figure, except eye), eagle's tongue.

Chapter 24

THE WHEEL OF FORTUNE

Key 10 is based on the illustration in *Ritual of the Sanctum Regnum.*

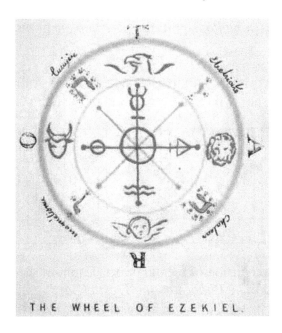

THE WHEEL OF EZEKIEL.

"The Wheel of Ezekiel is the type on which all the Pantacles of the Higher Magic are designed. When the adept is in the blessed possession of full knowledge of the Seal of Solomon's powers and the virtues of the Wheel of Ezekiel, he has sufficient experience to design talismans and Pantacles for any magical purpose.

The Wheel of Ezekiel contains the solution of the *quadrature of the circle* and demonstrates the correspondence between words and figures, letters and emblems; it exhibits the tetragram of characters analogous to that of the elements and elemental forms. It is a glyph of perpetual motion. The triple ternary is shown; the central point is the first Unity; three circles are added, each with four attributions and the dodekad [3 x 4 = 12]) is thus seen. The state of universal equilibrium

221

is suggested by the counterpoised emblems and the pairs of opposites. The flying Eagle balances the Man; the roaring Lion counterpoises the laborious Bull." – pp. 39 - 40.

Number 10

The tenth Sephiroth is Malkuth, MLKVTh (מלכות). It means *Kingdom*. A kingdom expresses the will and authority of its ruler. One Greek name for 10 was *pantelia*, signifying *all complete* or *fully accomplished*.

The Tarot Keys from 0 to 4 inclusive add up to 10. An inspection of these keys will show you a representation of the noun "Kingdom."

A correct comprehension or mental grasp (Kaph) of the ten aspects of the Life-power in *The Pattern on the Trestleboard* serves to place the ruling power in its right position in our thought. This ruling power is the Reality designated by the divine name IHVH (יהוה), Jehovah, comparable with the meaning of Jupiter of the Romans.

The title of Key 10 refers to Jupiter, the Greater Fortune in astrology. The Jupiter center is near the *solar* plexus, or the celiac plexus is a group of nerve cells situated in the abdomen behind the stomach. A Jupiter center's correct functioning brings about the perfection of good fortune.

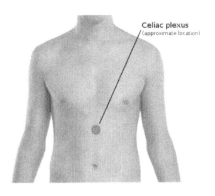

Celiac plexus
(approximate location)

This image was improved or created by the Wikigraphists of the Graphic Lab (fr).
Upper_body_front.png, Public Domain,
https://commons.wikimedia.org/w/index.php?curid=11211981

This organ, sometimes known as the abdominal brain, controls assimilation. Its occult functions have to do with activities in which we may synchronize our existence with the Life-power's universal cycles of self-expression.

Kaph – כ – West

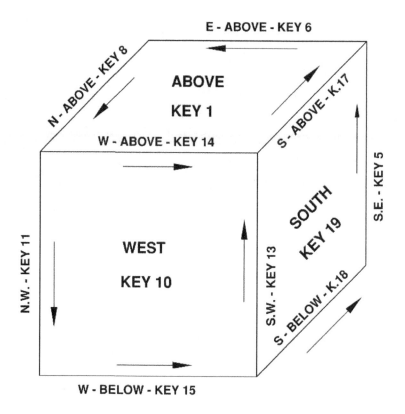

In the Cube of Space, the letter Kaph and Key 10 correspond to the direction West. This is the face of the Cube nearest the observer. Because closest to us, the western face represents those events and circumstances which, at any given moment, *are in the immediate present.*

What surrounds us now is the culmination of a stream of events coming out of the past. Thus the present situation represents the *end* of a cycle of preceding activities. Therefore, the present moment is symbolized by the direction West, the place of sunset, corresponding to the end of a "day." In occultism generally, the day stands for any time-period as in the first chapter of Genesis.

Key 10 is the direction West and is in contrast to Key 3, the Empress and East. Key 3 represents the first stages of a cycle of manifestation (sunrise). Key 10 represents the culmination of a stream of events (sunset) having their origin in Key 3.

However, a whole series of events is continuous with its origin or cause. Therefore, Key 10 is another aspect of the Empress. Thus the titles for Malkuth (Kingdom, 10th Sephiroth), *Bride,* and *Queen,* are words that describe the Empress.

The *connecting link* between the East and West, in the Cube symbolism, is the Mem (מ) or Key 12 line.

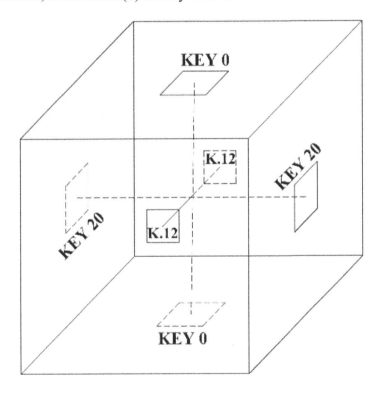

This line is attributed to Mem, the second of the three Mother letters associated with Water. Mem (מ) and Water is the root matter that links the origins represented by East to the consequences corresponding to West.

The Four Fixed Astrological Signs

In Key 10, the bull, eagle, lion, and man are supported by clouds to remind us that Jove and Jehovah are gods of rain and lightning and thunder. The four animals are the ones mentioned in Ezekiel and Revelation. Also, clouds are a symbol of power.

"With clouds, he covers light and thereby commands with forcefulness." – Job 36:32.

The lion corresponds to Yod (י), the first letter of IHVH (יהוה). The eagle is the second letter (ה). The man stands for the third letter (ו). The bull is the last letter (the second ה).

These living creatures are also related to the four fixed signs of the zodiac. The lion is Leo, the eagle Scorpio, the man Aquarius, and the bull Taurus. These are the 5th, 8th, 11th, and 2nd signs. Their numbers in the zodiacal series add to 26, which is the sum of the numeral values of the letters in IHVH (יהוה).

Leo - ♌	Scorpio - ♏	Aquarius - ♒	Taurus - ♉
Lion	Eagle	Man	Bull
י	ה	ו	ה

On Key 10, the figures are placed in the corners of the design to illustrate the statement. "In him, we live and move and have our being." – Acts 17:28.

These ideas are also present in a poem written for Zeus, the Greek equivalent to the Romans' Jupiter.

"Most glorious of immortals, many-named,
Almighty and forever, thee, O Zeus,
Sovran o'er Nature, guiding with thy hand
All things that are, we greet with praises. Thee
'Tis meet that mortals call with one accord,
For we thine offspring are, and we alone
Of all that live and move upon this earth,

Receive the gift of imitative speech."
—Cleanthes, Hymn to Zeus.

The same thought is in these lines from the *Kaivalya Upanishad*:

"Within me, the universe came into being Within me, the universe is established; Within me, the universe passes away — This Brahma, without a second, I myself am It."

Squaring the Circle

Squaring the circle is a problem proposed by ancient geometers. The challenge is to construct a square with the same area as a circle using a compass and straightedge.

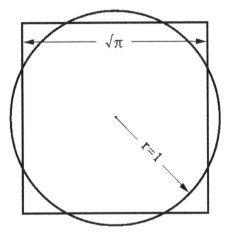

By Original PNG by Plynn9; SVG by Alexei Kouprianov - Pd-self image by Plynn9, Public Domain, https://commons.wikimedia.org/w/index.php?curid=1681996

It can't be constructed exactly but only approximated. Thus, the circle's squaring symbolizes the interchange between matter (square) and spirit (circle).

The value of pi (π) can be expressed as the fraction,

A closer value of pi is 3.1415926. Therefore the approximation 22/7 is 0.04% within the "actual" value of pi. There is no actual value of pi, just better and better approximations.

Therefore the circle and pi (π) are a symbol of the Infinite and Immeasurable. The square represents us, earthlings. Squaring the Circle is a symbolic representation of the interaction of Spirit and Humanity. Look at the image above with this idea in mind. It sends a message to your subconscious that you're interested in ideas associated with the symbol.

The Three Alchemical Principles

Mercury – Sulfur – Salt

In Key 10, at the top of the wheel is the letter, T. Under this letter is the alchemical Mercury. At the right, beside the letter A, is the symbol for alchemical Sulfur. At the left, beside the 0, is the barred circle representing alchemical Salt. Above the letter, R are the two wavy lines sometimes used by alchemists to symbolize Dissolution.

Mercury	Sulfur	Salt	Dissolution
☿	🜍	🜔	∿
Sattva	Rajas	Tamas	
Wisdom	Passion	Inertia	
Super consciousness	Self conscious	subconsciousness	

Mercury, Sulfur and Salt, the three "principles" of the alchemists, correspond to Hindu philosophy's three gunas, or qualities. Do not be confused by *principles* and *qualities* as used in the special senses here indicated.

Mercury corresponds to the Sattva-guna or Wisdom. In these chapters, we call it super-consciousness.

Sulfur corresponds to the Rajas-guna, or passion and desire, inciting to action. This is the main characteristic of self-conscious awareness.

Salt corresponds to the Tamas-guna or the quality of inertia. This is the dominant characteristic of subconsciousness.

Because this symbol of dissolution is also the sign Aquarius (♒), it may be understood to represent Humanity as the dissolver of the phantoms of illusion.

The Four Worlds of the Qabalah

In alchemy and yoga, *we learn to dissolve the various forms of appearance which surround us, extract their essence, assimilate that essence to ourselves, and project it in new forms modified by our creative imagination.* Here is the theory of practical occultism in a sentence.

In Key 10, the innermost circle is divided into eight sections. It is an alchemical symbol for the Quintessence, Spirit or Akasha.

The center of the wheel represents the First Unity. Thence all motion originates. The central POINT is the Archetypal World (Atziluth). The knobs also symbolize it at the top of the staff and crown of the Hierophant. However extensive that manifestation may be, it is the world where all the potencies of manifestation are concentrated into a single POINT.

Surrounding this center, the smallest circle stands for the Creative World (Briah) or mental plane. It's also symbolized by the top bar of the Hierophant's staff and the topmost of his three crowns.

The next circle is the alchemical symbols of the forces active in the Formative (Yetzirah) World. It's represented by the Hierophant s staff's middle bar and by the second of his three crowns.

The outer circle, containing letters that suggest the manifestation of the WORD, or the Logos, stands for the Material World (Assiah), or World of Action. This is symbolized by the lowest bar of the Hierophant's staff and the lowest of his three crowns.

The Wheel

The eight segments are divided into arcs of 45 degrees. 45 is the value of the ADM (אדם), Adam, the generic name for humanity. What is suggested is the essential spiritual being or Quintessence, is the same Life-power, which is the spirit of humanity.

The eight radii of this circle remind us that 8 is the number of Hermes (Hod, Mercury 8th Sephiroth), and Jesus (Ιησους).

I	η	σ	ο	υ	ς
10	8	200	70	400	200

$$Ιησους = 888$$

They indicate that the secret of mastering circumstance is to be sought because humanity's inner spirit is identical with the ruling power (Christos, the Anointed), which sets the wheeling activity of the cosmic cycles into motion.

The field wherein man may apply the Central Spirit's royal power is in the Formative (Yetzirah) World. We do this by combining the three alchemical principles in the Great Work, which dissolves all seeming obstacles by the "philosophical Mercury." Dissolution makes available the various energies locked up in the form.

The letters in the outer circle spell IHVH (יהוה), Jehovah, in Hebrew. In Latin, *Rota* means Wheel. The letters of ROTA may be arranged to form a sentence (in a barbarous Latin):

ROTA TARO ORAT TORA ATOR.

It means; The Wheel of Tarot speaks the Law of Ator. *Ator* is one Latin spelling for the name of the Egyptian goddess Hathor, personifying Nature and Venus. Thus the Law of Ator is the Law of the Empress in Tarot.

These letters are written in the outer circle to remind us that the Material World is the plane of the uttered WORD of the indwelling Spirit.

Descending Serpent

The serpent on the descending side of the wheel is yellow to represent light. Its wavy form symbolizes vibration. It stands for the descent of the Serpent Power into the field of physical manifestation. Thus it represents the involution of Light into Form.

Hermanubis

Hermanubis, the red figure rising on the right side of the wheel, stands for the evolution of form and symbolizes the average development of human personality. With a jackal's head, he has a human body to show that humanity as a whole has not evolved beyond the intellectual level. His ears rise above the horizontal diameter of the wheel. This suggests that through interior hearing (intuition - Key 5), humanity is beginning to know the cycle of evolution through which we are destined to rise.

The wheel segment between Hermanubis and the Sphinx contains Yod (ʼ), and Key 9, The Hermit. What completes humanity's unfoldment and develops powers beyond our intellectual level of consciousness is an organic change. To effect this change is to accomplish the Great Work, and Yod (ʼ) symbolizes that accomplishment. The perfection of the Work identifies the personal self, the Ego seated in the heart, with the Ancient of Days, the Silent Watcher of Key 9.

Sphinx

The Sphinx symbolizes the perfection of this identification. She carries a sword, the weapon corresponding to Air's element, the Formative World (Yetzirah), Zain (ז), and Key 6.

Her weapon stands for conquest in the Formative World, or plane wherein the Life-Breath's subtle forces are at work. The right discrimination affects this conquest.

The Sphinx combines the two principal elements in the symbolism of Key 8. She has a woman's head and breasts, combined with the body of a male lion. She is the union of male and female powers, the perfect blending of forces that appear to be opposed at lower levels of perception.

Summary

Key 10 represents all cycles of natural manifestation are cycles in One Power's orderly expression, which is identical with the innermost Spirit of Man.

The Kybalion is a statement having a direct bearing on the meaning of Key 10.

''The farther the creation is from the Center, the more it is bound; the nearer the Center it reaches, the nearer free is it.''

— The Kybalion, p. 179.

Chapter 25

ACTION - EQUILIBRIUM

Equilibrium is the basis of the Great Work. This doctrine is behind all the meanings of Key 11.

Consider the number eleven. Its digits are equal (1 = 1). Thus 11 is a glyph of balance or equilibrium. Hence it typifies equality, parity, symmetry, and poise. Eleven (11) is similar to the zodiacal sign Gemini (♊) and Roman numeral two – II. The idea of equilibrium implies that of duality. Balance, says Eliphas Levi, is the result of equalizing opposing activities or forces.

"Equilibrium is the result of two forces, but if these were absolutely and permanently equal, equilibrium would be immobility, and consequently the negation of life. Movement is the result of alternated preponderance — warmth after cold, mildness after severity, affection after anger— this is the secret of perpetual motion and the prolongation of power. To operate always on the same side and in the same manner is to overload one side of a balance, and the destruction of equilibrium will soon result. Everlasting caressing quickly engenders disgust and antipathy, in the same way that constant coldness or severity alienates and discourages affection in the end.

Principle of Polarity

The Kybalion states the same law: "To destroy an undesirable rate of vibration, put in operation the Principle of Polarity and concentrate upon the opposite pole to that which you desire to suppress." The same book gives this excellent summary of the Principle of Polarity.

"Everything is dual; everything has poles; everything has its pair of opposites; like and unlike are the same; opposites are identical in nature, but different in degree; extremes meet; all truths are but half-truths; all paradoxes may be reconciled."

Lamed – ל

Lamed looks like a serpent in motion. It represents the same force we discussed in Teth (ט) and Key 8. Teth is the *coiled* serpent; Lamed is uncoiled and active.

The verb *la.mad,* למד means learn or teach. It the root of the word, *tal.mid* תלמיד, meaning scholar. Also derived is *mal.mad,* מלמד, ox goad.

Thus, it suggests the idea of control, combined with that of incitement. An ox-goad impels an ox to move and keeps it on the road chosen by the driver.

The ox is Aleph (א), and Key 1, The Fool. We invite the superconscious Life-power into our lives and to enter into action. We do not exert any control over it or do anything to control its free and spontaneous activity. However, it *seems* like we do.

The Life-power *directs itself.* Key 11 and Lamed represents the seeming personal consciousness that functions to direct our activities. These functions *appear* to originate within us.

We know that the sun doesn't revolve around the Earth. But that doesn't stop us from telling time from the Sun's apparent position in the sky.

22nd Path of Lamed - ל

The 22nd Path is the Faithful Intelligence (Sekhel Ne'ehman). It causes spiritual powers to multiply. Through it, the Spiritual Ones are drawn close, and all find shelter in its shadow.

Ne'ehman (ןמאנ) means faithful, trustworthy, loyal, reliable; firm and sure. From the root, *Amen* (ןמא), meaning: so be it, surely; to be found true, and firm.

Amen is the title of the first Sephiroth Kether (כתר), the crown. The passage, *dwell or rest in his shadow* is similar to Psalm 91:1: "Whoever dwells in the shelter of the Most High will rest in the shadow of the Almighty."

Libra - ♎

In medical astrology, Libra governs the kidneys that maintain the chemical equilibrium of the blood. The organs eliminate and balance. They clear the bloodstream of the impurities produced by bodily action and maintain the proper balance of its elements.

Libra also governs the adrenal glands that sit on top of the kidney. These glands produce hormones that help the body control blood sugar, burn protein and fat, react to stressors like a major illness or injury, and regulate blood pressure.

In the Sepher Yetzirah, Libra, the Scales are attributed to Lamed. In the *Sepher Yetzirah*, 2:1.

The Three Mothers are Alef (א), Mem (מ), and Shin (ש). Their foundation is a pan (כף) of Merit (מ), a pan of Liability (ש), and the tongue of decree (א) deciding between them.

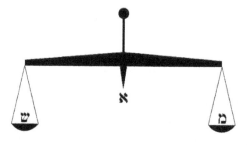

And the pan is spelled the same as Kaph (כף) in Key 10, The Wheel of Fortune.

The Pan of Merit (מ) is the Pillar of Mildness – Chokmah, Chesed, and Netzach. The Pan of Liability (ש) is the Pillar of Severity, Binah,

Geburah, and Hod. And the Middle Pillar (א) is Kether, (Da'ath), Tiphareth, Yesod, and Malkuth.

I mention in passing to hint at the interweaving of ideas that runs deep through the Kabbala.

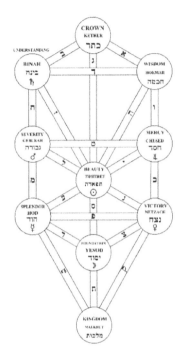

The ruler of Libra is Venus. Key 3, Venus, and creative imagination. All occult practice calls creative imagination into action. Yoga books are full of exercises in mental imagery. Modern metaphysical teachers make extended application of the same principle. Creative imagination is the basis of all practical work with the Tarot.

Imagination and Faith

Imagination builds faith. Real imagination— not mere fantasy— rests on the firm foundation of science. The *Arabian Nights* tales of the Magic Carpet give us a fanciful notion of flying. However, real creative imagination is founded on the observations made by Key 4, The Emperor. Measurement and observation build our faith in flying. With every advance in accurate weighing and measuring, creative imagination grows clearer and sees farther. Leonardo's sketches added to humanity's faith, though he never flew. But his research made valuable contributions to the science of aviation.

The Arabian story-teller contented himself with flights of fancy. He rendered no service to the cause of the conquest of the air because he had no real faith in our ability to fly.

Faith is a prime requisite for the accomplishment of the Great Work. Without faith, you can do nothing. You must have confidence in the principles whereby you operate. You must have faith in yourself. Hence occult schools make their pupils familiar with the lives and achievements of adepts who have completed the Great Work. This builds faith. Study the lives of Jesus and Buddha. In what they said and did, the principles of the Great Work are explained and exemplified.

Saturn in Libra

Saturn (♄) is exalted in Libra (♎). Saturn represents the power of limitation, which makes possible the manifestation of specific forms. The power of limitation is the active power at work in *Karma*. It expresses itself to us as undeviating justice. Hence the Saturn power has its highest manifestation in the Great Work, enabling us to control Karma.

We can make a complete conquest of his future. We can make whatever Karma we choose. Some persons are so afraid of "making bad Karma" that they do nothing to improve the conditions. Others are afraid of "interfering" with Karma. Don't worry about that; it can't be done.

You can generate new Karma, but you cannot change immutable law nor interfere with it. You must reap what you sow, but you may select your seeds and determine the nature of tomorrow's harvest.

As for today's weeds among the wheat, use your discrimination. You can put even bad Karma to good use if you are ingenious.

People who "invite their Karma" and immediately have all sorts of unpleasant experiences, which they bear with a proper facial expression of uncomplaining martyrdom. These people think that Karma is identical to sorrow and disaster. However, their imagined evils are faithfully reproduced by subconsciousness. These self-deluded martyrs have not called down their Karma from a Pandora's Box of afflictions from the Lords of Destiny. They have indulged their imaginations in making negative patterns, and what they get is what they have made.

Karma means *Action* or *Work*. We cannot escape from Karma because there is no such thing as inaction in all the universe.

The fruit of "inaction" is the loss of faculty and function because what is not used atrophies. This loss of power in *action in the wrong direction*. Usually, we work harder to fail than to succeed — harder. Thus Madame Blavatsky wrote: "Inaction in a deed of mercy is action in deadly sin."

Recall the admonition from Ecclesiastes 9:10 "Whatever your hand finds to do, do it with all your might."

This does not mean you should exert as much force in picking up a pin as you would lift a crowbar.

"With your might" means you must apply your *full* power to whatever you do, whether the expenditure of energy is small or great. This takes *concentration,* which is *limitation.* Saturn's power, for concentration, eliminates every distraction that takes force away from the work at hand.

COLORING INSTRUCTIONS

YELLOW: Between curtains, in the background.

GREEN: Surrounding square on the crown; cape over shoulders.

BLUE: Sleeves (same shade as the canopy of the chariot in Key 7).

INDIGO: The letter T on woman's breast.

VIOLET: Curtains (not ropes, tassels or fringe), oval, round neck, veil connecting pillars of the throne (a light violet for this veil).

GRAY: Throne and dais.

GOLD: Balances, sword hilt, rings holding ropes on curtains, outline, and peaks of the crown.

STEEL: Sword blade.

WHITE: Shoe, square on the crown, panels beside T on woman's breast.

BLONDE: Hair.

RED: Circle in the square on the crown, garment (not cape or sleeves), ropes tassels, and fringes on curtains.

Chapter 26

JUSTICE

The background of Key 11 is yellow, like that on Keys 1 and 8. The Law of Equilibrium is applied through the directive activity of self-consciousness (Key 1) and using the Serpent Power (Key 8).

Curtains and Throne

The two curtains suggest duality and polarity, and their symmetrical arrangement typifies balance. Their folds are similar to the drapery of the High Priestess and suggest vibration. Their violet color is complementary to the yellow Air background. Violet is associated with Kaph (כ) and Key 10. This means that the mechanical aspect of universal manifestation symbolized by the Wheel of Fortune veils the living, conscious IDENTITY.

The throne repeats the symbolism of the pillars of the High Priestess and the veil between them. In Key 11, the pillars are part of the throne and are surmounted by pomegranates instead of lotus buds to show that the activity represented by Key 11 has arrived at the stage of fruition.

Crown

A triple ornament surmounts the crown. This refers to the letter Shin (ש), shown on Key 20, in close correspondence with Keys 2 and 11. The triple ornament represents the Serpent Power. When this power is exalted, it releases human consciousness from the limitations of three-dimensional interpretations of experience.

The circle and square on the front of the crown refer to the movement of Spirit within the physical form. This detail is connected with Key 10, which shows a wheel or circle moving in space bounded by the Zodiac's four fixed signs (Bull, Lion, Eagle, and human face).

Collar

The ornament on the breast of Justice combines a T-cross with an ellipse. The cross is indigo, the color associated with Saturn. This detail hints at the mathematical elements combined in Key 21. It is also a reference to the exaltation of Saturn in Libra.

Sword

The pointed blade of the sword has the same underlying meaning as the ox-goad. The sword is of steel, the metal of Mars. Whenever the Venus force in Libra comes into play, the Mars force is also active. Venus and Mars are complementary. The activity of one always excites the action of the other.

The hilt of the sword is a T-cross. Thus the uplifted hilt is another symbol of the exaltation of Saturn in Libra. Exaltation means *to raise*. The sword-hilt is gold of the Sun. This is a hint of the alchemist's transmutation of "lead" into "gold." Saturn also represents limitation and form. The Sun stands for light and radiation. When the power of restraint is used positively, it is combined with the radiant energy of the Sun. Thus *enlightenment exalts form*.

Zain (ז) corresponds to the sword, which cuts off. It symbolizes the physical and mental eliminative processes. Recall that Libra governs the kidneys, the organs that maintain the blood's chemical equilibrium by eliminating waste. Psychologically, the sword's meaning is: *Use right discrimination to rid yourself of everything useless, to free yourself from attachment, prejudice, resentment, and regret.*

Scales

The scales represent weighing and measuring, or the exercise of mental powers related to mathematics. The pans of the scales are semicircular. Hence each semicircle stands for 11 since 22 is the number representing a complete circle.

Thus, the balance's pans represent the equilibration of the 11 pairs of complementary activities represented by the 22 letters and Tarot Keys. The pans are golden to show that all these activities are modes of the single force, radiant energy, and physically manifested as a solar force.

The length of the cross-bar and the lines supporting the scales are equal. Thus seven equal straight lines are shown. They refer to the seven aspects of the Life-power represented by Keys 1, 2, 3, 10, 16, 19 and 21. These correspond to Mercury, the Moon, Venus, Jupiter, Mars, the Sun, and Saturn, which relate to the seven alchemical metals and the seven chakras in a human body. Again, the seven Keys also correspond to corresponding to Hebrew letters and the six sides and interior center (Saturn) of the Cube of Space.

Key		Planet		Chakra	Cube of Space
1	ב	Mercury	☿	7	Up
2	ג	Moon	☽	6	Down
3	ד	Venus	♀	5	East
4	כ	Jupiter	♃	3	West
5	פ	Mars	♂	2	North
6	ר	Sun	☉	4	South
7	ת	Saturn	♄	1	Center

The seven equal lines remind us of the seven-sided figure, or heptagon, which appears in alchemical diagrams. This heptagon is the geometrical basis for constructing the seven-sided vault described in the Rosicrucian *Fama Fraternitatis*.

In Key 11, the seven lines' arrangement indicates a square (4) combined with a triangle (3). Note also that the lines hold the pans of the scales form two triangles (6). By their arrangement, the seven equal lines hint at the number 10 (4 + 6 = 10) and a direct presentation of 7.

In occult arithmetic, 10 and 7 are related because the sum of the numbers from 1 to 7 is 28.

$$1 + 2 + 3 + 4 + 5 + 6 + 7 = 28 \qquad \text{or } \Sigma = 28$$

This is called the Theosophical Extension.

The Theosophical Reduction of 28 is 10 (2 + 8 = 10). What is weighed and measured by the scales of Justice is the complete manifestation of the personal activities symbolized by Key 7. The activities seemingly originating in the field of personality are also cosmic operations. Hence the chariot moves because it is on wheels, and the wheels represent what is symbolized by Key 10. The Law of Karma is the consequence of the rotation of the cosmic cycles.

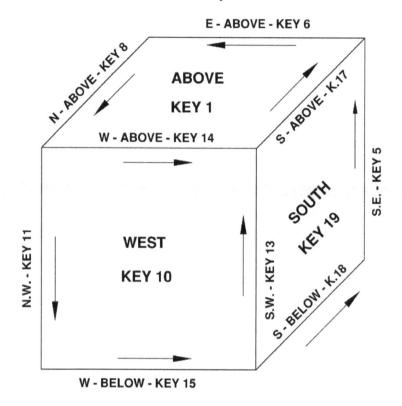

The direction assigned to Lamed and Key 11 is North-West. It connects North (Mars) and West (Key 10).

On its left-hand, or north side of Key, 11 is the uplifted sword of Mars. On the other hand, Justice is the scales, whose two semicircular pans, fitted together, would make a sphere or wheel (Jupiter and Key 10).

Thus, Key 11 and Lamed's symbolism are directly connected North (Mars) and West (Jupiter).

North-West connects the west end of the line North with North-Below (Key 9 and Yod). West symbolizes the completion of a cycle of activity. It follows that Key 11, joining the *western* ends of the lines corresponding to Keys 8 and 9, represents the culmination of the activity symbolized by these two Keys.

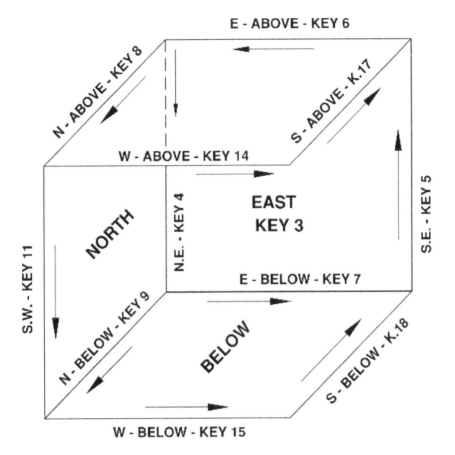

E - ABOVE - KEY 6

N - ABOVE - KEY 8

S - ABOVE - K.17

W - ABOVE - KEY 14

N.E. - KEY 4

EAST
KEY 3

S.E. - KEY 5

NORTH

S.W. - KEY 11

N - BELOW - KEY 9

E - BELOW - KEY 7

BELOW

S - BELOW - K.18

W - BELOW - KEY 15

Key 8 has to do with *consciousness*, and Key 9 with *subconscious* activities that reach completion in what is represented by Key 11. The modification of Karma, by right discrimination and right judgment, applied to work or action, is the outcome of processes typified by Keys 8 and 9.

Key 11 and the line North-West also joins the north ends of West-Above's lines (Samekh and Key 14) and West-Below (Ayin and Key 15). The explanation of them will wait until we come to these Keys.

247

Venus' clothes

The cape of Justice is green, the color of Venus. In the Tarot correspondences, green is also the color of Libra.

The woman's robe is red, a color compliment to green. It symbolizes the Mars force, which energizes the muscular system. The symbolic meaning of the robe relates to what enables us to work.

Throne

The dais and throne are stone, meaning that the Law of Equilibrium is operative even in the mineral kingdom. For many persons, the physical plane is the only one in which they have any direct sense-experience. Tarot tells us that if we interpret our physical plane experience correctly, we shall learn all that is necessary to know to begin using the Law of Equilibrium.

That which is above is as that which is below. One does not need to sense higher planes to see the law at work.

Summary

This week consider your actions more carefully than you have ever done before. Go about your daily tasks earnestly, no matter how trivial they may seem. No one ever did great things well who had not first done well with small things.

Go about your work in a poised, quiet manner. When you sit down to study, sit still. Teach your body the meaning of balance.

Fear not. Dismiss anxiety. Banish the mood of haste. Whatever you do, remember that every personal action is a particular expression of the perfect Life-force. Above all, train yourself to fashion clear forms for your desires and look upon these mental images as realities.

Chapter 27

REVERSAL

The symbolism of Key 12 is to the Law of Reversal as Key 11 to the Law of Equilibrium. This law's application is expressed as the wise's mental attitude, which is the exact reverse of popular opinion — that which the wise set high value is nothing to the average man. Thus the first Tarot Key is The Fool and numbered Zero.

The series of Tarot Keys is intended to effect a reversal of the superficial, mistaken interpretation of the universe that holds the ignorant in bondage. Superficially, the man in Key 12 is in bondage and suffering. However, Key 12 is a symbol of the state of absolute freedom.

Mother Letter Mem - מ

Mem is the second of the three Mother letters in Hebrew. In *the Sepher Yetzirah*, 3:2,

Three Mothers: Alef Mem Shin (אמש)
A great, mystical secret
covered and sealed with six rings
And from them emanated Air, Water, and Fire
and from the Fathers, descendants.

Let me explain this passage with a table.

Element	Mothers	Fathers
Air	א	ו
Water	מ	י
Fire	ש	ה

The six rings are the six directions, up, down, east, west, north, and south.

The three Father Letters Yod (י), Heh (ה) and Vav (ו) form the name of God IHVH or יהוה. The four-letter name of God, Tetragrammaton, is the name of God in the World of Rectification. These are the four worlds of creation, Atziluth, Briah, Yetzirah, and Assiah. Five worlds if you include the Adam Kadmon.

Before the *World of Rectification* or *Tikun* (תקון) was the *World of Chaos* or *Tohu* (תהו) mentioned in the first chapter of Genesis. The World of Chaos was ruled by Emesh (אמש).

"There is, however, an aspect of creation that existed before the Sefirot. In this stage, the proto-Sefirot existed as simple non-interacting points. In the language of the Kabbalists, this is known as the Universe of Chaos (Tohu). In this state, the Vessels, the proto-Sefirot, could neither interact nor give one another. Since they could not emulate God by giving, they were incomplete and could not hold the Divine Light. Since they could not fulfill their purpose, they were overwhelmed by the Light and 'shattered.' This is known as the 'Breaking of the Vessels.'" - *Sepher Yetzirah*, pp. 140-141

Water – Reversal – Subconsciousness

Water symbolizes the Law of Reversal because water reflects everything upside down. Only a person who has experienced the reversal of consciousness pictured in Key 12 can understand what is meant by "Water."

From the chapters on the High Priestess, we know Water is related to subconsciousness. Subconsciousness is the substance of every form in the universe—the ONE THING from which all things are made. Consequently, Mem (מ) is the *Mother Deep* or *Root of Nature*.

The universal subconsciousness is also your subconsciousness. Its creative powers are those which you govern by suggestion, as explained in *Seven Steps*.

One thing that makes the mental and occult practice seem difficult is supposing that the work demands some intangible mental power exertion. This power must be pitted against the inertia of physical reality. This "matter" surrounding us seems to be so dense, resistant, and hard to move that most persons find the idea impossible that mere *thinking* can have power over external conditions.

Surface appearances do not deceive the wise. They see themselves surrounded by things that have neither the solidity nor inertia the unaided senses report. They understand that the densest substance and the lightest gases are *forms of energy*, built up from tiny, widely separated "drops" of the "Water."

Thus, the wise do not face the difficulty that besets those who believe their senses report concerning their environment. A practicing magician knows there is no difference between the energy which takes form as thought and the energy which takes the shape of a diamond, a piece of metal, or any physical object. The wise know that thought-forms are centers of more intense and lasting activity than material things.

The element Water is a substance that is electrical in nature. This knowledge enables an individual to effect a reversal in his environment. We can free our minds from subjection to appearances through this reversal, which prevents most persons from using mental imagery to change conditions for the better.

The 23rd Path of the Stable or Sustaining Intelligence

The 23rd Path is the Sustaining Intelligence (Sekhel Kayam). It is the power sustaining all the Sephiroth.

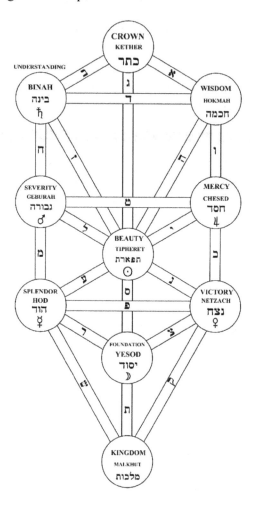

Mem (מ) is the Mother Letter of Water from which the father letter, Yod (י), came forth. Together they spell מי, *yom*, meaning ocean, sea. This word is numerically 50, which is the number of Nun (נ). In Ancient Egypt, Nun was the primordial waters of chaos (Tohu) from which creation came forth. Therefore the element Water is the sustaining power of the Universe and the Sephiroth.

Number 12

The number 12 is almost inexhaustible meanings. It is similar to number 7. 12 is the *product* of 3 and 4 (3 x 4 = 12), and 7 is the *sum* (3 + 4 = 7).

Twelve is the number of astrological signs. Seven is the number of planets known by the ancients. Together, the signs and planets are used to measure time.

Since 12 is composed of the digits 1 and 2. We read the digits in a composite number from right to left. Therefore, 12 expresses the manifestation of 2 through the agency of 1. In Tarot, 2 is the High Priestess, and 1 is the Magician.

Hence 12 suggests an outpouring of the powers of subconsciousness (2) through the fixation of the conscious mind's ability of attention (1). Precisely this is what the Hanged Man typifies.

Samadhi

When concentration is prolonged, the effect produced is what Hindus call *Samadhi*. Samadhi derives from the root sam-a-dha, which means *to collect* or *bring together*, and thus it is often translated as *concentration* or *unification of the mind*.

Samadhi is a deep trance and the *suspension* of most of the bodily functions. The inner result is a direct experience of super-consciousness. The union of personal consciousness with the universal is attained by practices that quiet the mind and suspend chains of associated ideas.

The title of the Key, the Hanged Man, refers to the result of such practices. Without changing its meaning, we might call it the *Suspended Man*.

"Man" is derived from the Sanskrit root *Manas*, meaning mind as the thinking principle. Therefore, Key 12, the Hanged Man, suggests the suspension of personal mental activity. This is achieved by concentration.

When this suspension of personal activity is affected, there is a release of the marvelous subconscious powers that make themselves manifest in the "works of power" performed by adepts.

As a result of even momentary experience of the superconscious state, one's whole attitude toward life becomes the reverse of the average human being. They who have this experience know themselves to be vehicles or instruments of the cosmic Life-Breath. Gone forever is the delusion that personality is, or can be, separate from the sum-total of cosmic activity.

The words of Jesus, "Of myself, I can do *nothing*," express the mental state of Samadhi. This is not a confession of weakness. It is the recognition that there is no form of personal activity, which is not an expression of universal forces and laws. Instead of lessening the importance and value of personality, this consciousness enhances one's estimate of the personal vehicle's worth. It shows that personality, though it can do nothing of itself, is the indispensable agent whereby the One Life's powers may be expressed.

Neptune - Ψ

Key 12 is assigned to the planet Neptune. Astronomers discovered it in 1846. However, its existence is known to occultists. Hence they made a place for it in the Tarot series. Neptune is the planet of inversion and is thus related to Key 12.

Neptune rules inspiration, psychometry, and mediumship. It is also connected with drugs that produce unconsciousness and hallucinations. Some of these drugs affect chemical changes in the blood, which make possible an imperfect perception of higher forms of consciousness.

Be on your guard here. Drugs can open a temporary gateway into the higher consciousness. Never make experiments of this kind.

These chemical substances enter the bloodstream and stimulate the brain centers through which the higher consciousness is experienced. However, these drugs can be destructive to the delicate tissues of the nerves and brain.

The fact that narcotic drugs do enable one to experience superconsciousness points to an important conclusion. Those who experience Divine Consciousness does so because of a *chemical change* in the blood. This change, however, must be effected from within the physical organism, not by outside agencies.

Since the bodily processes are entirely under the control of subconsciousness, your body's necessary chemical changes are being brought about by the work you are doing in your Tarot study.

When you look at the Tarot Keys, study the chapters, and carry out the instructions, you provide subconscious patterns on which to work. Subconsciousness brings about the required modifications in your body chemistry healthily and safely. Ultimately, as a result of these chemistry and nerve structure changes, you will experience the consciousness pictured by Key 12.

Summary

In many respects, Key 12, the Hanged Man, is one of the most important Keys. As you color it this week and during your regular periods of study, be sure to make a note of any impressions you may receive.

Many highly advanced humans are at all times using Tarot as a focus for their meditations. Because they are illuminated men and women, they are like high-powered broadcasting stations. Then you work attentively and receptively with Tarot; you are likely to pick up some of the ideas set forth by members of the Inner School.

Soon you will learn to distinguish these thoughts from the ideas developed through the deductive process in your field of subconsciousness. You may even receive a clear impression of the source whence these flashes of illumination come to you. Always have a pencil and paper at hand when you work with the Tarot Keys. Then you will be ready to record anything you may get in this way.

YELLOW: Slippers, halo round head.

BLUE: Coat. (Not crescents, buttons, belt or stripe down the front and round neck). Same as a canopy, on Key 7.

GREEN: Grass.

BROWN: Scaffold, hill slopes at the base of trees,

GRAY: Background.

SILVER: Crescents, belt, buttons, and front stripe. Hair of man, and rope by which he is suspended.

RED: Hose.

Chapter 28

THE HANGED MAN

The gallows are shaped like Tav (ת). The two vertical lines of the letter are a tree-trunk, each having six lopped branches. They correspond to the twelve signs of the zodiac and twelve types of personality. The intimation is plain. In the state of mental reversal, personal peculiarities are reduced to a minimum (the branches are lopped), and the emphasis falls on the Inner Self that is our true Spiritual Identity.

Samadhi

Tav (ת) is on Key 21 because it represents the inner meaning of Tav. In the state of Samadhi, or the suspension of *personal* consciousness, an adept in concentration becomes aware of the real nature of the universe. This is depicted in Key 21, The World.

To reverse one's mental attitude is to have a new world-view, which sees the universe as a dance of life, full of joy and freedom. Furthermore, the Hanged Man's suspension from Tav suggests that one realizes the complete dependence of personality on the universal life in this state of consciousness.

Since Key 12 is related to Water, a mirror that reverses the images upon it. Therefore Key 12 is a reversal of 21 to indicate that the state of Samadhi reflects the freedom depicted in Key 21 as the World Dancer. It appears in Key 12 to be a state of restriction or bondage. That is to say, the appearance shown by Key 12 is the reverse of the inner reality.

In Samadhi, the personal vehicle is in a state of motionless trance. The physical body is cold, the heart-beat slow, and the respiration almost imperceptible. Body functions are in a state of suspension.

Interiorly, adept experiences the bliss of union with the Central Reality of the universe. That Central Reality is a focus of intense activity, though itself at rest. Here the limitations of language force us into the use of paradox.

Tav is associated with the direction *Center*. The Temple of Holiness, which stands in the center, supports the six directions of space. Thus Key 12 indicates that the state of Samadhi is one of union with the supporting Center of all things.

Critics say that Samadhi is selfish. That sitting motionless in meditation is an escape from the responsibilities of life. Some people seek to escape from reality by mystic practices; others rush madly from one form of occupation to another.

A true adept is never idle, even though his physical body may be in a state of motionless trance. Samadhi is union with the sustaining principle of all manifestation, and a sage in this condition is sharing the burden, responsibility, and the joy of *cosmic administration*. Thus we find Tav is attributed the Administrative Intelligence, which directs the motions of the planets, leading them all in their proper courses.

Cube of Space

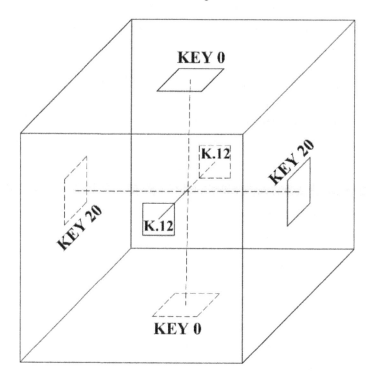

Mem and Key 12 is attributed to the line that connects east and west on the Cube of Space. Mem is the root of Water, which is the stream of substance that flows from the mental origins represented by East and Key 3.

This stream of substance enters into manifestation as the system of related events forming the cosmos' mechanism. In the west, Key 10 symbolizes the expression of this force as the Wheel of Fortune.

Tome - תם

The Cube of Space center is *final* Mem (ם) combined with Tav (ת). This word תם, *tome*, means wholeness, perfection, purity, and innocence. With different pronunciations, *Tam*, meaning to be finished, completed.

In Ancient Egypt, *Atum* is a creator god whose name means Complete One and the Finisher of the World, which he returns to Nun's watery chaos at the end of the creative cycle.

Crossed Legs (4) and Arms (3)

The legs of the Hanged Man form an inverted figure 4, suggesting Reason. His body, arms and head for an inverted triangle corresponding to number 3. The symbolism here is a correct statement of the situation depicted.

As we learned in Key 4, the Emperor, the triangle over a square symbolizes alchemical Sulfur.

In Alchemy, the Soul is the Sulfur principle because it is a unique expression of the Life-power. Sulfur is the active male principle and creates change. In Key 12, the Sulfur symbol is upside down suggests personal thoughts are actively suppressed.

The practices which lead to mental reversal are based on a rational grasp of Reality. That is, at the *center of human personality is the Universal Life of God.* This Law is a corollary to the Law that the *Life-power is present in every point in space* - omnipresent.

This realization results from a subconscious response to the seed-idea that the Divine Presence is central to our personality. This idea is a suggestion which subconsciousness elaborates and effects subtle changes to our body. Brain cells are stimulated. And through the activity of these brain centers, which begins as little more than a rational grasp of the principle, there comes an ecstatic experience of the I AM's Real Presence. To the glory of this experience, every great mystic has borne witness.

The four over the three also shows the subordination of imagination (3) to the reason (4). Most persons permit reason to be dominated by imagination.

Let reason determine what mental images shall occupy your field of attention. Let your mental imagine flow around the idea of the importance of your personality in the Administration of the Cosmic Order. That is, you're an instrument of the Primal Will to Good. This is not an exercise in egotism — quite the contrary.

Most persons rationalize their uncontrolled imaginations, which are at the mercy of race thought. Therefore, suggestions are based upon external appearances. Not so the adept pictured in Key 12. His subconsciousness is always under the direction of the reasoning self-consciousness. He is not the slave of moods, nor swayed by race-thought. When storms of passion toss about others, he remains unmoved. The Constituting Intelligence, pictured in Tarot by the Emperor, is the ruling principle of every detail of his life experience. By clear mental vision, he sees,

1. That there is only ONE POWER.

2. That the ONE POWER is centered everywhere,

3. That the ONE POWER is the central fact behind every mask of personality.

4. Therefore, whatever is done, is accomplished by the One-power, which acts *through* a person. And since the same power is the energy that forms the "universe," it must be true that whatever seems to be done by a person is performed by the sum-total of cosmic forces, operating through the personal instrument.

Hanged Man Clothes

Generally speaking, clothes represent the equipment or powers at the disposal of the personality.

The Hanged Mans' jacket is blue of Water and is like the robe of the High Priestess. The lunar crescents forming the pockets emphasize that subconsciousness is the container of the powers and stored-up experiences. The ten buttons suggest the 10 Sephiroth on the Tree of Life.

The jacket's belt and trimming suggest the combination of circle and cross, with the cross uppermost. A cross on top of a circle is a symbol of Mars. This hints that what seems to be a motionless suspension of activity is an intense expression of force.

The halo surrounding the Hanged Man's head suggests that he is an embodiment of the One Light. His hair is white, like the hair of the Emperor and the Hermit. However, the Hanged Man's face is young; he is Ancient of Days as a youth of endless summers.

Water Channel

Below his head, the ground is hollowed out, as by a watercourse. This is also a reference to Mem (מ). His head from the eyes to the top of the skull is below the soil's surface from which spring the trees. Thus we are shown that his vision and his brain functions are active *below the surface*.

This is what differentiates an adept from most persons. Adepts see through the surface of things. They discern laws hidden below illusive appearances.

Summary

The whole figure represents a pendulum at rest. Thus, the tree trunks are like the pillars of Key 2, the sphinxes of Key 7, and the pillars of the Hierophant and Justice thrones. The Hanged Man is unmoved and immovable. He knows that no *person* ever thinks, says, or does anything. An adept knows that the ONE IDENTITY is the only Thinker, Speaker, Actor. They realize that their personality is supported by the Central Principle of the universe, symbolized by the Tav-shaped gallows.

This week, practice checking your thoughts to see how many times your first thought's reversal is more in line with Ageless Wisdom's teachings. Be on your guard against subtle rationalizations. One of the most typical forms of rationalization is that which makes some course of action seem to be reasonable when, in reality, it is just the opposite. An overworked example is a desire for something. Often we persuade ourselves that we can't do without the object of our desire. This is imagination above reason, and we delude ourselves. This week, maintain alert watchfulness for rationalizations.

Chapter 29

TRANSFORMATION

Many superstitions are connected with the number 13 as a symbol of bad luck and disaster. Like so many things in occultism, we shall learn that 13 and Death have other meanings.

Both the number and the title relate to the Law of Transformation, which brings about dissolution and change. Minds dominated by race thought fear change, not because change is usually adverse, but because its outcome is unknown. Such persons fail to realize that life could not exist without continual change and that even if it could, its monotony would be unbearable.

Number 13

13 is the number of AChD (אחד), *achad*, which means "unity," and AHBH (אהבה), *ahebah*, love The Unity, the One Power from which all things proceed, is also the Love Power, which is the cause of all attractions and affinities.

We think of the Love Power as being chiefly concerned with reproduction. Thus Key 13 is attributed to the sign Scorpio (♏), governing the reproductive organs. Scorpio is the natural ruler of the 8th House associated with sex, death, and transformation. The same Love Power, which leads to birth, controls the physical changes resulting in dissolution and death. The Love Power governs both the beginning and the end of our physical activities.

There are not two antagonistic powers, one making for life, and the other for death. There is only a single power, which has a twofold manifestation. Consider this statement and meditate upon it.

Death

Humans fear death because they do not know the meaning of this transformation. "Dissolution is the secret of the Great Work." The dissolution of form is necessary for growth. When forms break down, energy is released to be utilized for further development.

Stone disintegrates to form soil, which springs the vegetable kingdom. Animals eat vegetables and incorporate their essences into a higher type of organization. We eat animals and plants and build the cells into our bodies. If we learn a secret which is available for all who are willing to work, we can do more. We liberate ourselves from the conditions of physical existence and master the energies which build our body. When mastery is achieved, we can maintain our bodies beyond the ordinary span of human life. Furthermore, in this mastery's full perfection, we can disintegrate our physical body at will and reintegrate it. When this stage of development is reached, as the world knows death, is at an end.

This is a fantastic statement. Possibly it is expecting too much to assume you will accept this teaching at this stage of your progress. Whether you agree or not, be sure you know this teaching. In time, you will have firsthand knowledge of this truth by performing the experiments demonstrating its accuracy.

With this instruction, you are beginning these experiments now. You have been taught the importance of forming the right mental images. Therefore visualize yourself as having a body that readily responds to the willpower you express. Your clear picture of a changed organism, which will be a perfect and beautiful body, both in function and appearance, has suggestive power that subconsciousness accepts.

In response to that suggestion, subconsciousness is *now* setting in motion processes that lead to the desired transformations. You do not need to tell subconsciousness *how* to do these things. It already knows. Tell it *what* you want it to do, and make your picture as clear and concrete as you can.

Thus you will triumph eventually over physical death. We already triumphed over death because *humans do not die*. Those who are prejudiced refuse to examine the evidence. The lazy don't take the time to trouble themselves with facts. However, the evidence is abundant and convincing.

Humanity is immortal and can never die. Though our bodies change and disintegrate a thousand times, *we* remain. You are approaching when you will know this as others that have gone this way before you.

24th Path of Nun - נ

The 24th Path is Imaginative Intelligence (Sekhel Dimyoni). It gives a form to the imaginations of all Living Creatures.

Imaginative is Dimyoni (דמיוני). It also means *likeness* and *fantasy*. The first to letters spell Dam (דמ), meaning blood. The last four letters are numerically 76. Words with this value are:

1. *Sod* (סודו) – his secret.

2. heh.vohn (חביון) – the hiding place.

The work of the 24th Path has to do with modifications of the blood. That transformation is brought about by the right use of fantasy and imagination.

Letter Nun - נ

As a noun, the letter-name *Nun* (נון) means "fish." As a verb, it signifies "to sprout, to grow, to propagate." For centuries, the fish has been a symbol of Christ, the immortal principle in every one of us. It is when we grow "to the measure of the fullness of the stature of Christ" that we approach the comprehension of life. The first moment of superconsciousness, of true Self-realization, is mystically called the "birth of the Christ-child" in human personality.

The noun "fish" is closely related to "propagation" because fish are prolific breeders. This fits the idea of propagation is intimated by the Scorpio's attribution to the letter Nun and Key 13.

Sexual Energy

Scorpio governs the sexual organs, which is the force used in reproduction and is related to the liberating, transforming the power of dissolution. Do not be misled. The doctrine has nothing in common with the pseudo-occultism of certain free-love cults. We speak of a *force*.

Ordinarily, this force is utilized in the reproduction of the species. It may be applied to higher purposes. It may be used to change your consciousness so that you will *know* yourself to be immortal. It may also be used to modify your body's metabolism so that you may renew it continually, or, if you so desire, dissolve it instantly and as quickly reconstitute it.

Be careful not to get false ideas. We suggest no abnormal restraint of the sex function. We do not recommend celibacy. Individual instruction for the Scorpio force's higher direction is reserved for those who have demonstrated their fitness to receive such information and use it wisely. It will come to you when you are ready for it.

The information you're receiving aids your subconsciousness brings you to the stage where you are qualified to undertake more advanced work. The purity of thought and action are essential. What you learn from these pages is sufficient for the present.

Mars rules Scorpio, which is the driving force of reproduction. Mars also rulers Aries (♈), symbolized by Key 4. In medical astrology, Aries governs the head and brain. Aries is the *Day* throne of Mars, while Scorpio is the *Night* throne. Aries is a Fire sign, and so it's a Day sign, while Scorpio is Water and associated with Night.

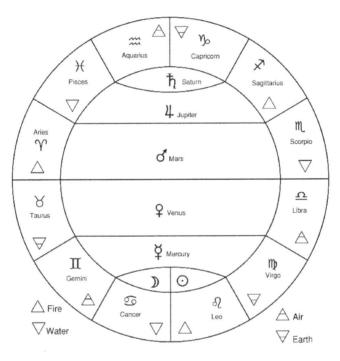

When the Mars force, working in the darkness and concealment of Scorpio, is raised so that it energizes brain centers ruled by Aries, it brings one into the daylight of the clear vision of Reality represented by the Emperor.

According to modern astrology, Uranus is exalted in Scorpio. In Tarot, Uranus is the Fool, representing superconsciousness. The highest expression of the Uranian influence in human personality results in first-hand knowledge of immortality. This is brought about through the activity of the Love Power.

Death and inheritance are connected with the horoscope's eighth house, the "natural" house of the eighth sign, Scorpio.

Our most precious heritage is the power that ordinarily manifests itself in bodily death.

This power, when we misunderstand and misapply, it results in disease and death. However, it is also the power whereby we may experience perpetual health and immortality. It is the power of life and growth to all who know and obey its law. To those who disobey it, is it the instrument of death and destruction.

Summary

Give a great deal of thought this week to the ideas of dissolution and change. Learn to welcome change and overcome the fear of it. The future holds what you have earned, conformity with past action, and patterns you are now making. Welcome it with a smile.

Key 13 Coloring Instructions

YELLOW: Sun, band on man's crown.

GREEN: Leaves and rosebush.

BLUE: Stream.

BROWN: Scythe handle.

STEEL: Scythe blade.

WHITE: Skeleton, rose, the cuff on hand in the center,

BLONDE: Woman's hair.

GOLD: Points on man's crown.

RED: Background.

Chapter 30

DEATH

On the surface, the skeleton of Key 13 is a conventional representation of the Grim Reaper. To the initiated, it's a reminder that our bones are the foundation of every motion. Because our muscles are attached to our bones, we can walk, move our hands and feet, and so on. Even the involuntary muscles are connected with the skeleton and could not move otherwise. Key 13 shows the foundation of all our physical activities. Symbolically, Death symbolizes the origin of growth and development.

The Seed

One-power, specialized in the body's reproductive functions, is the *seed power* shown in the key's upper left-hand corner. This little seed is composed of two ovals, that is, of two zeroes.

From the smaller oval, five rays extend toward the limits of the larger one. The two ovals are joined so that they are one. Here is a simple hieroglyphic for the process of manifestation.

The inner and smaller oval is the source of radiant energy, differentiated as Ether, Fire, Water, Air, and Earth. This energy fills the space enclosed by the larger oval, which is one with the smaller oval. This expresses a fundamental doctrine of Ageless Wisdom:

The inner power projects itself, or a seeming extension of itself, as space – the larger oval. This power fills space with forms of energy whose combinations constitute the body of the Universe.

Copy this italicized statement into your notebook. Read it several times. If you can, add to it some thoughts of your own. In due course, you will come to understand that it is a concise and accurate statement of the way the universe comes into being.

OBTW.

The ratio of the two ellipses' (ovals) diameters is roughly 2.7 to 1. This number jumps out at me because it's close to 2.71828... which is Euler's number or "e." The number e is a famous irrational number and is one of the most important numbers in mathematics.

limit $= (1 + 1/n)^n = e = 2.71828...$
As n approaches ∞

That means that as the number n approaches infinity, it gets closer to the value of e. For example n = 1000.

$$(1 + 1/1000)^{1000} = (1.001)^{1000} = 2.7169$$

Euler's number e is called the *natural language of growth* and rate of change.

The Skeleton

The skeleton twists at two points, above the pelvis and at the neck. This would be obvious were the bones covered with flesh. It is a posture no contortionist could imitate. The force here symbolized must be twisted, or reversed, to perform its highest function.

The skeleton walks from north to south, from the darkness of ignorance to the light of perfection. It represents the framework of all progress — the disintegration of form for the sake of releasing energy.

Scythe

The handle of the scythe is shaped like an English T and the Hebrew Tav (ת). Thus the handle of the scythe is connected with Key 21 and Saturn.

The scythe blade is shaped like a crescent, suggesting the moon and referring to subconscious powers symbolized by Key 2. The blade is steel, the metal of Mars. The red background is another reference to Mars.

The River

The river flows toward the sun. It starts in the north and makes a bend so that it also flows eastward.

The bend in the river has the same significance as the twist in the skeleton's spine. It intimates a change of direction in the current of energy. This river begins in the robe of the High Priestess and makes a waterfall in the Empress' garden. As an exercise, trace its flow through the other Tarot Keys.

The Rising Sun

As the end of personal existence, the idea of death is usually associated with the west and with sunset. In this Key, the sun is rising in the east. This suggests that power called death is the power of life. Every dissolution of form brings about the birth of new ones.

The rising sun is in the East is connected with Daleth (ר), and the Empress. Meditating on this relationship will deepen your understanding of Key 12, which precedes Key 13. Note that the digits of 12 add to 3. The rising sun refers to the dawn of higher consciousness in the state of Samadhi symbolized by the Hanged Han. This dawn of new knowledge is what is behind the transformation shown by Key 13.

White Rose

The white rose is the planet Uranus and has the same meanings as the rose in the left hand of the Fool.

The rose represents desire. Its thorns symbolize pain. Its bloom typifies beauty and joy. It is white to intimate that we align it with the Primal Will through the desire nature's right cultivation. Then our desires will be conscious expressions of underlying tendencies in the cosmic order.

Rose represents the number 5 because roses have five, or some multiple of five, petals. 5 is the number of adaptation and adjustment, and self-consciousness is the unique human expression of Life by adaptation.

Thus 5 is the number of humanity, who embodies the personal factor which carries the development of natural forces beyond the mere averages, which are characteristic of the sub-human and subconscious levels of being.

Geburah is the Sphere of Mars is the 5th Sephiroth on the Tree of Life. The mastery of the Mars force is a work of adaptation, symbolized by the number 5.

Woman's Head

The woman's head at the lower-left corner is a symbol of Understanding, Binah. This is the 3rd Sphere on the Tree of Life.

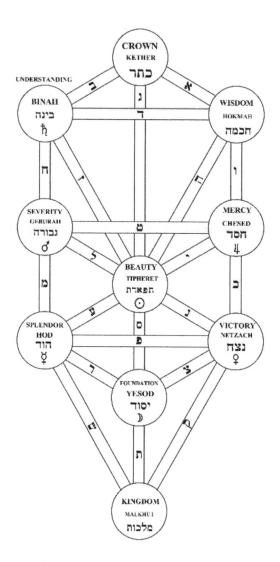

Understanding or Binah is the Divine Mother. The perfection of the Great Work, the Queen (Malkuth, 10th Sephiroth) and the Mother (Binah) is made one.

Man's Head

The man's head represents Wisdom (Chokmah, 2nd Sephiroth) and Beauty (Tiphareth, 6th Sephiroth). Father, is termed Wisdom, and the Son, is called Beauty. Remember that the Father and the Son are ONE, and their unity is intimated here.

276

Hands and Foot

Three hands are shown. Two are active and springing up from the earth. The third is passive, resting palm down on the surface of the ground. The active hands represent the new works that result from the transformation indicated by Key 13. The passive hand is a reference to Yod (ʼ), the Great Hand.

Pisces (♓) rules the feet. Only one foot is shown to symbolize the end of the Piscean Age or Dispensation.

Also, the white cuff is symbolic of the fall of the clergy class. Scorpio rules secrets. The Aquarian Age is all about instant communication. Dark to Light is painful but necessary for the healing process.

These details of the three hands and the one foot are in strict conformity with the esoteric Tarot, which has never been published. They also agree with the Tarot shown in Court de Gebelin's *Monde Primitif* and reproduced in Papus' *Tarot of the Bohemians*, and *The Key of Destiny*, by Dr. and Mrs. Curtiss.

Summary

For good reasons, much has been left to your intuition concerning this Key. These chapters are not a proper medium for practical instruction in reversing the Mars force's currents. We believe enough has been said to point you in the right direction. If you study this chapter, with Key 13 before you, many valuable insights should present themselves to you, especially in meditation.

Your subconscious mind understands pictorial symbolism. It is the one universal language transcending the limitations of human speech. Key 13 tells the secret of secrets and passes on to you our inheritance from the wise who have gone this way before us.

It is a secret that kills the old mistaken conceptions of personality in the scheme of things. It is a secret that makes one free from the "last enemy," giving us the direct perception of life eternal.

As you progress in the path, this will become to you more and more an open secret. As you begin to understand it, you will also appreciate the reasons for the careful reserve concerning it, which is characteristic of all wise instruction.

Those who know this secret has in their hands a power that might be used to overturn the world. No person learns it until they are truly prepared. This includes *ethical* preparation so that there is no temptation to misuse this power.

For the present, school yourself to know that change is never your enemy. Strive to become one of those of whom the *Bhagavad-Gita,* Chapter 2, says:

"The wise in heart mourn neither those who live nor those that die. Nor I, nor thou, nor any of those, ever was not, nor ever will not be, forever and forever afterward. All that doth live lives always! To man's frame, as there come infancy and youth and age, so some their raisings-up and laying down of other and of other life-abodes, which the wise know, and fear not."

Chapter 31

VERIFICATION

Samekh - ס

The letter name Samekh (סמך) means to prop, bear up, establish, uphold, sustain. As a noun, it means a tent-peg, which makes the tent firm in its place. The lesson of Samekh is to be reliant on the loving-kindness of the One-power to sustain us. Samekh is a test.

25th Path of Samekh - ס

The 25th Path is Experimental Intelligence (Sekhel Nisyoni). It is the primary test through which all the Merciful Ones (Chasidim) become skilled.

Note that the path begins in Yesod (9th Sephiroth), Foundation or Basis— also designated as the Sphere of the Moon. Remember that all representations of Water in Tarot begin with the robe of the High Priestess. Bear in mind also what was said in *Seven Steps*, that mind-stuff at subconscious levels is based on all forms of embodiment.

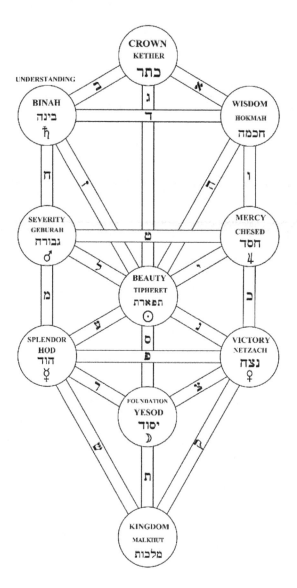

The Path of Samekh connects Tiphareth to Yesod. From previous lessons, we learned that our environment is shaped by the subconscious mind-stuff generated by humanity. In the Path of Samekh, theories are put to the test. Your skills are tested. Yes, the universe is mental, and energy follows thought. However, theory and reality are two different things. In this path, your abilities are developed through trial and error.

Verification

This path's meanings are related to the verification principle, which is the keynote of this chapter.

Most of the instruction given so far consists of theory. This is an essential part of your training; you must be well grounded in theory before practice.

You must learn the terms. Nevertheless, these theories must be *established* and *supported*. They must be verified before they can become part of your working equipment. They must be tested. Their *temper* must be *tested* to the utmost.
Application is the touchstone whereby all our knowledge must be tested.

This point differs from many systems of occult instruction. It is *practical*. You will be given directions as to how to test and apply these theories.

Already you have made a start if you have carried out faithfully the exercises given with these chapters. They are intended to help to shape your attitudes toward yourself and your brothers and sisters here on earth. Realizing humanity's nature and unity is *absolutely essential* for magic's successful practice in its authentic and highest forms.

These exercises are also intended to accustom you to link up the various ideas depicted by the Tarot Keys, both with one another and with your experience of life.

However, this does not mean that you only need a recipe or set of directions to practice the magical art, which you routinely follow. The magical art includes transforming your personality and raising or expanding your consciousness until you perceive the principles and laws operate. The great trial is testing yourself. Tarot represents *your* states of consciousness. The principles it depicts are those governing your life. They emanate from the *One-identity*, which is your innermost SELF.

The letter Samekh represents the trial, the probation, the purgation and purification of your personality, to the end that it may become a fit channel for the expression of the One Force. Thus the Law of Verification brings about the establishment or foundation of the House of God. As you progress with your studies and perform them, you are at the same time undergoing subtle tests that prove your fitness to carry on the Great Work.

See to it that you take this enterprise seriously. You have announced yourself as a candidate for Truth. The truth will be revealed to you when you have proved yourself ready for it.

Your first test is the earnestness with which you apply yourself to the preliminary instruction. This is the real purport of the following passage from the Book of Tokens:

"Thus am I as one who testeth gold in a furnace.
And this aspect of my being
Presenteth to the unrighteous
A face of wrath.

Yet by this purgation of fire
Do I uphold and sustain thee
In every moment of thy life.

Behold, I am he who testeth thee
With many subtle tests.

Wise art thou if thou knowest
That the subtle serpent of temptation
Is in truth the Anointed One
Who bringeth thee to liberation."

Note the reference to wrath and a serpent. These are both connected with the letter Samekh and with the underlying meaning of Key 14.

Three Serpent Letters

Lamed ל – Teth ט – Samekh ס

In Key 8, we see the serpent coiled, symbolized by Teth (ט). In Key 11 is Lamed (ל), the serpent uncoiled and active, its head erect, and its tail is pointing downward. Samekh (ס) shows the completion of the tail's upward movement toward the serpent's mouth. Samekh is a reversal of the symbolism of Teth.

Teth shows the Serpent Power as it is before we have learned how to direct it. Lamed shows it at the half-way stage toward mastery. Samekh shows the result of perfect control.

The serpent biting its tail is a symbol of eternity and wisdom. It suggests circular movement by its shape.

In the Sepher Yetzirah, Samekh (ס) is assigned Sagittarius (♐), ruled by Jupiter (♃). Sagittarius means *archer*, and its symbol is an arrow. Like Aries and Leo, Sagittarius is a Fire sign. Jupiter rules Sagittarius because the fiery power (♐) is directed and controlled using the Law of Cycles or Rotation, pictured by Key 10.

This fiery activity is a form of intense vibration. The Serpent Power is vibratory. It is the desire-force, which is the energizing principle behind all we do. It can be destructive when not wisely directed. Wrath or anger is its most characteristic destructive emotional manifestation.

Yet, it is the power that leads to freedom and is the force that destroys limitations and impediments to free expression. It is the tempering, cleansing energy that gets rid of all impurity and error in our consciousness. To the objects of its disintegrating activity, it is terrible, but the wise perceive its beneficence.

Number 14

The number 14 represents the principle of reason (4) expressed through the agency of concentration (1). The verification of hypotheses arrived at by reason is carried out using concentration. Concentration focuses on the vibratory activity of the Serpent Fire at a specific point in the brain.

The means whereby concentration is accomplished is symbolized by the Magician, directing power from above toward a plane below— his garden.

The digits of 14 add to 5, the number of the Hierophant. The goal of verification is reached by following the instruction imparted by the "still, small voice" of Intuition. Five (5) is the number of adaptation and desire. The proper adjustment of the tremendous force of desire, through intelligent direction, results in attaining the higher consciousness.

Sacrifice and Zeal

The clue to the inner meaning of all this may be found in the word DBCh (דבה), *debakh*, "to sacrifice," which is numerically 14.

Nobody ever attains to perfection without sacrifice. Those who know the value of their objective feels no sense of loss when they rid themselves of encumbrances, which interferes with their progress. In the early stages of the Great Work, one is called upon to make decisions that appear to involve sacrifice. Experience demonstrates the falsity of such appearances. Experience shows that every act of wise elimination makes possible the expression of a more considerable measure of power. At first, though, some of the tests are hard to meet.

They who fail are usually the persons who assert that there is nothing in Ageless Wisdom's premises. In a sense, they are right. There is less than nothing for the lazy, the double-minded, fearful, and who lack the courage to face periods of seeming failure. Those who seek the highest must-have zeal. They must be in fiery rebellion against the limitations and bondage of ignorance.

To carry on against odds that seem hopeless, we must be filled with an intense, one-pointed desire to demonstrate by experience concerning humanity's inner nature.

Zeal, however, is not enough. No one was ever liberated because they had a burning desire for freedom. The fiery force of the desire nature must be directed intelligently, to this Key 14, Temperance is a symbol.

Temperance

Temperance includes the thought of being able to manage one's appetites and desires. Also, Temperance, by its ancient definition— "the act of tempering or mixing."

In metallurgy, the object of tempering is to increase the strength and reduce brittleness. In the Great Work, this is attained by the proper mixture of opposite forces, by applying the Law of Equilibration and balance, shown in Key 14.

As you color the Key14, consider the symbolism carefully. By this time, Tarot should begin to speak to you even before you have read the detailed analysis of its symbolism. No study can exhaust the meanings of the Tarot. What is written here is intended to put you on the right track of correct interpretation. There is a unique personal message for you in every key because you have accumulated a store of experience in the age-long development of your personality to its present stage of growth. This treasure is below the surface of your consciousness. The Tarot can evoke from subconscious depths all you need to know.

Write down what Key 14 means for you. Next week, compare your findings with the analysis of the symbols given in Chapter 32.

COLORING INSTRUCTIONS

VELLUM: Crown over mountain peaks. Yods over the eagle, torch flame (interspersed with red to show that it is fire), lion's eyes, the path from mountains.

BROWN: Lion (see instructions for Key 10) eagle (except beak and legs), torch handle.

BLUE: Pool, and stream from the vase.

GREEN: Grass.

ORANGE: Ornament on the head of angel; vase.

VIOLET: Mountains in the background. Dilute the color so that the mountains will not be a violent purple.

GOLD: Background; star on the angel's breast. (Use yellow, if not gold.)

WHITE: Dress.

BLONDE: Angel's hair; beak, legs, and talons of an eagle.

RED: Angel's wings. These are highlighted with blue.

The rainbow is a succession of bands of color. Begin at the upper side of this are with violet, then blue, green, yellow, orange, and red.

Indigo, the color of Saturn, is hard to show it clearly. It is between blue and violet. If you have artistic skills, try adding the 7th color.

Chapter 32

TEMPERANCE

The central figure of Key 14 is the angel Michael (מיכאל), which means "Like God." He is the angel of the Sun and the direction South and the archangel of the element Fire.

On his brow is a solar symbol. One foot rests on water, a symbol of the cosmic mind-stuff. The other foot is on land, a symbol of concrete manifestation.

The angel is a symbol of the Higher Self that is indwelling in every human being. He is not the One-Identity, but the Life-Breath of that One-Identity, centered in the heart of personality. Most people think the pronoun "I" refers only to the personal self as a separate and independent entity. Others suppose themselves to be guided or overshadowed by some divine or angelic presence. They regard it as separate from the One-Identity, and also separate from the personal ego.

The esoteric doctrine is that one's feeling of "ego" is due to the focusing of a ray of the fiery Life-Breath of the One-Identity within the personal organism. The fiery Life-Breath is in continual circulation between the personality and the One-Identity from whence it originates. Just as the electricity is in uninterrupted flow between the light bulb and the dynamo at the power station, we are continually connected with the One-power source.

יהוה - Divine Name of Tiphareth

On Michael's white robe is the Tetragrammaton, Jehovah, יהוה. *In Gates of Light,* by Joseph Gikatilla, IHVH יהוה is assigned to Tiphareth, the 6th sphere on the Tree of Life.

Among names Of Tiphareth are,

Name	Hebrew	English	Meaning
Ben	בן	BN	Son, offspring
Melek	מלך	MLK	King
Adam	אדם	ADM	Humanity

Tiphareth is the seat of the personal ego. It is the manifestation of our essential humanity (Adam), the Divine Son (Ben) of the One-Identity.

7-Pointed Star

The seven-pointed star on the angel's breast is a figure that cannot be drawn perfectly using a straight edge and compass. To make a 7-pointed star requires trial and error before a good approximation is made. Thus, the 7-pointed star is a symbol of mastery.

Freemasonry says the compasses are used to circumscribe our desires and keep our passions within due bounds. The compasses are the Masonic symbol for controlling the fiery desire force, which is represented by the circular form of the letter Samekh (ס).

Can you take this hint? The seven-pointed star represents skill in wielding the compasses. But this star is on the angel's breast, to remind us that the ability to manage the desire nature depends on the "Knowledge and Conversation of the Holy Guardian Angel."

To obtain this skill, we must receive instruction from the angel. We put ourselves in a position to receive the angelic message when we devote ourselves to the work of making experimental verification of the real presence of the Higher Self at the heart of our personal lives. Such devotion brings us into harmony with the Universal Order, expressed by the cycles of the heavenly bodies or celestial spheres.

The Great Work completes the expression of the laws of nature. It is an *artistic adaptation of the laws of nature* by humanity. Without our labor, this work never comes to its full fruition. "Nature unaided always fails," says an ancient occult maxim. All human action results from a series of transformations of the One Energy. When that Energy is expressed through human thought, word, and deed— intelligently directed — that fulfillment is possible. *The Great Art requires the agency of human personality.*

Sagittarius - ♐

The wings of the angel are fiery red, with blue highlights. Sagittarius is a Fire sign, and in the Tarot attribution of colors, blue is Sagittarius. The symbol of Sagittarius is an arrow, suggesting aim, will, purpose, intention. Additionally, the 9th House belongs to Sagittarius in the Natural House System. The 9th house has to do with long journeys that expand the mind, higher education, religion, and philosophy.

With the quest for knowledge comes the need for "verification." Hence Sagittarius has to do with long journeys (*the travels in strange countries* of Masonry.)

Sagittarius is connected with high aspirations of the human heart, which lead us away from "this world" of false appearances into the country, strange, alas, too many, which is our true home.

Torch

The torch is a symbol of fire, and from it falls five Yods upon an eagle. The Yods refers to the five differentiations of the Life-power into the five subtle principles of sensation. They have the same meaning as the radiating lines in the oval shown in Key 13. Yod (ʼ) is numerically 10, and five Yods are 50. And 50 is the number of Nun (נ) and Key 13.

Furthermore, since they are Yods, they indicate a connection with Key 9. The fire is the subtle fire generated in the Virgo (♍) region of the human body.

The five flames are directed toward the head of an eagle, a symbol of Scorpio (♏). The Great Work has to do with modifying the phase of the Life-Breath, concentrated in the nerve centers connected with Scorpio.

This hint is one of the most carefully protected secrets of alchemy. Its full meaning cannot and must not be put into plain words, lest the unprepared misuse the knowledge. But if you verify with your own experience the Tarot teachings, you will fully develop this seed-thought. With your comprehension of the secret, you will understand the necessity for keeping it a mystery undisclosed to the profane.

Vases

The vase represents what alchemists call the "vase of art," In Philalethes' *Fount of Chemical Truth*, we read:

"When we speak of our vessel and our fire, we mean by both expressions, our water, nor is our furnace anything diverse or distinct from our water. There is one vessel, one furnace, one fire, and all these make up one water. The fire digests, the vessel whitens and penetrates, the furnace is the bond which comprises and encloses all, and these three are our Mercury."

This cryptic language refers to personal *consciousness*, which is 3-fold,

> Spirit - the Fire.
> Soul - the Vessel.
> Body - the Furnace.

These three constitute our "Mercury" or human *self-consciousness* and is represented by the vase. The vase is held in the angel's hand to show that the Great Work cannot succeed unless the human personality *is taken in hand* by the Higher Self or Holy Guardian Angel.

The vase's water pouring refers to Mem (מ), and the doctrine symbolized by the Hanged Man. In Key 14, the Purified Water, or reversed personal consciousness, is poured out on a lion. Through suspension of the false notion of personal independence, one understands the correct function of personality as an instrument for the Divine WILL.

This change in thinking is carried into subconsciousness, as shown in Key 8 (Leo, the Lion). In medical astrology, Leo rules the heart. And when the angle takes us by the hand, *a change of heart is brought about.*

A new activity is instituted at the heart center. Understand this as written. Here are no blinds, no figures of speech. This change an anonymous German philosopher alludes to when he says: "Fire and flowing water are contrary to one another; happy thou if thou canst unite them: let it suffice thee to know this!"

Rainbow

The rainbow symbolizes the differentiation of the vibratory activity of light into color. When the water of consciousness is mingled with the cosmic Life-Breath, it manifests the rainbow of promise. The colors of the rainbow are the colors of the planetary centers.

The rainbow represents the harmonious combination of the alchemical metals.

Planet	Metal	Chakra	Color[1]
Mars	Iron	2nd	Red
Sun	Gold	4th	Orange
Venus	Copper	5th	Green
Mercury	Mercury	7th	Yellow
Moon	Silver	6th	Blue
Saturn	Lead	1st	Blue-violet
Jupiter	Tin	3rd	Violet
[1] Tarot Scale			

The rainbow also refers to the occult *use of color as the most effective means to bring greater power into our human field of operation.* Using color, we can use vibratory activity to modify external conditions.

The rainbow also confirms Key 14 to Samekh (ס) and Sagittarius (♐). In Hebrew, for Sagittarius is (קשׁת), *quesheth*, the Bow.

The path in Key 14 rises between twin mountain peaks, which symbolize the Sephiroth, Wisdom, and Understanding; it ends beneath Kether, the Crown of Primal Will.

Cube of Space

In Chapter Thirty, no mention was made of the direction assigned to the letter Nun and Key 13 because we wished to bring this into closer correspondence with Key 14.

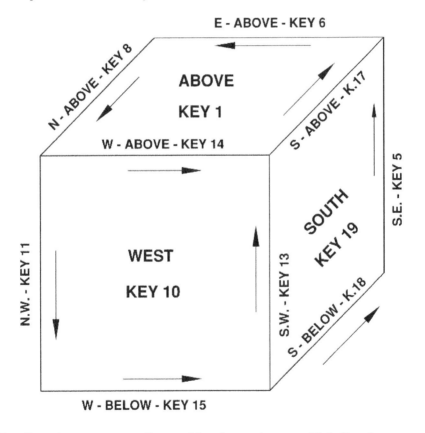

The direction corresponding to Nun is south-west. This line is opposite south-east, corresponding to Taurus, just as the sign Scorpio is opposite to Taurus in the zodiac.

Since Key 13 and Nun are the south-west face of the cube, it corresponds to the Wheel's ascending side in Key 10 and the rising figure of Hermanubis. Key 10 has to do with the ascending scale of evolution, or physical development, which is an expression of Scorpio's reproductive forces.

The reproductive forces include the bonds that form molecules and the sexual activities of plants and animals. Through these processes, the Life-power provides itself with finer and finer vehicles of expression. At last, the human organism appears, and it goes through progressive refinements. It is the sex drive or libido that drives our development. Our progress to the goal of illumination is conditioned by our understanding of our sex drive's significance.

By controlling the *libido,* we may go beyond the position of Hermanubis in Key 10 and rise to the point of conscious union with the Higher Self. Thus the cube symbolism shows the ascending south-west line terminates at west-above, assigned to Samekh and Key 14.

The west-above (Key 14) line begins at the top of the north-west line, assigned to Lamed and Key 11. The current of energy in west-above moves from north to south. But the flow of energy in the north-west moves from above to below. Although west-above joins the north-west to south-west, *it receives no influence from the line north-west.* The current energy in the north-above line (Teth and Key 8) moves from east to west.

At the northwest upper corner, Teth, Lamed, and Samekh's lines meet and the current divides. Part of it flows down (north-west line). Part flows southward (west-above. Note that the letters Teth (ט), Lamed (ל), and Samekh (ס), by their serpentine form, represent three aspects of the Serpent Fire.

Since the current energy in the south-west line moves upward, it contributes nothing to the west-above line flow. Therefore Key 14 (west-above) receives energy from the line corresponding to Teth (Key 8), but none from the line of the letter Nun (Key 13).

In the symbolism of Key 14, Leo's lion is on the left side of the angel, and the eagle of Scorpio (Nun) is on the right side. The angel in Key 14 is between the lion and the eagle, like the cube's corresponding lines.

Only the head of the lion and his forepaws are shown, and his body rests horizontally, with the hindquarters nearer the east than his head. The eagle's whole body appears in the picture and stands in a vertical position. Thus, the lion and eagle's placement correspond to the positions of the lines to which these animals are assigned. This careful attention to detail indicates that great adepts worked out the Tarot.

Also, the west-above line represents an activity carried on at the level of self-conscious awareness. Recall the top of the cube corresponds to Beth (ב) and the Magician.

Knowledge and Conversation of the Holy Guardian Angel is the Aim of the Magician. The self-consciousness activities are directed towards experimental verification of the truth that your personal life is under the angel's guidance and direction in Key 14.

Understand, this verification does not at all bring about such guidance and direction. The most ignorant man, deluded by the illusion of separateness and independence, is under its guidance, as is the most illuminated sage. Every human being is led and guided by the Holy Guardian Angel. Only a few are consciously aware of this. To most people, the Holy Guardian Angel presents himself as the dreadful central figure in Key 15, the Devil.

Summary

This week, test yourself. Ask yourself such questions as:

Does my belief support me in the various crises of my daily experience?
If not, what does?

Who does what I do, thinks what I think, and feels what I feel?

Are my studies and work transmuting the base metal of my personality into the gold of attainment?

Are my desires becoming purer, my mental processes clearer, my intuitions better defined?

Ageless Wisdom is not a creed or belief system. It is not an escape from reality into a mirage of glittering generalities. Nor is it a doctrine that puts aside until after death all hope of verifying its fundamentals. Plainly and explicitly, it declares that its principles of human knowledge and experience are tested.

Ageless Wisdom warns all who approach the Path of Attainment that it is not for cowards or dabblers. To the courageous, enthusiastic, and persevering, it offers evidence that admits no denial. It points out the way to attaining first-hand knowledge and shows how to follow that way.

Ageless Wisdom refuses to communicate the higher aspects of its knowledge to persons who have not made their bodies and minds ready to receive such communication. It never attempts the impossible feat of transmitting to those who are not prepared any part of those inner mysteries. Ageless Wisdom remains hidden by the veil of ignorance from those unready to look upon the face of truth.

Chapter 33

BONDAGE

Key 15, the Devil, depicts a man in a woman in bondage. But this is an illusion based on superficial appearances. The gross, repellant surface of this Key represents the illusion. You must see through the illusion to find Key 15's real meaning.

LVX – Light in Extension

Let us begin by examining the number 15. In Roman numerals, this is X (10) and V (5). These are the last two letters of the word L.V.X. That designates the One Force we concentrate by acts of attention. Therefore, XV is L.V.X., minus the L.

The L is Lamed (ל), which means "to instruct." As a noun, Lamed means shepherd's staff, which is an instrument to direct a flock. L.V.X. minus L suggests the absence of the equilibrating, directive power symbolized by Key 11. Hence from the number XV suggests that Key 15 represents the One Force, as it operates apart from human knowledge and direction.

XV is also composed of the numbers 10 and 5. Key 10 (X) is the Wheel of Fortune, which symbolizes the *mechanical* aspect of the One Force's cosmic manifestations.

Our conception of the universe as a mechanism has been built from our observations of the seasons' cycles and other recurrent phenomena. Most of the observations responsible for mechanistic theories and philosophies are in *fields below the human level*. According to the law of averages, the phenomena observed seem to be the working of a blind aggregation of forces.

This law of averages seems to be at work in the survival of the fittest. As evolution progresses, this law seems to work with somewhat diminished force. A poet once wrote of the Life-force. "How careful of the type it seems, how careless of the single life." In the lower forms of life, countless numbers are wiped out of existence. Only the strongest survive. Thus nature perfects her species.

It's different with humans. The survival of the individual takes on increasing importance because a new principle is at work. Key 5 pictures this new principle. It is consciousness that is hidden by the mechanical appearance of the universe.

Through the superficial examination of the environment, the ignorant build in their mind the conception of mechanism symbolized by the Wheel of Fortune. When we turn our attention inward, toward the center of our existence, we discover the indwelling presence of the Great Revealer, the Hierophant.

Thus X (10) in XV represents the world of outward appearances, through which humanity gains knowledge of the outer aspects of the One Force manifestation. V (5) in XV stands for the subjective world of consciousness whence humanity derives their knowledge of the *significance* of the whirling cycles of change.

By combining these two kinds of knowledge, X and V, we find inside ourselves guidance, enabling us to control our environment. We wage a successful war against sickness, poverty, and death. The war is not over, and sometimes the battle seems to favor the forces of darkness than light.

Do not be dismayed by the terrors of this age of transition. Whether we like it or not, The One-Life is the master chess player that will ensure that humanity evolves into a more enlighten and free species. Victory is assured.

The enlightened minority can act as channels for the superior powers whereby the automatic forces of nature, below the human level, may be controlled and directed constructively.

Advanced humans have long foreseen this era. For centuries they have been preparing to bring into manifestation the *New Order of the Ages* is one of the mottoes of the Great Seal of the United States. As a result of their endeavors, forces are being brought to bear, which will enable all humanity to exorcise the Devil by adding L to XV and making V *central*, as in the word L.V.X.

Since the middle of the nineteenth century, the Inner School is actively bringing about wider dissemination of Ageless Wisdom. Now is the time for humanity to gain greater control of themselves and their conditions.

Today thousands are ready for instruction, where hundreds only were prepared in former times. The enlightened are still the minority and will be for decades, or even centuries, to come. The main difference now is the time has arrived when aspirants may, in many parts of the world, work openly without fear of persecution by the Church or State. While the Old Order falls in ruins, they are making ready for the New Era of light and freedom, which is to witness a great advance toward the liberation of ALL humanity.

By theosophic reduction, 15 adds to 6 ($1 + 5 = 6$). Compare and contrast Keys 15 and 6. They contain similar details so that it seems that Key 15 is a caricature of Key 6.

Fifteen (15) is theosophic extension (sum) of the numbers from 0 to 5 ($0 + 1 + 2 + 3 + 4 + 5 = 15$). However unlikely it appears on the surface, we may understand that the Devil sums up the previous Tarot Keys from the Fool (Key 0) to the Hierophant (Key 5), inclusive.

Also, 14 is related to 5 because 1 and 4 add to 5. Since 15 is the theosophic extension of 1 to 5, there is a connection between Keys 14 and 15. Put both Keys before you and see how many relationships you can find by comparing the two Keys.

The 26th Path is the Regenerating Intelligence (Sekhel MeChudash). By it, the Blessed Holy One regenerates the World of Creation.

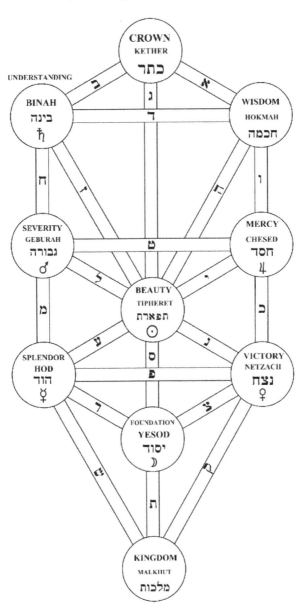

Consider these words carefully. They are clues to what is meant by "creation." For "regeneration" suggests that the beginning of a cycle of creation is a renewal of activity related to other cycles preceding this beginning.

Consider the meaning of Ayin (ע) as a fountain. A fountain is a spring where water nourishes the growth of plants. Where there is a fountain in a desert, there is an oasis. Usually, it is ringed with trees and looks like an eye in the face of the landscape when viewed from a height.

The fountain does not make the water that flows from it. It is the beginning of a little stream that trickles. This small stream joins itself with others until they all unite in a river that ultimately reaches the sea. The fountain renews but is fed by rain falling from clouds, formed by evaporation from the ocean. The fountain is not the source. It is merely a point at the commencement of a particular cycle.

In a magical manuscript of the sixteenth century, quoted by Eliphas Levi in *Transcendental Magic*, that among the powers and privileges of an adept:

"Ayin – To force Nature to make him free at his pleasure."

When we see through appearances, we find the underlying Laws in action. Through intelligence adaptation of these laws, the world is made new.

Since the Path of Ayin connects Hod to Tiphareth, Ayin is the Guardian on the Threshold from one perspective. The last test before entering the Sphere of Tiphareth.

Ayin - עַ

The letter on Key 15 is Ayin. As a pictograph, it's an eye. The letter name Ayin (עֵין) means, *appearance, sparkle, gleam*; a *fountain*; read causally; to consider, think over, and look carefully.

The eye is one of four bodily "fountains," the other three are mouth, skin, and urethra. Sweating removes heat from the body, urine eliminates toxins, and the eye produces water during grief or pain. All have to do with cleansing or purification.

For ages, the All-seeing Eye is a symbol of Deity. Thus Key 15 must have something to do with certain aspects of the One-Power. And this One-Power is a fountain of manifestation or source of creation. Add the meaning of Ayin's appearance, suggesting that the One-Identity is the source of the forms and appearances.

The eye as the organ of vision hints at a relationship between Ayin and sight, to Heh (ה) and Key 4. The sense of sight, important as it is, is also a source of manifold illusions and deceptions. We must make mental adjustments to interpret correctly what we see. For example, while standing on the deck of a ship as it leaves port, it appears the land is moving away from us.

Diablos – The Devil

Our eyes deceive us only if we let them. This deception connects Ayin and Key 15 with the Devil. In Greek, diablos, διαβολος, means slanderer, backbiter, an accuser.

An old proverb says appearances are deceiving, and Jesus counseled his disciples to avoid judging by appearance. In the New Testament, the Devil is called the "Father of Lies." That is the source or principle of falsehood, confusion, error, fallacy, and mental disorder.

The Devil represents the fundamental error whence all other falsehoods proceed. This is the error of supposing that "Matter" as opposed to "Spirit." Or the mistake that the physical world is the only reality and that "Spirit" is no more than an intellectual abstraction.

Maya – Illusion

The Sanskrit word for matter is *Maya*, and one of its meanings is "illusion." The Asian philosophers interpret the objective, phenomenal world as an unreal phantasmagoria of ever-shifting appearances.

Ageless Wisdom reconciles these conflicting interpretations. The outer world may be Maya, or illusion, in one sense of that term. However, "Matter" is the "appearance" of "Spirit," as it enters the field of name and form. It is not possible to separate the *appearance* from the One Identity's reality, which is making the appearance.

Error creeps in when we try to establish a separation between the appearance and may be termed the "appearer." The seeming Two are One; they are not in opposition to each other.

Temptation

In Matthew 4:1, "Jesus was led by the Spirit into the wilderness to be tempted by the devil."

This verse provides an important clue to the mystery of Key 15. Note that the Spirit did the leading for the specific purpose of *testing* Jesus with temptation. Remember what you have learned concerning the need for *verification*. The Devil appears to have some good use.

In Job 1:6: "Now there was a day when the sons (offspring) of God came to present themselves before Jehovah, and Satan came also." Satan is not prohibited from coming into Jehovah's presence. He is one of the companies of the Sons of God or *Beni-Elohim*.

In Qabalah, the Beni-Elohim is the choir of angels associated with Hod and the Sphere of Mercury. These angles are related to the consciousness represented by Key 1, The Magician. The "Mercury of the Sages," human self-consciousness, makes contact with its environment through the senses, especially sight.

What must we conclude from all this? First, the appearances that deceive us are *necessary* for the manifestation of the Life-power. Furthermore, to attain our full stature as human beings, so that we are in a position to force nature to make us free at our pleasure, we must be subjected to tests and trials of our faith. These trials are imposed on us by appearances.

The "mystery of evil" is no mystery to those who have met and passed the trials of faith. Those who have passed this test say in that experience, all consciousness of evil vanishes.

Some may say, "All very well, but I am acutely aware of the economic, political and social evils of the present day. I have the same shortcomings myself, and most of the people around me are not much better. No amount of fine theory will erase the slums, cure diseases, and empty prisons."

Granted. The way of life leads to the realization of humans' correct place in the scheme of things does more than banish evil. We become centers of expression of a power that transmutes semblances of evil into manifestations of positive good. Thus the magical manuscript quoted ends with these words:

"The wise man rules the elements, stills tempests, cures the diseased by his touch, and raises the dead ... The initiates know, and as for others, whether they deride, doubt, or believe, whether they threaten or fear— what matters it to science or us?"

Until we experience the higher order of knowing, we may have difficulty with evil's various appearances. We may wonder why appearances are often deceiving. But even without this higher knowledge, reason will take us far. Logic forces us to attribute the manifestation of the visible universe to a Primal Will-to-Good. Thus it follows that even if appearances are deceiving, the *appearance itself* is necessary for the perfect manifestation of the Life-power.

The manifest universe may be Maya. However, Maya proceeds from a wise, good, and all-powerful Source. Then, whether we can explain it or not, we are forced to conclude that the power that deceives the mind and originates all sorts of delusion is somehow useful. Maya, therefore, is part of the universal order.

This involves no denial of the various appearances of relative evil. Nor does Ageless Wisdom narcotizes us into an indifferent acceptance of these appearances at face value. The people who have done most to banish illness, sorrow and pain from other people's lives are the ones who bear witness to the higher reality, in which all consciousness of evil disappears.

Capricorn - ♑

In the fifth Chapter of *Sepher Yetzirah*, Ayin (ע) is attributed to Capricorn. Saturn (♄) rules Capricorn, the planet of limitation and restriction. Mars (♂) is exalted in Capricorn or has its highest field of expression. Thus Key 15 is a symbolic representation of a power which both binds and liberates.

In its binding aspect, it creates form. All form has specific limitations. The release of energy is shown in Key 13, Death. Key 13 and Nun (נ) are attributed to Scorpio (♏), ruled by Mars. Key 13 represents the operation of the Mars force that dissolves forms. In Capricorn, these different aspects of One Reality (binding and liberation) are brought together.

Summary

Form necessitates limitation, and in our experience, the limitation is bondage. However, the very limitations which gall us may become spurs to action which sets us free.

Layout the first column of Keys [shown horizontally to save space]. The exercise of concentration (Key 1) puts into operation the law of suggestion (Key 8), which results in a renewal of consciousness that releases us from bondage (Key 15).

When the force of Mars, represented by the red robe of the Magician, is brought to bear through concentration, it brings about a regeneration that dissolves the appearances of limitation.

In the Short or *Raavad* version of the *Sepher Yetzirah*, Ayin is assigned to Mirth. The perception of incongruous causes laughter. That is, *not in harmony or keeping with the surroundings or other aspects of something.*

Mirth is but a step from the truth that joy results from understanding the discrepancy between appearances of limitation and the reality that we are the One Identity's immediate agent. Experimental verification of this truth brings an experience of the most intense bliss.

There is an old saying, "The Devil is God as He is misunderstood by the wicked." It means that the monstrous figure in Key 15 symbolizes our ignorant ideas of Reality's true nature. When we have false opinions concerning our place in the scheme of things, this ignorance is the real Devil. They who set their feet upon the ancient Way of Liberation learn how to banish the Devil and destroy his works.

Key 15 Coloring Instructions

As you color Key 15 this week, notice that this hideous figure is an impossible combination of contradictions. Never did this nightmare shape exist outside the realm of disordered fancy, and it never can.

YELLOW: Insignia above cross below navel of the devil. The male and female figures' hair, the torch flame, and the male figure's tail are yellow, shot with red.

GREEN: Tail of female figure.

BROWN: Feathers, legs, and horns of the devil, torch handle, foreground, body, and wings of the devil (this is more effective if a little gray be mixed with diluted brown to give a dull, earthy color).

WHITE: Star, beard, horns of male and female figures.

STEEL: Chain and ring.

RED: Cross on the devil's body, grapes on the female figure's tail, the devil's eyes. (Also note what is said under Yellow.)

Chapter 34

THE DEVIL

The black background of Key 15 represents darkness. It is a symbol of ignorance. It also refers to Saturn, the planet ruling Capricorn.

The central figure is an androgyne goat, having the wings of a bat, the arms and hands of a man, and an eagle's legs and feet. The wings refer to the Devil's title of "Prince of the Power of the Air." It indicates subtle energy in the atmosphere, which is one of the powers controlled by practicing magicians.

The eagle's legs and feet refer to the sign Scorpio (♏), ruled by Mars (♂), which is exalted in Capricorn (♑). The Scorpio forces must be purified in test and trial fires if we are released from bondage.

The arms and hands of the monster show a gesture resembling the Magician. The difference is that the uplifted hand is open and bears on its palm the symbol of Saturn, signifying limitation.

The gesture of the Devil's right hand is also a contrast to that of the Hierophant. The Devil seems to be saying, "What is visible, what can be grasped by the senses, is all there is." This is the underlying fallacy of materialism and is the cause of man's worst limitations.

The inverted torch in the Devil's left-hand burns wastefully and gives little light. It is typical of the false light of pseudoscience. It also represents the blazing torch of revolution and rebellion.

On the Devil's body, just below the navel, is a symbol of Mercury (☿). It refers to the subtle processes of digestion and assimilation under Mercury's influence in Virgo that is brought under intelligent control. This work combines mental processes, indicated by the yellow upper half of the Mercury symbol. The red cross forming the lower half of the symbol represents biological responses or reactions.

The Devil's eyes are red, the color of Mars. The eyes emphasize the meanings of the letter Ayin (ע). The red eyes refer to Sight attributed to Heh (ה), and Aries (♈), ruled by Mars.

Inverted Pentagram

The inverted pentagram between the Devil's horns is the evilest sign of black magic. The essence of black magic is a mental inversion, rooted in the belief that the Self of an individual is dominated by the elements composing their physical environment. Thus the inverted pentagram is a symbol of falsehood because it is never true that Spirit can be dominated by matter.

The Half Cube Pedestal and Bound Figures

A cube often symbolizes this world. Therefore the pedestal is a half cube representing the imperfect understanding of the physical world. At the front of the pedestal is a large ring. To it are fastened chains that bind the two smaller figures.

These typify the human conscious (man) and subconscious (woman) minds. The bondage of delusion is a consequence of man's erroneous interpretation of the nature of the physical universe.

The hoofs, horns, and tails of these little prisoners intimate that delusion bestializes man.

On the Cube of Space, Key 15 is represented by the line West-Below. This line connects the lower ends of the North-West and South-West lines. It designates an activity working at the subconscious level.

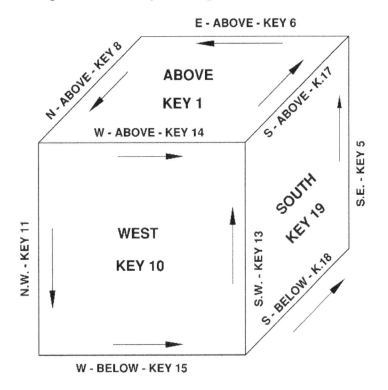

In the Cube of Space, Key 15 represents the operations of Key 10, at work on subconscious levels of manifestation. It represents the subconscious element in the Law of Rotation.

Key 15 shows how the power represented by the High Priestess (Below) manifests itself in the Law of Rotation (West). The Law of Rotation operates Below the level of conscious awareness.

The current of energy in this line moves from North to South. It combines the current passing from East to West along the North-Below line with the current passing from Above to Below along the line North-West.

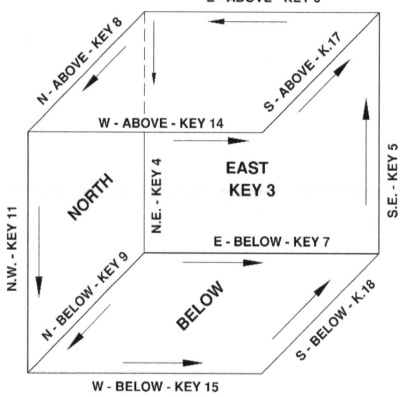

W - BELOW - KEY 15

Key 15 represents an activity that combines the forces of Key 9 with Key 11. Here is a clue to the practical meaning of Key 15. It shows us that whatever is represented by the Devil's symbolism combines Virgo and Libra's secret forces.

The line West-Below is opposite the line East-Below. The latter is assigned to the Chariot and Cancer (♋), which is opposite of Capricorn (♑). Furthermore, the line West-Below is diagonally opposite the line East-Above, and we have seen this opposition in the symbolism of Keys 6 and 15.

In practical occultism, Key 15 represents a force that combines the energy released into the physical organism through the Virgo (♍) region's functions, with power specialized by the adrenals and governed by Libra (♎).

All these forces are phases in the operation of the One Force. Each stage is distinct and has its peculiar characteristics. For example, we may think of the One Force as electricity, which is specialized through electro-mechanical devices into various kinds of activity. Passing through the filament of an electric lamp, it manifests as light. Sent through the coil of a stove, it becomes heat. One manifestation enables us to read at night. The other warm a room or cooks a meal. But we do not try to read by the light of a stove, nor prepare dinner over an electric bulb.

To speak of anything so obvious may seem out of place for the instruction of intelligent men and women. It is necessary because so many believe that one only needs to contact the One Force's central source to accomplish all things.

We have been asked what good there is "all this technical knowledge." Often the question is put by a person describing themselves as an "advanced student." They have spent years reading occult literature and have been members of one or more "very occult" societies.

Failure to grasp this principle accounts for the lack of success of many earnest students. *Practical* occultism is as full of technicalities as exoteric science. Our conquest of the inner world is made by the same kind of procedures which has brought about our conquest of the outer world.

Eliphas Levi describes the Astral Light as,

"This electromagnetic ether, this vital and luminous caloric, is represented on ancient monuments by the girdle of Isis, which twines in a love-knot around two poles, by the bull-headed serpent, by the serpent with the head of a goat or a dog, and by the serpent biting its tail, emblem of prudence and Saturn. It is the winged dragon of Medea, the caduceus's double serpent, and Genesis's tempter. Lastly, it is the devil of exoteric dogmatism, and is the blind force which souls must conquer, to detach themselves from the chains of earth."

Nachash

In Genesis, the tempter is called NChSh (נחש). *Nachash* means "brass," an alloy of copper and the metal of Venus. The number of *Nachash* is 358, the same as MShICh (משיח), Messiah, and signifying Christos.

What is hinted at by this numeral identity? The agency of temptation and that of release are the same. The Life-power is the cause of both bondage and liberation. When we do not understand them, the laws of the Life-power's self-expression seem to be our adversaries. When we come to know that all manifestation proceeds from the One Identity, we discover that a reversal of relationship is possible so that what seems to be against us is transformed into the means for our release from restriction.

Eliphas Levi speaks of the Astral Light as blind; he employs a subtlety of language. The force is blind only so long as we are unaware of its true nature. When we see the truth, this power becomes the vehicle of our vision. Hence it is connected with Ayin (ע), the Eye.

The secret of release is to get the pentagram right side up. Human's monstrous creation, the Devil, is none other than God, as God seems to individuals who have an upside-down conception of the *One Identity*. To know the One Self dwelling in the heart of each individual dispels the delusion that the elements dominate the spirit. When this delusion is overcome, evil's powerlessness becomes self-evident, and the Devil's works are destroyed.

Learn to laugh at appearances. Laugh at the notion of a Devil. The most effective resistance to error is ridicule. Laugh at the Devil, and he and all his angels will flee.

Chapter 35

AWAKENING

Key 16 is the second stage of spiritual unfoldment. It is the awakening of the nightmare of bondage. The first stage, represented by Key 15, is the realization of bondage's nature: ignorance. And when we understand the truth, the lightning flash illuminates the darkness, and the bad dream is over.

Key 16 is a picture of destruction, but the source of the destructive power is the Sun. The disintegrating force comes forth like a streak of lightning. It refers to the flash of superconsciousness, which constitutes the first awakening.

It is the first moment of clear vision, after which we are never again quite the same as we were before. It is like the hatching of a chick from an egg. Another life opens before it. So it is with us. At the moment of sudden illumination pictured by Key 16, we receive an initiation, and from then on, we see the world with different eyes. We belong to a new order of creatures.

Destruction is the Foundation of Existence

In *The Book of Tokens*, the meditation on the letter Peh (פ) says:

"Verily destruction is the foundation of existence.
And in the tearing down thou seest
Is but the assembling of material
For a grander structure."

A little observation will convince you that destruction IS the basis of existence. Our entire lives are spent in the disintegration of forms for the sake of building up other forms.

Disintegration releases power. The food we eat, the clothes wear, the automobiles we ride in are all in the process of destruction from the first moment we put them into use. Many engineers have a strong Mars in their natal chart. Building a road requires blasting rock and cutting down trees.

In the experience of spiritual unfoldment, awakening is distinctly a destructive process. All the wrong thinking and acting must go. The false sense of personal will, of personal autonomy, of personal self-action, must be destroyed.

It is not an easy process; when one is forced to recognize that some of their most cherished beliefs are false, the consequent readjustment is not easy. The wise in every age have testified that this destruction is a gathering of materials for a grander structure.

In the first chapter of John, "In the beginning was the Word, and the Word was with God, and the Word was God. He existed at the beginning with God. God created everything through him, and nothing was created except through him. The Word gave life to everything that was created, and his life brought light to everyone."

This passage refers to the power which you have been studying since the first chapter of *Seven Steps*. This power is not only the source of the forces used in creation, integration, and reproduction. It is also the forces that manifest in the opposites, destruction, disintegration, and death.

In *The Book of Tokens*, under Peh (פ), which means "the mouth as the organ of speech," states:

"I am the mouth, whence issueth the breath of life;
I am the all-devouring one
Whereunto all things return."

It is the power active in the disintegration of the old forms of personal consciousness. It rends the veil which hides the truth from our eyes. The teaching that this breaking down of form is fundamental in the process of the Life-power's self-manifestation.

The practical magician has to learn that to reach any goal requires first breaking down the conditions that stand between you and your Aim or heart's desire. To find release from the chains that bind us, we must learn how to break them.

The time to begin breaking down the old limiting forms is *now*, not in the future. You have already made a good start. You are aware of your limitations. You are making an effort to transcend them. This is witnessed by the fact that you have followed the instruction thus far.

As you proceed, other practical methods for combatting your limitations will be given to you, and things of splendor will unfold within you. Your first step is to apply in your daily life the principles represented by the Tarot Keys. Your aim is to build those principles into the structure of your being.

Number 16

The number 16 says as much. Right discrimination, the principle represented by Key 6, is necessary for this work. Apply this principle through acts of concentration, typified by Key 1, and you will find that each day's experience brings you some measure of the awakening so strikingly pictured in Key 16.

Superficial observation will not suffice. You must give attention to the meaning of your thoughts, desires, and actions. Thus you apply the principle of limitation (concentration) to overcome the limitation.

Those who are proficient in concentration rarely place themselves in embarrassing situations by rash and unconsidered action. We think before we act and then act wisely.

Peh - פ

As a pictograph, Peh is a mouth. The letter name Peh (פה) also means mouth and synonymous with speech. It also means command, orifice, opening, entrance, end, extremity, border, edge (of a sword), the womb. All these words are related to ideas related to *openings*.

In *The Hebrew Letters*, Rabbi Ginsburgh says that speech is the power to enter the *here and now*. The correct use of language is to direct the forces of nature by making words the tools of organized thought.

The Tower

Some old versions of Key 16 are named, The House of God, The Fire of Heaven, and the Lightning-struck Tower. Tradition says it refers to the fall of the Tower of Babel. In the Biblical story, Babel was built as a tower to heaven. God confused humanity with the introduction of new languages. When we try to use words to define superconscious states, which are beyond words, the inevitable result is confusion.

27th Path of Peh - פ

The 27th Path is the Perceptible or Felt Intelligence (Sekhel Murgash). Through it, the senses of all living beings under the zodiac are excited.

Mur.gash (שגרומ) is from the three-letter root rah.gash (שגר), meaning to roar, rage; to be excited. With different vowel points, the same letters spell *reh.gesh*, meaning, feeling, emotion, sense, sentiment.

Rabbi Kaplan translates *mur.gash* as *palpable*, which means,

1. A feeling or atmosphere so intense as to seem almost tangible.

2. Able to be touched or felt.

The 27th Path is not subtle. This particular specialization of the Life-power is hard to ignore or miss.

OBTW.

In Hebrew, most words are derived from the root words of two or three letters. Then other letters are suffixed to denote possessive (his and hers) or plural.

If you're interested in Hebrew, do a web search for "prefixes in Hebrew." Better yet, take a class. In six months to a year of study, you can learn all the Hebrew you need for the Western Mysteries.

For the study of Hebrew, purchase Reuben Alcalay's, *The Complete Hebrew English Dictionary*. It's a five-volume set and worth its weight in gold.

And for a beginning Hebrew language study, *The First Hebrew Primer.*

The planet Mars is related to Key 16 through Peh (פ). Mars is the god of war and bold action. Mars is the driving force behind all successful activity. The way the Mars force manifests in us depends on whether we direct it or permit it to control us, thus inducing rash and foolish activity.

The Mars force is the propulsive energy of desire. The direction of desire is not repression. No one without powerful desires and emotions ever attains to the heights of mastery. When you repress the Mars force, it sooner or later breaks loose in a burst of terrible destruction. Do not suppress desire; instead, find a positive outlet for its energy.

The channels through which the desire force finds expression usually are under our conscious control. It is perfectly natural to manage the desire-nature. Key 1, The Magician, shows how. Formulate your desires, using intelligent discrimination, and then bring them into manifestation by concentration. Make your mental images of the desired result sharp and clear so that subconsciousness receives a definite impression. Then the activity of the dynamic Mars force will make your dreams come true.

This week, as you color Key 16, observe its details. Try to get some hint of their deeper meaning, and make a note of whatever ideas may come to you.

COLORING INSTRUCTIONS

YELLOW: Two bands a crown that looks like a rope; star; the crown of woman. The Yods are yellow, with a tongue of red in the general shape of a Yod in the lower right corner of each. A preponderance of red, shot with yellow, makes them more realistic.

BLUE: Dress of woman; hose of man.

GOLD: Crown, except yellow parts; lightning-flash.

GRAY: Tower, clouds (heavy storm clouds, as in Key 10).

BROWN: Cliff. The top of the cliff is a lighter brown.

BLONDE: Woman's hair.

RED: Boots & coat of man, shoes of woman. (See also under yellow.)

Chapter 36

THE TOWER

The lightning-flash in Key 16 is a reference to the *Book of Formation* 1:6:

Ten Sefirot of Nothingness.
Their vision is like the *appearance of lighting*.
Their limit has no end.
And His Word in them is *running and returning*.
They rush to His saying like a whirlwind
And before His throne, they prostrate themselves.

Thus, the lightning-flash symbolizes the power of the creative Word and Peh (פ) attributed to Key 16.

The flash comes from a solar disk to show the active force at work is a phase of the Life-power, despite the destruction wrought by it. The disk is in the same corner as the white Sun in Key 0, The Fool. It is a symbol of Kether, the Crown, as the source of everything. One of its titles is "The Profuse Giver."

One of the teachings in the Kabbala is God is Good. God seeks to give you as much good as you can take. And when the cup overflows, it's the lightning bolt of Key 16.

The lightning-flash is drawn so that the bolt traces a path down the Tree of Life.

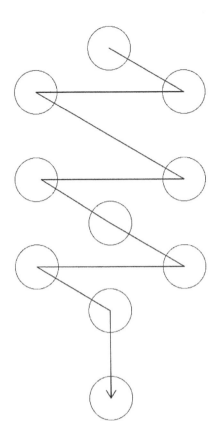

2nd Stage of Spiritual Unfoldment

Concerning the second stage of spiritual unfoldment, the lightning indicates the sudden illumination, or flash of inspiration, which comes to us when we have faced our problem boldly. We have concentrated on our problem with the full force of our attention, and the Life-power does not disappoint and rewards our efforts.

Tower

The tower is built of brick of 22 layers. Since there are 22 Hebrew letters, this represents a structure built on the wrong use of speech.

The tower is a structure of human error and ignorance, yet it is still a House of God. Our personalities, even though they are structures that incorporate our false notions, are still Temples of the Living God. Our bodies' inadequacy is caused by the influence on subconsciousness of our wrong thinking, expressed by erroneous use of words.

Hence the lightning-flash of true perception is felt in the body. There must be a period of physical readjustment before our bodies can be vehicles to express the higher levels of consciousness.

Crown

The crown knocked off the top of the tower is a symbol of will-power. Kether, the Crown is the Primal Will. However, the crown of the tower is false. The crown of personal will tried to usurp the Primal Will and failed. Its failure is adorned on top of the crown as four letters M.

In Hebrew, M is Mem (מ), is numerically 40. And 4 Mems is 4 x 40 = 160. The number 160 is QN (קן), *Cain*. Cain is the first murderer, and personifies false will power. The idea is that every person has a will of his own, separate from the Cosmic Will.

True knowledge begins with a flash of perception, which makes us realize that our personal experience is part of the total expression of the Life-power's activity. However brief this flash maybe, it overthrows the notion of a separate personal will; it also disrupts mental structures based on the error that we live our lives in perpetual antagonism to the universe and our neighbors' lives. This lie is behind every murder. It is eradicated by even the briefest perception of the fundamental unity of all that exists.

The Man and Woman

The falling man is self-consciousness; the woman is subconsciousness. The flash of inspiration upsets all our former conceptions of the nature of personal consciousness and reverses our old ways of thinking.

In Key 16, the figures are clothed because they hide their true nature from each other. The man is in a state of ignorant separateness. In this connection, clothes are symbols of shame and sin.

Red Shoes

A shoe is a symbol of base desires. Normally in the Tarot, shoes are yellow to symbolize our desires are under intelligent control. Because in the Tarot color scale, yellow is Mercury and Key 1, the Magician – self-consciousness.

The man and woman have red shoes to symbolize that their base desires (shoes) are being led by their passions – Mars (red).

The red shoes remind me of a quote from the Egyptian Bronzebook.

"These are the signs and times which shall precede the Destroyer's return. A hundred and ten generations shall pass into the West, and nations will rise and fall. Men will fly in the air like birds and swim in the seas as fishes. Men will talk peace one with another; hypocrisy and deceit shall have their day. Women will be as men and men as women; passion will be a plaything of man." The Book of Kadmis 3:7

Twenty-two Yods are suspended in the air. The ten on the right of the tower are arranged like the Tree of Life. The twelve on the left are arranged as a figure eight with Yods in the center of the ellipse. These Yods stand for the 22 letters of the Hebrew alphabet because every Hebrew letter is an aspect of the letter Yod (ʼ).

These Yods float in the air to represent the sum-total of cosmic forces. They also symbolize the Creative Word and the powers of human personality.

They are shown hanging in space because none of these forces has a physical foundation. This idea is the reverse of what is suggested by the rocky, isolated peak on which the tower is erected. Note that this peak is the same brown color as the Devil's body.

The average person thinks their life has a physical basis. They suppose it to be sustained by food, air, water, and their environment's various physical forces. Ageless Wisdom says the Life-power is the basis of all manifestation, physical or otherwise. It does not deny the importance, much less the actual existence, of the physical plane. It does say that the physical world is an expression of the powers of spiritual life. Thus it declares instead that material existence is caused and maintained by the Life-power.

It is true that special physical conditions must exist so the human personality may function on earth. It is NOT true that these conditions are the *cause* or *support* of human personality. The true cause is the Life-power; the Life-power manifests itself in every physical condition and physical force. The conditions are the effects. They are NOT the cause of manifestation.

Thus Ageless Wisdom holds causation to be vital rather than physical. This idea is not in fashion. Nevertheless, it is *demonstrably* true. Nor is it less true because few people living can make the demonstration.

Not every person can play a concerto. Those who have musical talent and devoted themselves to hours of practice can do so. Many people who have practiced the laws of life and become skilled in applying them can control physical conditions, which seems miraculous.

Such people have command because of their regenerated bodies, which enables them to do extraordinary things. Yet these masters were at one time as much in the dark as we seem to be. They met the same problems and difficulties that we are encountering. They supposed causation was physical, and they thought they were "going it alone." Like the tower, their house of personality was built on a peak of selfish isolation, and it was crowned with the usurper's belief in the personal will.

Then there came a day when, like lightning, a flash of clear perception reversed their opinions. Darkness closed around them again, for, at this stage of spiritual unfoldment, the light is not continuous. However, they remembered what they had seen and created a radical change in their fundamental conception of life.

We must make the same change, but we have to pass through the same experience before making it. If you have had this experience already, you will understand the more profound implications of Key 16. If you have not had it, this chapter will help prepare you for the sudden, terrible, yet wonderful awakening which will end your dream of separation and bring you near the beginning of the Way.

Peh (פ) is assigned to North, the place of greatest symbolic darkness.

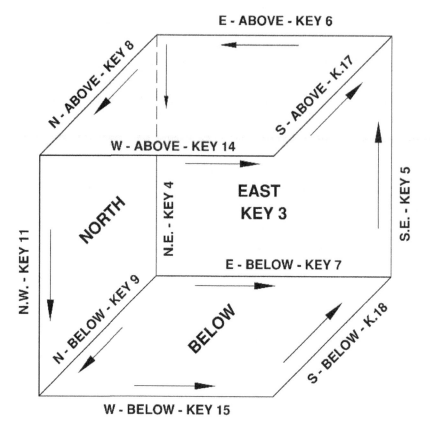

Compare this darkness symbolism with the black pillar on the left or north side of Key 2 and the black sphinx on Key 7. Note that the pillar marked with Beth (ב) is associated with the idea of *strength*, and also as *severity*. This is suggested by the grim expression of the black sphinx in Key 7.

Darkness, North, and strength are ideas associated with powers that are veiled in darkness. However, these are powers that bring release and enlightenment. These forces are liberating. What inspires fear and terror in the mind of a savage is what a civilized man employs to set himself free from limitations.

Standing near a lightning bolt is an awe-inspiring experience. However, electricity is the willing servant of human intelligence that sends words and pictures around the world.

This is why the Emperor faces north. Human reasoning is always concerned with the unknown, with what is concealed from the average mind. Those who conquer their fear of darkness can discover the secrets it hides. It will bring us to light.

By ideas associated with Mars and North, the wise hint at electricity. The occult force symbolized by a flash of lightning is the basis for those inner modifications of the personal vehicle, which result in enlightenment. A serpent also represents this aspect of the vital cosmic electricity. In Key 6, a serpent on the north side is winding around a Tree of Knowledge of Good and Evil. In Key 10, a serpent is descending on the north side of the wheel.

North is the place of the unknown. Therefore the perspective of Key 16 is the observer in the south looking north.

This puts North-East on the right side of Key 16 and North-West on the left side, with North-Above at the top and North-Below at the bottom.

Summary

The power that arouses terror in ignorant minds is the same power for our enlightenment or awakening.

The Mars force stimulates desire. Devote yourself this week to a study of your desires. Most of us are beset by a veritable mob of miscellaneous desires. Many of them are unimportant, weak, and fleeting. An enlightened have few desires, but those they have are deep, powerful, and one-pointed. Such a human shoots straight at their mark, permitting nothing to deflect their purposeful aim. Their thoughts dwell on what they have decided to be and do. Their mind pictures it clearly. Their activity is directed to its attainment.

Select your most important desire. Do not allow less important ones to interfere with it. Yielding to the influence of small desires dissipates energy you can apply to truly important work.

This practice is difficult, easy as it is to describe. To bring the desire nature completely under control takes a long, steady drill. On this account, do not drop the practice at the end of this week. Keep at it continually. Desire is the power that achieves, and the art of directing this power is based on all kinds of mastery.

Chapter 37

REVELATION

The third stage of spiritual unfoldment is *Revelation*. Revelation is *unveiling, disclosure, and discovery*. The seeker does not discover the truth. It is made for them. We receive the revelation. We do not lift the veil of Isis. She unveils herself.

Thus Key 17 pictures an operation above the level of personal human consciousness. The physical senses do not perceive disclosures made at this stage. They are not conclusions reached by the reasoning mind, based on observing externals. Quite the reverse. These revelations come when the reasoning mind is wholly stilled and the senses sealed.

Tzaddi - צ

Tzaddi is assigned to Key 17. Tzaddi, as a pictograph, is a man lying on his side. The letter name *Tzah.dee* (צדי) means, side. The related verb Tzah.dah (צדה), means, wait, waylay, lurk, ambush, and do by design. Ernest Klein adds "fishhook" to the meanings of Tzaddi. Therefore Tzaddi is related to research or hunting for an answer.

The quest is for something not yet realized. It is a groping, a feeling one's way, a "fishing" for something. Thus, Tzaddi (צ) symbol stands for an agency or instrument whereby one endeavor to solve problems. It symbolizes the means that once follows a clue for discovering secrets or solving a mystery.

The 28th Path is called the Natural Intelligence (Sekhel Mutba). It completes and perfects the nature of all that exists under the revolution of the Sun.

Mut.ba is from the root, *tah.vah* (עבט) meaning, to sink; to coin, impress; to be drowned. The same letters are *teh.vah* mean, nature, character, element, and substance. And also, *tee.vah*, to put a ring on, to be ringed.

The meanings imply that nature is like the impression made on wax by a signet ring. The quote from 32 Paths of Wisdom says that all things are under the sun's orb. And the orb (ring) of the Sun is the twelve signs of the zodiac which are impressed upon our personalities.

Meditation

The *Book of Formation* assigned *thought* to Tzaddi and suggest *meditation*. As the English *contemplate,* it implies the marking out of a field of observation, limited in extent, wherein the whole force of attention may be brought to bear on some object of thought.

Patanjali defines meditation as "an unbroken flow of knowledge in a particular object." The symbolism of Key 17 agrees with this definition. Meditation is close, continued thought. It is a deep reflection. It is a continual dwelling on one *central* idea, diving down into the mind's depths for the various associations connected with the main thought— that is, fishing for the truth.

Such associations of ideas are the basis of Tarot practice. You will find this carried out even further when you come to the detailed study of the Tree of Life and its correspondences.

Keys 1, 2, and 3 symbolize the fundamentals of the process. First, the selection of an object on which attention is fixed (Key 1). Second, the associative activity is represented by Gimel (ג) and Key 2. Third, mental imagery development, the basis of understanding (Key 3 and Daleth ד). These are the mental aspects of the meditative process.

Meditation has specific tangible results and employs physical energy. Tzaddi, as a fish-hook, gives a hint as to the physical part of meditation because *fish* in Hebrew is Nun (נ), and the *hook* is Vav (ו).

In the letter name Nun NVN (נון), Nun and Vav are combined. In the Sepher Yetzirah, Nun is assigned to Scorpio (♏) and Key 13. Vav is Taurus (ו) and Key 5. These two signs are opposites and complement. Mars rules Scorpio. Venus rules Taurus. These are also complementary planets and chakras in the human body.

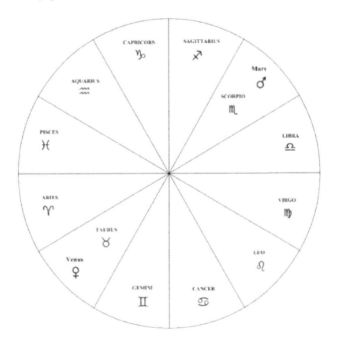

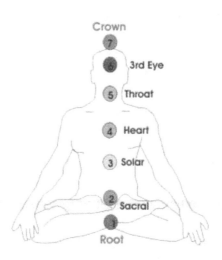

	Chakra	Planet			Chakra	Planet
1	Root	Saturn		5	Throat	Venus
2	Sacral	Mars		6	3rd Eye	Moon
3	Solar	Jupiter		7	Crown	Mercury
4	Heart	Sun				

In meditation, the force which ordinarily expresses itself through sexual energy (Mars) is *raised* and becomes active in Venus (Taurus) chakra in the throat, which includes the hearing centers in the brain. The resulting stimulation of these centers enables one to become aware of the Hierophant's Inner Voice. The Hierophant is the Revealer, and Key 17 is a symbol of the Revelation.

The numeral value of the character Tzaddi (צ), is 90. This is also the value of Mem (מים) corresponding to Key 12, The Hanged Man. In Hebrew gematria, words that have the same numerical value are related.

A fish-hook is an instrument for lifting fish out of the water. Alchemical Water is a symbol of the universal subconsciousness, the Great Sea in which all things have their origin.

Key 12, the Hanged Man, is synonymous with the Suspended Mind. It signifies the suspension of personal consciousness as a result of profound meditation. In Sanskrit, this suspension is called Samadhi. Samadhi is said to lead to the revelation of the highest truths. Note that a fish-hook is suspended from a line so that it hangs. This makes a fish-hook useful.

In meditation, by keeping the stream of consciousness flowing to some particular object. We gather impression after impression from that object. Our minds take the form of that object. We become identified with it. Thus we become aware of the object's inner nature. It reveals itself to us.

The object of meditation is usually some problem. As one must have the right bait to get fish to bite, so one must have a definite meditation object. The reason for meditating is to solve the problem.

Because it *is* a problem, it appears to be the adversary of the person who is meditating. It may look like the Devil himself, but we know this is only the first appearance and disregard it. We know the solvent power of consciousness and apply it.

In meditation, the first is to silence the superficial activity of personal consciousness. A fisherman sits quietly, so one in meditation must learn to wait patiently until the fish of thought takes the hook. The hook is always a specific question. It is not a passive meditation. The mind is active.

We do not discover the truth. However, our mental attitude must be one of the *active* quest. We must not be content merely to sit still in the hope of enlightenment. Quiet we must be, but at the same time *intent* on receiving light on our problem — as the poet says, we must *invite* the soul. We can hear the Hierophant's voice in this attitude, and he will speak distinctly and definitely.

As we become skilled in meditation practice, it's easier to find the specific problem that gets our attention. In Ancient Egypt town of

Sais is a statue of Isis. On it, an inscription reads, "I am all that has been and is and shall be, and no mortal has ever lifted my garment."

No mortal can lift her veil. However, it is raised again and again by Isis for those who are truly prepared to behold the vision of her lovely presence.

Nature does not hide from us. The veil which conceals the truth is the veil of human ignorance, the foolish belief in his separateness and mortality. The practice of meditation may remove this veil.

Number 17

The number 17 is composed of the digits 7 and 1 — seven (7), standing for the power which is expressed. One (1) is the agency through which that power operates. Key 7, The Chariot, is a symbol of the receptivity that is necessary for meditation. The Path of Wisdom associated with Key 7 is the Intelligence of the House of Influx. It is something that flows down into the field of personal consciousness when we are quiet and receptive. It is what does the work in meditation.

Those who want to meditate must be keenly aware that personality is only a vehicle for Life-power. They must understand that the Life-power, being the *Word* or Creative Speech, finds expression in *all* forms.

Because this *Word* is seated in our hearts, we can receive its disclosures of truth. Key 1, The Magician is the means whereby truth so disclosed can be put into practical application. We are the transformers of our environment by our perceptions of reality. Whether we apply our power wisely or unwisely, **we are all magicians**, projecting our magic circle of circumstance by our mental imagery. When we understand this truth about ourselves and act upon it, we find release from every kind of bondage.

In the Sepher Yetzirah, Tzaddi is assigned to Aquarius, the water-bearer. It's an alchemical symbol for dissolution. Therefore it is directly connected with the ideas of Key 13, Death. Also, Nun (נ) means fish and related to water.

Also, if you look at the Aquarius constellation, where the water pours down is Southern Fish.

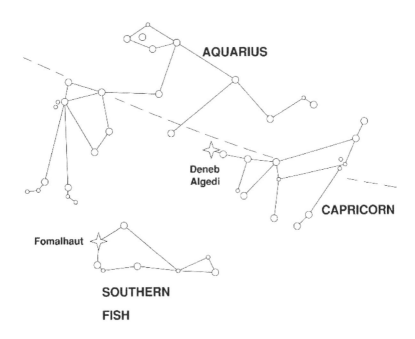

In the corners of Keys, 10 and 21 are the fixed signs of the zodiac. Aquarius is the Man. Humans are great fishers for new forms of truth. We are the possessors of the Universal Solvent of the alchemists. The Universal Solvent is human consciousness, concentrated and directed in meditation. Utilizing this, we may solve every problem.

Uranus and Saturn rule Aquarius. Key 0 is Uranus (The Fool (Key 0). Saturn is the World (Key 21). This suggests the practice of meditation eventually finds answers to every question, from the abstract (Key 0) to the concrete (Key 21). Many ideas are connected Saturn and Uranus as co-rulers of Aquarius. Seek to find them in meditation.

The Star

The title, The Star, refers to the universal Light-energy which condenses itself into stars. It is the reality behind their physical forms. There is more on this subject in the next chapter.

Summary

This week develop the exercise you began last week. *Formulate your desires into specific problems.* Focus upon them, the spotlight of your consciousness. Make every detail clear and definite. Then fish and meditate.

Do not try to think about your problem's probable solution. Rather let the stream of consciousness flow, as it were, past your point of observation. Notice the ideas which seem to rise to the surface. Reject them unless they show some definite relation to the central idea of your meditation. Keep your objective always in view.

Key 17 Coloring Instructions

YELLOW: The central star.

GREEN: Grass, leaves on a tree.

BLUE: Background, pool, water from, vases. Deeper shade in ovals on vases and stripes around their necks.

VIOLET: Mountains. (Note that there are rising hills before the peak.)

ORANGE: Vases (except stripes, ovals, and handles).

WHITE: Smaller stars, vase handles, the stripes across ovals on vases, except the stripes colored red, the highlights on the water.

BROWN: Tree trunk,

BLONDE: Hair. It can be done beautifully by putting a little darker shade over the shading lines.

FLESH: The woman's body.

RED: Top band over oval on a vase at the left of card: lower band over oval on the vase at right; the bird on the tree.

Chapter 38

THE STAR

The great yellow star stands for the Quintessence (Fifth Essence) of the alchemists. The eight-spoked on the Fool's dress, the Wheel of Fortune, and this eight-rayed star are all emblems of the Quintessence, Spirit, the power behind the energy transmitted to their world-systems by suns. Note that the star has eight short secondary rays. You will find these rays meaning developed in the symbolism of Key 19.

Seven Lesser Stars

The seven lesser stars are also eight-rayed to show that they are manifestations of the same Quintessence. They also represent the seven alchemical metals and chakras, which are centers through which the One Force manifests itself in the human body. Recall from the last chapter.

Metal	Planet	Chakra
Lead	Saturn	Root
Iron	Mars	Sacral
Tin	Jupiter	Solar
Gold	Sun	Heart
Copper	Venus	Throat
Silver	Moon	3rd Eye
Mercury	Mercury	Crown

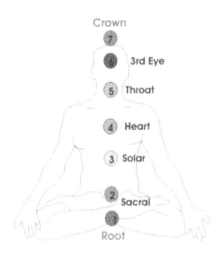

Concerning the development of these centers, much has been published. However, forcing the development of your chakras is a risky business. It's best to have a teacher that can monitor you.

Even worse is a book filled with time-wasting nonsense. With the easy availability of information, one must use discrimination to separate the wheat from the chaff.

Certain aspects of the instruction must be kept secret until the student is ready. Thus we admit that in these chapters, we hold back information. On the other hand, we give you no "blinds" of false interpretation, nor do we waste your time with fruitless practices. When you have taken the preliminary steps in your training, you will discriminate and find teachings that work for you.

Nude Woman

The nude water-bearer is Isis-Urania (Ουρανιη). Ourania (Urania) was named Muse of astronomy and astronomical writings.

She represents truth, and the practice of meditation reveals the truth without disguise. Hence she is nude. Her legs are bent at 90 degrees. Ninety (90) is the number of goodness, virtue, and Tzaddi (צ).

Notice also her legs from the shape of Tav (ת), which is the ruler of Aquarius (♒).

Her body's weight rests on her left knee and is supported by earth, representing physical existence. Urania maintains her balance with her right leg while her foot rests on the surface of the pool. This means that something occurs during meditation, which gives to unstable mind-stuff, symbolized by water, solidity, and stability like the physical world. This is the alchemists, *fixation of the volatile.*

Two Vases

The two vases represent self and subconsciousness, like the two ministers in Key 5 and the man and woman in Key 6. The ellipses on the sides of the vases represent the zero sign. Spirit, or Akasha. Only two ellipses are shown, but there are four, signifying the expression of Spirit through the four worlds and the four elements.

From the vase falls a stream that sets up waves in the pool. The waves are concentric rings, like the circles on Key 10. These waves represent the activity set up in subconsciousness by meditation.

From the other vase, a stream falls on land and divides into five parts. This represents the purification and perfection of the senses, employing meditation. Not that the woman lifts the vases. That is, the two modes of personal consciousness are taken in hand by the angel. Also, note that water comes from the pool and goes back to it.

Mountain

The mountain in the background is the same as the one in Keys 6 and 8. It represents the Great Work's perfection, which is human's conscious control of the inorganic forms of the Life-power's self-expression. This control begins with the mastery of our mind and body to become open channels for the outflow of the higher aspects of the Life-power's consciousness.

When this preliminary work with the personal vehicle is completed, the culmination of the Operation of the Sun manifests as mastery of the patterns of the inorganic world. This appears to the uninitiated to be a mysterious miracle-working power. However, the adept knows that this power is latent in all humanity and seeks those ready to take the journey to the mountain-peak of mastery.

Tree

The tree in the middle distance refers to the human nervous system. The upper part of the tree is the brain, and the trunk represents the spinal cord, and the sympathetic nerves and ganglia. The 36 leaves represent the three decans of ten degrees in each zodiac sign (12 x 3 = 36).

The bird perched in the branches is an ibis, a fishing bird sacred to Thoth. This is Hermes of the Greeks and Mercury of the Romans. In Key 17, Hermes' bird reminds us that meditation is begun and supervised by the self-consciousness pictured in Key 1, The Magician. The ibis is red to show that the mind focuses on its desire (red).

Tzaddi and Key 17 is line South-Above. Key 17 represents the southern half of Key 1, where we see a table with ceremonial magic implements.

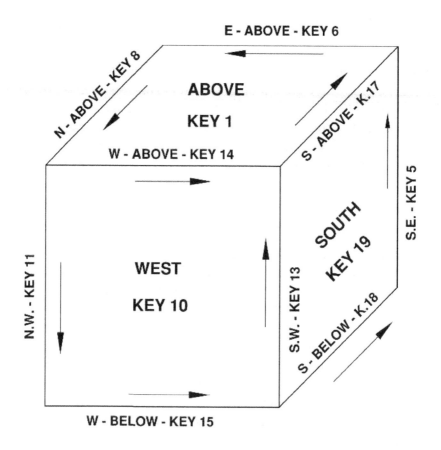

Ceremonial magic is one form of meditation because everything done in a magical ceremonial emphasizes the ritual's central idea or seed-thought. In this connection, Chapter 6 has this to say:

If you learn to concentrate, make your mental imagery clear and definite. If you make accurate observations from which you draw correct inferences, the seed you plant in your subconscious garden will bear fruit in your personality's renewal and regeneration.

Review this Chapter 6 with an emphasis on what it has to say about subconsciousness.

Symbols, colors, scents provide ambiance. For example, Thursday is Thor's day. And Thor is the Norse god similar to the Roman Jupiter. Sitting on my desk with the cap off is a cedarwood oil because cedar is a tree governed by Jupiter.

All these associations focus your mind on a central idea. Then you do something with the information, like opening a bottle of cedarwood oil on Thursday. That's ritual.

Back to the Cube of Space.

Cube Currents

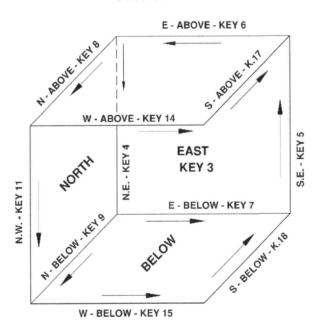

Line North-East (Key 4), the current is downward. Line South-East (Key 5) moves upwards. In the line East-Above (Key 6), it moves from South to North, as seen by careful inspection of the key's symbols. East-Below (Key 7) runs from North to South, like the river in the picture.

345

Notice you can trace a continuous line around the boundaries of the eastern face of the cube. Start with Key 4 from Above to Below.

Then through the line East-Below (Key 7), moving North to South.

Then Below to Above in the South-East line (Key 5).

From South-East corner, through the line East-Above (Key 5), back to the North-East top corner.

On the North face of the cube, it is impossible to trace a continuous line for the current in lines North-Above (Key 8) and North-Below (Key 9). They both move from East to West. The North-West (Key 11) current runs top to bottom like the North-East line (Key 4).

It is also impossible to trace a continuous path around the western face because West-Above and West-Below both carry currents from North to South (Keys 14 and 15).

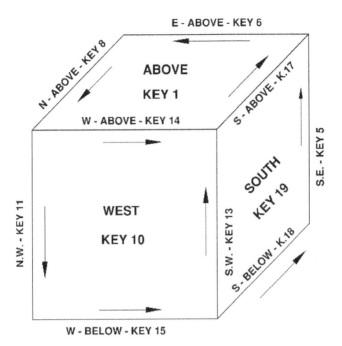

E - ABOVE - KEY 6

N - ABOVE - KEY 8

ABOVE

KEY 1

W - ABOVE - KEY 14

S - ABOVE - K.17

S.E. - KEY 5

N.W. - KEY 11

WEST

KEY 10

SOUTH

KEY 19

S.W. - KEY 13

S - BELOW - K.18

W - BELOW - KEY 15

On the cube's upper face, we may trace a continuous line, starting from any corner. East-Above (Key 6) moves from South to North,

North-Above (Key 8) the current runs from East to West.
West-Above (Key 14) moves from North to South.
South-Above (Key 17) carries a current from West to East.

No continuous line may be traced around the lower face because the lines East-Below and West-Below both move from North to South.

Also, no continuous line is drawn around the south face because South-East and South-West lines move from Below to Above. The line South-Below and South-Above carries a current from West to East.

The South-Above (Key 17) joins the lines South-West (Key 13) and South-East (Key 5). Thus Key 17 and Tzaddi (צ) joins Nun (נ), the fish, to the line of Vav (ו), the hook (see Chapter 37).

Observe the current from the line West-Above (Key 14) and South-East (Key 13) meet and mix. This indicates that the forces represented by Keys 15 and 14 blends in Key 17. In every act of right meditation, Scorpio's secret force (♏) is aimed by the arrow of Sagittarius (♐).

The line South-Above (Key 17) ends where it meets the South-East (Key 5) line. Since the current moves upward, the force carried by Key 17 cannot move downward against the current in the line South-East (Key 5).

At the end of successful meditation, one receives a Hierophant's revelation, which relates to some eternal principle that bears directly on the problem.

Then, the current from the South-Above line passes into the East-Above, symbolized by Key 6. The revelation is part of their conscious awareness. This enlightenment then contributes to the exercise of discrimination pictured by Key 6.

At this time, we shall not follow the course of the cube boundaries further. The alert reader will make their discoveries by applying the principles outlined.

Key 17 - Observers Perspective

Case states in Chapter 3,

Except for Keys 16, 17, 18, and 19, the observer right corresponds to the direction south. The left is north. The background is east. The foreground is west. Remember this because it is an essential clue to the meanings of many Tarot symbols.

However, Case doesn't mention the observer's perspective in the last three Keys. I'm not sure what they are, so I leave the readers to speculate for themselves.

Summary

Continue your meditation practice this week. Begin by giving five minutes to letting the image of Key 17 make an impression on your subconsciousness. This Key is a picture of what adepts know about meditation and gives your subconsciousness definite suggestions, which will make it easier for you to meditate successfully.

Consider this passage from The Book of Tokens. It contains an important secret concerning Key 17.

"Thinkest thou, O seekers for wisdom.
That thou bringest thyself into the Light
By thine own search?

Not so.
I am the HOOK,
Cast into the waters of darkness.
To bring men from their depths
Into the sphere of true perception.

Entering that sphere.
They must die to their old selves
Even as a fish cast upon the land must die;

Yet do they die only to live again.
And what before seemed life to them
Now weareth the aspect of death.

Men think they seek me.
But it is I who seek them.
No other seeker is there than myself.
And when I find mine own,
The pain of questing is at an end.
The fish graspeth the hook.
Thinking to find food.
But the fisherman is the enjoyer of the meal."

Chapter 39

ORGANIZATION

Key 18 symbolizes the 4th Stage of Spiritual Unfoldment.

Stage 1: Key 15 – After one has realized that the condition of bondage to appearances is an illusion;

Stage 2: Key 16 – The flash of spiritual illumination overthrows false structures of wrong thought and action;

Stage 3: Key 17 – Then comes a quiet period like the calm, which follows a storm. During this quiet, new relations come to us through meditation.

After this, begins the process of organization.

The term organization means the organization of the various parts of the human body into a higher type of organism than that are not spontaneously provided by evolution.

The practical application of the teachings of Ageless Wisdom is aimed at changing the human organism. Creatures in the evolutionary scale below humans have a limited ability for self-modification. Animals and plants brought under the influence of humanity are considerably modified in a relatively short time. However, they tend to revert to the original types when the cultural influence of man is removed.

The alchemist, *Great Art*, is concerned with producing a finer, sensitive, and responsive human body type. This is not affected by genetic changes or selective breeding. Our will and imagination's direct action upon our flesh and blood is that the transformation is effected.

This transformation is accomplished by the working together of universal forces. It is not merely a consequence of personal efforts. However, the culmination of the Great Work requires the introduction of the personal factor. No one accomplishes this work until they see, understand, and apply the laws and forces involved in transforming their substance. The alchemists call this "The Operation of the Sun."

The exercise of the imagination accomplishes this. Imagination is what makes clear and definite our desires and aspirations. Mental images are the patterns that we pass into subconsciousness, the body's builder and the controller of all its functions.

If our patterns are clear, definite, and keep intact, subconsciousness will build a body to correspond to them. This does not mean that we can sit still and do nothing but hold mental images. This, alone, will not transmute our bodies. When our pictures are vivid, they provide patterns for bodily transformations and *urge us into action*, which brings about the necessary changes.

For example, a child wants to be a concert pianist. This image dominates their actions so that the child willingly goes through hours of practice, which would be drudgery to an unmusical person. The practice affects the muscular structure of his hands, arms, and legs. It causes subtle changes in the centers of sight and hearing.

It affects many other groups of nerves and muscles. Eventually, the child grows and becomes what they imaged. By action corresponding to the imagination, the child builds the specially conditioned body, which is characteristic of a pianist.

The same principle holds in every activity that requires a skill. Everything that we achieve is accomplished through action. This skillful activity is made possible by the changes and development of our organic structure.

Whatever your desire, you will achieve it when you have built a physical vehicle that can transform the Life-power into the particular kinds of action corresponding to your mental imagery.

Number 18

The number 18 expresses the potency of the number 8, working through 1. Thus 18 represents the Law of Suggestion symbolized by Key 8 as being applied through the directive activity of attention typified by Key 1.

Review Chapter 2 of *Seven Steps* in connection with this study of Key 18. The chapter's teaching on subconsciousness should often pass through the conscious mind. Each review reinforces upon subconsciousness a deeper imprint of your conscious realization of these facts. *When subconsciousness knows that we understand what it can do, it works better.* Advanced adepts remind themselves continually of this and invented the Tarot for this purpose.

About the organization of a finer and more responsive physical vehicle, Lamarck, wrote:

"The production of a new organ in an animal body results from the supervention of a new want continuing to make itself felt, and a new movement which this want gives birth to and encourages… The effort may be in large measure unconscious and instinctive, but must in large measure be conscious, being made with a mental purpose to produce some desired result."

29th Path of Qoph - ק

The 29th Path is Physical Intelligence (Sekhel Mugsham). It depicts and establishes the growth of all physical bodies incorporated under the Zodiac.

Physical is from the root, geh.shem (גשם), meaning substance, matter, and a rain shower. The same letters with different vowels are, *gee.sham*, to carry out, realize, effect, execute.

Key 18 pictures a shower of 18 Yods. Yod is 10, so 10 x 18 = 180, the number of degrees in a semicircle. Because the sun follows the apparent path of a semicircle from east to west during a day, 180 is a symbol of the "day," or incarnation period of a personality.

Qoph - ק

The Ancient Hebrew Language and Alphabet state that Qoph is a pictograph of the Sun on the horizon. However, it can be just as easily the Moon on the horizon.

The letter name Qoph (קוֹף) means ape, and some sources suggest that the shape of Qoph is a monkey with a tail hanging down. With different vowels, the same letters spell Quf, meaning the *eye* of a needle, a *hole* for an ax, *aperture* and perhaps a *knot*.

"The origin of the glyph shape of qōp (𐤒) is uncertain. It is usually suggested to have originally depicted either a sewing needle, specifically the eye of a needle (Hebrew קוֹף and Aramaic קופא both refer to the eye of a needle), or the back of a head and neck (qāf in Arabic meant 'nape.'" – Wikipedia

Some of the most important organs in the body are in the back of the head. This part of the brain houses the posterior lobes of the cerebrum and cerebellum. The Occipital lobe of the cerebrum contains the sight center. We literally see with the backs of our heads.

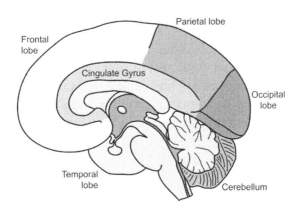

By NEUROtiker - Own work, CC BY-SA 3.0,
https://commons.wikimedia.org/w/index.php?curid=2653584

Just below the cerebrum's posterior lobe are a knot of nerve tissues called the *medulla oblongata*, uniting the brain to the spinal cord and its branches in the spine. Thus, the medulla connects the higher centers of sensation, thought, and action, located in the head, and the subordinate centers located in the body. The medulla itself is indeed a knot, presenting many intricate problems to anatomists and physiologists. Many of these problems are unlikely to be solved by those who depend on ordinary methods of investigation.

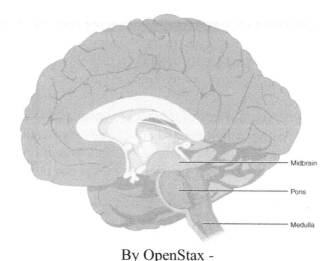

The medulla governs respiration, regulates the heart, and contains the principal center that controls blood circulation throughout the body. Besides these, it has other functions of basic importance to the maintenance of the organism. Thus the knot of nerve cells at the back of the head is really what keeps us alive, for its functions are carried on without interruption, even while we are asleep.

Sleep

In *Sepher Yetzirah*, Raavad version, Qoph is assigned to sleep. Qoph is the consciousness that remains active during sleep. Sleep is the period of rest and recovery during which the waste caused by the day's activity is eliminated, and new materials are woven into the bodily structure.

While we sleep, the plans and thoughts we have been concerned with during the day are ripened and brought to maturity. Night brings counsel. Many a problem has been solved subconsciously during the night. Our mental processes continue at subconscious levels, even while the cells of the upper brain are resting.

It is during sleep that our aspirations and efforts are built into the organic structure. We have thought and done during the day, influencing the body while we are sleep. This is why it is advantageous to review each day before falling asleep. We see where we have fallen short, and we vigorously determine to do better the next time we find ourselves in a similar situation. We intensify the effect of all our well-doing by this mental repetition of our daily actions and thoughts. Then, before slumber, we bring before us, as clearly as we can, the image of that which is our highest and most genuine desire. By this means, we build our aspirations into our flesh and blood, impressing our dominant desire on every cell.

While coloring this week, make yourself familiar with the details of Key 18. The number 18 add to 9 (1 + 8 = 9), and 9 is the Hermit. Review the two chapters on Key 9, emphasizing the functions of the Virgo area of the human body. Note that Keys 9 and 18 are both night scenes, and both have the suggestion of height and a path leading to that height. This will prepare you to understand next week's chapter.

COLORING INSTRUCTIONS

YELLOW: Moon and rays; path. Yods same as in Key 18.

GREEN: Grass in the foreground. (Note that this does not reach the towers.)

BLUE. Background, pool.

GRAY: Towers, wolf, stones round pool.

VIOLET: Crayfish, mountains. (Dilute for mountains.)

BROWN: Dog, plains between the grass and the mountains.

WHITE: Tower windows, highlights on the pool, wolf's fang.

Chapter 40

THE MOON

Key 18's title, The Moon, refers to subconsciousness and its powers of duplication, reflection, reproduction, and energy turning back to its source. Key 18, therefore, symbolizes the Path of Return.

This Key symbolizes an ancient maxim. "First the stone, then the plant, then the animal, and then the man." At the lower end of the path by the pool are several stones. Nearby are the pointed leaves of a water plant, looking like arrows and suggesting aim and aspiration. The vegetation also continues in the field beyond. Climbing onto the path is a lower form of animal life, a shellfish, and a little farther along are a dog and a wolf. Then come the towers, human structures, but the path continues beyond them.

Pool

The pool is the same as that of Keys 14 and 17. It is the great deep of cosmic mind-stuff, which emerges the dry land of physical manifestation. From it, all forms proceed, both inorganic and organic.

The Animals

The crayfish is a hard-shelled crustacean with a shape similar to a scorpion. This resemblance is one of the reasons for selecting this creature as a symbol. That which rises, and makes the whole journey along the Path of Return, is the force of the sign Scorpio (♏). The crayfish represents, on the negative side, selfishness, crabbedness, obstinacy. As a positive symbol, it represents purpose, courage, determination, and a little stubbornness.

The shellfish typifies the early stages of unfoldment, wherein the student thinks they are separate from the rest of nature. Hence, the crustacean wears a shell of armor.

The dog and the wolf belong to the canine family. The wild wolf is a natural production, apart from human interference and adaptation. The dog is the result of modifications in the wolf by human thought. Men tame wolves and modify the structure of their bodies by crossbreeding. This detail in the symbolism is a direct allusion to control the body consciousness and develop specific patterns formulated by human intelligence. Therefore, the wolf is a symbol of Nature, and the dog is a symbol of Art.

The Path

In medical astrology, Pisces (Key 18) rules the feet, and this is suggested by the yellow path left by the feet of those who have traveled before.

The path goes between two extremes. It is the way of balance, the way or method which goes neither too far toward artificiality nor toward the error that everything should be left to natural impulse.

The path progresses over the undulating ground that is a succession of ascents and descents. Advance along the Path of Return is not an unbroken upward climb. As we traverse it, we attain one eminence after another, and after surmounting some lesser peak, we seem to go downhill for a time.

We cannot climb all the time. In the Great Work, there is periodicity. It is a work of the Moon and the Sun. In this operation, there is waxing and waning, flux and reflux, rest, and activity. Assimilation, or taking in, must be balanced by expression or giving out. Periods of intense effort must alternate with periods of relaxation. A bow always is drawn. It never speeds the arrow.

The path rises over the rolling ground. As we advance, there comes a time when the lowest point of descent is a higher level than the peak of the previous attainment. To all of us, there come times when we cannot climb. If we do not understand the law, we become discouraged. The one thing needful is to keep facing toward the goal and keep walking.

Towers

The towers are the work of man. They have battlements and form a gateway. The suggestion is that each tower is part of a wall, not shown in the picture. The wall represents the ordinary limits of human sensation and perception. However, it is not a final boundary. A vast region of experience extends beyond it. Many have entered that region, and their footsteps have marked a path where we may follow.

The Moon

The Moon is with 16 principal and 16 secondary rays, though some of the top's secondary rays are not shown. Thus there are 32 rays, which is the number of paths on the Tree of Life. The 32 Paths include the 10 Sephiroth, and the 22 connecting paths represented the Hebrew alphabet and the Tarot Keys. Therefore, the moon's rays indicate the sum-total of cosmic forces at work in the field of human personality.

In Hebrew, the Moon is LBNH (לבנה), *L'vah.nah*. Using its letters, it spells four other words.

Hebrew		Transliteration	Meaning
לבנה	LBNH	*L'vah.nah*	The Moon
לב	LV	*Lav*	*the heart* as the seat of knowledge, *understanding, thinking, midst, center.*
לבן	LBN	*Lo.ven*	White, blankness
בן	BN	*Ben*	son or offspring
בנה	BNH	*Bah.nah*	To build, establish

This esoteric analysis of the word *L'vah.nah*, suggests:

1. In the heart of the son (humanity) are to be found the sources of beauty;

2. It is the aspect of the Life-power the alchemist calls the "white work" of the Moon that conceals the secret of building the mystic temple of regenerated humanity.

Eighteen Yods fall from the Moon onto the path. In the colored Keys, they are red and yellow, to intimate the combination of solar energy (yellow) with the vital force in the blood (red).

In other versions of Tarot, these Yods are replaced by drops of blood. They suggest that the powers of subconsciousness are developed by changes in the blood's chemical constitution. The body is built from elements in the bloodstream, and the chemistry of blood is controlled by subconsciousness, the Moon in Key 18.

The Way of Attainment is the Path of Return. Beyond is the Source. What is before us in the future is also what is behind us in the past. This is one meaning of the saying, "The last shall be first, and the first shall be last." When the cycle of evolution is completed, the end and beginning are one.

The path leads to a summit where the Hermit of Key 9 stands. Ancient teachers say the path is narrow, meaning that concentration is required for those who follow it. It is a life balanced between the conditions of nature and modifications that are made possible by art.

The beginning of the Way is in the realm of the familiar and commonplace. The path leads, by stages, from the known to the less-known, and from the less-known to the unknown. Every great Master of life has followed this path to its goal. The path is the path of physiological reorganization. The goal is true Self-recognition, correct perception of the universal I AM, and mental identification with that One Reality.

On the Cube of Space, Qoph (ק) and Key 18 correspond to South-Below. The current in this line moves from West to East, that is, from *appearances* to *causes*. Pisces is the South-Below line, ruled by Jupiter (West face), and where Venus (East face) is Exalted.

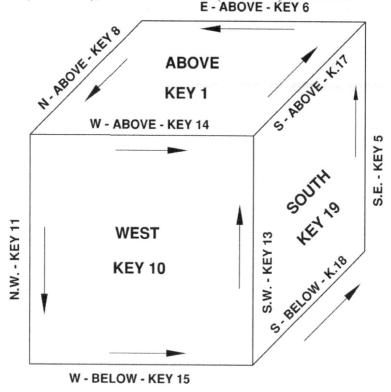

This line receives no influence from the South-West line because this current of energy moves upward. South-Below gets a stream of influence from the line West-Below, corresponding to Ayin (ע), Key 15, and Capricorn (♑).

Note that the current in South-Below communicates its influence to the line South-East (Key 5). Mental identification with the One Reality is symbolized by Key 5. This identification results from the reorganization expressed by Key 18.

Summary

This week begin your practice of reviewing your day's activities just before going to sleep. Record your gains and failures in your diary. Your attainments are steps in your progress toward Self-realization. Your failures warn you what to avoid in the future.

Never muse long on your failures. Remember that what we call "sin" is nothing but "missing the mark." Do not worry. Worry is the concentration on the negative appearances of life. If you are given to worry (focusing on a negative), you can concentrate. Change the polarity of your thoughts and emotions. Before you fall asleep, impress subconsciousness with the most positive images of good you can fashion. Persist in this practice. You will sow seeds that subconsciousness will build into a new and better bodily structure.

Chapter 41

REGENERATION

The fifth stage of spiritual unfoldment, symbolized by Key 19, is the new birth from natural humanity into spiritual humanity. Every ceremonial presentation of the process of regeneration employs this symbolism of rebirth.

In the natural man, the powers of subconsciousness are stifled and perverted by the negative suggestions implanted as a result of erroneous thinking. By applying the correct conscious self-direction, we become a new-born being, one "twice-born." In this new birth, the physical body is transformed. The practical method which effects this change is concisely summarized in the injunction, "Be transformed by the renewing of your mind."

Meditate on these words. The new birth is a very real process, a deepening inner realization of humans' status in the cosmic order. It is a degree of adeptship that of liberation from the limitations of physical matter and circumstance. It is also a grade of conscious identification with the One Life.

It is not final. It is a stage where material resources are under the control of the adept. It is not full liberation. The person who reaches this grade still feels like a separate or distinct entity.

In a sense, they have become childlike and experience the fulfillment of the promise, "A little child shall lead them." In this stage, physical forces are dominated by the adept's will because they are an unobstructed vehicle for the power of the One Will, which has ruled these forces since the beginning.

The 30th Path is called the Collective or Inclusive Intelligence. By it, astrologers study the Laws that govern the stars and the zodiac to perfect their knowledge.

The Sun holds the solar system together. The revolution of the planets around the Sun is the principle behind astrology.

Resh - ר

Resh, as a pictograph, is a head. Resh is associated with ideas of *top*, *beginning* of something, and *foremost* in rank. It suggests taking the lead, as the head of a government or a pupil ahead of their class.

Resh, as a head, suggests power. The ideas of completion and accomplishment are indicated by a phrase like "to bring to ahead."

The Operation of the Sun

In both Testaments, the Bible calls God the "sun of life and light," In other sacred books, the sun is an emblem of Deity. In alchemical writings, the Great Work is the operation of the Sun. The Sun is also the symbol for alchemical gold, of which Eliphas Levi wrote:

"The gold of the philosophers is, in religion, the absolute and supreme reason; in philosophy it is truth; in its visible nature it is the sun, which is the emblem of the sun of truth, as that itself is the shadow of the First Source whence all splendors spring; in the subterranean world, it is the purest and most perfect gold. For this reason, the search after the *magnum opus* is called the search after the Absolute, and the Great Work is itself called the 'work of the sun.'"

The correspondence between the sun and gold is a clue to the whole Hermetic mystery. Thus Sendivogius says the Philosophers' Stone is gold digested to the highest degree. Similarly, *The Golden Tract* says:

"The reader now knows that the substance of our Stone is neither animal nor vegetable, and that it does not belong to the minerals or the base metals, but that it must be extracted from gold and silver, and that our gold and silver are not the vulgar, dead gold and silver, but the living gold and silver of the Sages.

In its physical manifestation, this living gold is the sun's radiant energy, which is truly the First Matter of the Great Work. The alchemists say the First Matter has as many names as there are things on earth. It swims with the fishes in the sea and flies with the birds in the air. Compare their doctrine with the following summary from Tyndall's twelfth lecture on HEAT.

Every tree, plant, and flower grows and flourishes by the grace and bounty of the sun. As surely as the force that moves a clock's hands is derived from the arm that winds up the clock, it is surely all terrestrial power derived from the sun.

Except for volcanoes' eruption and the ebb and flow of the tides, every manifestation of power, organic and inorganic, vital and physical, is produced by the sun. Its warmth keeps the sea liquid and powers storms. The Sun lifts the rivers and glaciers the mountains. Every fire that burns and every flame that glows dispenses light and heat originally belonged to the sun. Every shock and charge in its application, or misapplication, is an adaptation of the sun's energy in war. The Sun blows the trumpet, urges the projectile, and bursts the bomb. The sun rears the vegetable kingdom, and through it, the animal. The sun forms the muscle, blood, and brain. And remember, this is not poetry, but fact.

The same essence takes a million hues and shapes and finally dissolves into its primitive and almost formless force. The sun comes to us as heat; he quits us as heat, and between his entrance and departure, the multiform powers of our globe appear. They are all special forms of solar power — the molds into which his strength is temporarily poured in passing from its source through infinitude."

In Tarot, this All Power is often represented as water. As Levi says, "It is substance and motion simultaneously; it is a fluid and a perpetual vibration." And alchemists, speaking of this spiritual radiance as the First Matter or Primal Substance, declares, "If you call it water, you will not be wrong."

The wise who compose the Inner School has transmitted their knowledge of this living, fluidic radiance down through the ages.

The First Matter

The spiritual, fluidic, golden water of the alchemist may be perceived as any other phenomenon in nature. Hence the Sages state they have seen their First Matter with their own eyes and have touched it with their hands.

They say their First Matter is seen by all, though known by few. It is something within the range of our physical senses. Its effects are perceptible by ordinary sensations, but not every person knows the significance. Ageless Wisdom is a record of those who, looking in the right direction, *have seen into* something which the uninitiated only *look*.

Heart Chakra

In the human body, the point of the entrance which admits this living radiance into the field of personality is a group of nerve cells forming cardiac ganglion or plexus. The cardiac plexus is a network of nerves by the base of the heart. Cardiac branches form it from both the sympathetic and parasympathetic nervous systems.

This ganglion controls the heartbeat. The undifferentiated Life-power enters the body through this center as an electric current comes into the building through the main switch. The sun-center nerve cells charge the bloodstream as it passes through the heart, with this current of radiant energy. Persons having a subtle vision can see these vibrations as they enter our bodies through this "main switch."

In astrology, the Sun rules Leo ($\mathfrak{N}$), which governs the heart. Therefore Key 19 (The Sun) is the dominant force manifested by the process in Key 8, Strength (Leo).

Additionally, the Sun is exalted or raised to its highest expression in Aries ($\mathcal{P}$), attributed to Key 4. What is pictured by the Emperor is the highest manifestation of what is symbolized by Key 19.

Number 19

The number 19 stands for the expression of the power symbolized by 9 through that symbolized by 1. In Tarot, this is the force represented by the Hermit through the activity of the Magician.

The Hermit represents the Universal Will, the single free will-power of the One Identity. The Magician represents the plane of personal self-consciousness. Thus, number 19 denotes the One Will (9) expression through human self-consciousness (1).

Key 19 is the 5th Stage of unfoldment called, Regeneration.
Regeneration is healing. The alchemist's medicine of the metals is
also referred to as the *ehben*, "Stone."

The first two letters of *ehben* spell Ab (אב), meaning "father," and the
last two spell Ben (בן), meaning "son" or "offspring." Thus *ehben*
(אבן) signifies the union of the Father (God) and the Son (humanity).

Consider the separate letters of *ehben*. Aleph (א) is a symbol of the
Life-Breath, typified by Key 0, The Fool. The second is Beth (ב),
representing self-consciousness, and Mercury, the Magician. The
third is Nun (נ,ן), corresponding to Scorpio, and Key 13. Add together
the numbers of Keys 0, 1 and 13, which is 14 - Temperance.

Key 14 symbolizes the knowledge and conversation of the Holy
Guardian Angel. When we establish communication with the Higher
Self, we enter into a state of conscious recognition of the truth that the
Father (אב) and the Son (בן) are in perfect union.

We enter into this consciousness through an influx of the All-Power
(Key 0) into the field of self-consciousness (Key 1). Then it is
directed to subconscious levels to modify the operation of the serpent-
power or Scorpio force. Thus the Magician cultivates flowers in his
garden, and flowers are the vegetable kingdom's reproductive organs.

The Scorpio force or libido is raised and sublimated. It awakens brain
centers that bring us into the higher order of knowing, in which the
Father (Ab) and the Offspring (Ben), instead of being perceived as
separate, are seen to be in perfect union. This conscious realization is
not only the "Stone," but also the "Medicine," for it heals all diseases
of mind and body. Sometimes it is called the Medicine of Metals
because the alchemical metals are the seven chakras pictured by Key
17. The Medicine of the Metals heals the chakras, and their powers
equilibrated.

The result is a physiological, as well as a psychological, transformation. The adept's body chemistry is changed. The subtle structure of the cells composing their organism is altered. Thus we become *newly born* or regenerated.

Summary

As you color Key 19, fix its details to more easily follow the explanations in the next chapter. Keep up the practice of reviewing the day's activities. Still, this week endeavor to intensify your realization that the whole *physical* aspect of these activities is, as Tyndall explains, really a transformation of solar radiance into all the multiform events and things of your daily experience.

COLORING INSTRUCTIONS

YELLOW: Sun and rays, sunflower petals.

GREEN: Grass (the circle should be darker than the rest of the grass), leaves.

BLUE: Background. (This should encircle the rays extending from the sun. Like those on the sun's face in the Key, blue projections should extend inward from the edge of the circle toward the sun. Make these projections very short.)

BROWN: Sunflower centers.

GRAY: Wall.

ORANGE: Yods.

BLONDE: Hair of both children.

Chapter 42

Key 19 – The Sun

The central figure in Key 19 is a radiant solar orb with a human countenance to signify the Sun is a living and conscious being.

The Sun has eight salient or pointed rays. Thus the lines passing through the center of the circle form rays similar to the circles of the Fool's dress, the eight spokes of the Wheel of Fortune, and the great star lines in Key 17. The same power is represented by all these symbols since their geometrical properties are identical.

In Key 17, the secondary rays of the greater star are seen again in Key 19. These secondary rays form eight curved or wavy rays of the sun. It suggests the development of power. The nature of this development is indicated because curved lines represent feminine aspects of the Life-power. Key 19 shows the equal development of masculine (salient) and feminine (wavy) forms of universal radiant energy.

48 Beams

Besides these larger rays, 48 beams are shown, in groups of three, each group placed between a salient and a wavy ray.

These lines refer to the One Force's expression in activities of integration, preservation, and disintegration. Their number, 48, reduces to 12 (4 + 8 = 12) but is also 4 x 12. This suggests a connection with Key 12 and the Law or Reversal operation symbolized by that Key in the four phases of matter – Fire, Water, Air, and Earth.

Again, the salient rays are masculine, refer to the solar radiance and the alchemical sun. The wavy rays are feminine and refer to the lunar current of the Life-power.

The number 48 is the value of *ko.kav* KVKB (כוכב), meaning star and the planet Mercury. Hence the three types of rays extending from the solar disk hint at the combination of the sun (salient), moon (wavy), and Mercury (48 beams). This, plus the sun, has a human face, suggesting the Operation of the Sun. The alchemists say, "The Great Work is performed by the Sun and Moon, with the aid of Mercury."

This work is the regeneration of human personality, and its perfection gives us the Stone (*ehben*), described as something that cannot be made, save by God's grace. Attaining this goal requires that our efforts are combined with an influx of power from the superconscious level of being.

125 Lines

Around the disk of the sun are 125 short lines. This is cube of 5, or 5^3 or 5 x 5 x 5 = 125. It represents the power 5, exercised in a threefold manner, or through the entire three-dimensional world. Five (5) is the number of the pentagram, a symbol of the dominion of Spirit over the elements. Therefore 125 is symbolically the extension of dominion through every part of nature.

This dominion is the Stone and Universal Medicine. ABN (אבן), the Stone, corresponds to Keys 0, 1, and 13 so that Key 14 sums up one aspect of the Stone. Since the digits of 14 add to 5, the number of the Hierophant, we see that there is a connection between Key 5 and the Stone.

The Knowledge and Conversation of the Holy Guardian Angel (Key 5) is the continuous intuitive perception of reality, which we receive through the function of interior hearing. Hence we enjoy both knowledge and *conversation*. Furthermore, 14 is the value of the word ZHB (זהב), *zah.hav*, gold.

Gold is symbolized by the sun in Key 19, and in Key 14, the same gold is the solar disk gleaming on the forehead of the angel Michael.

In Key 19, the solar orb human features are intended to show that it is a symbol of living, conscious intelligence. The ancient occult doctrine holds that all celestial bodies are vehicles of intelligence. As a synthesis of the active forces entering into the composition of human personality, the sun is shown as a living power, not merely physical energy.

The Sun is a power like unto ourselves. We have something in common with it. It enters intimately into our lives. Our lives are part of a series of transformations of solar energy. This energy constitutes a circuit. Energy comes from the Sun, flows through our bodies, takes form in our activities, and then *flows back to the Sun again*. These series of transformations were initiated by the Sun long before our bodies were formed and will continue long after they return to dust.

OBTW.

Dust in Hebrew is *ah.par* (עפר). It is numerically 350 and *seh.khel* (שכל), intelligence, and consciousness. It is also the number of *sah.peer* (ספיר), sapphires, and a beam or ray of light from the Sun. So dust is not so bad; it's another form of stone. Recall this quote from the *Egyptian Bronzebook*.

"Is a stone a thing unchanging, or is a star always a star? Who among you, people of ignorance, can see the bond between star and stone? Yet, there is a kinship in all things. The stars hanging above are not wholly apart from the heart of man. – Book of Manuscripts 11:9.

Thus the solar energy shines in us, and our energy shines in the sun. There is a difference in the degree of radiance, but the sun and humans are lights on the same circuit of spiritual energy. This is a central doctrine of Ageless Wisdom, and it has significant practical consequences.

There are 13 Yod shown falling from the sun, to suggest the ideas of Unity and Love. Because unity is *eh.chad*, (אחד); love and affection are *a.h'vah* (אהבה) are numerically 13. Also, Key 13 is Death, Scorpio, and the reproductive force.

Yod is assigned to Virgo, Key 9, and the Law of Response. It is the secret activity associated with Virgo is active

Therefore, these Yods are a symbol of the Scorpio and Virgo forces' combination, which brings about the state of regeneration wherein Unity and Love are made manifest through us.

Sunflowers

There are five sunflowers. Four are open. They are symbols of four stages in the evolution of form — the mineral, vegetable, animal, and human kingdoms. The unopened sunflower represents the kingdom of spiritual humanity, composed of regenerated men and women. This kingdom goes as far beyond that of the natural man as that of the natural man goes beyond that of the animal.

The four sunflowers representing the kingdoms already in full manifestation are turned to face the children as if they are suns to which they turn for life and light. The idea suggested is that the kingdoms of nature are turning to, and expressing their dependence on, the regenerated humanity typified by the children.

The fifth sunflower turns toward the sun above, for it and the children symbolize the same thing. It represents a state of being as yet in its earlier stages of development, in the bud, but not in full bloom. Thus at present, it is dependent on the working of universal forces than on any embodiment of those forces in human personality. The natural man and the three kingdoms below are dependent on the newborn spiritual humanity and receive their sustenance through the spiritualized and regenerated members of the human race. Spiritual humanity turns to that which is above.

The wall behind the children is stone. Thus it represents forms of truth instead of the forms of error shown as the tower's bricks in Key 16. The stone is a wall and has five courses to show that it is built of materials drawn from sense experience. Those materials are aspects of truth or reality. On this point, Ageless Wisdom is explicit. It does not deny the fact of sense-experience. Even though our senses do not give us a full report, the report is accurate as far as it goes.

Most persons believe there is no truth beyond what we learn through physical sensation. By limiting themselves to sensation, they build an artificial barrier that halts further progress. Thus the wall says: "Thus far, and no farther, shalt thou go." Key 19 gives intimations of another way.

The children are nude. Thus they repeat the symbolism of Key 17, where we see nature unveiling herself as truth. In Key 19, we see humanity so identified with that same truth that it has nothing to conceal.

Someone may say, "What about the secrecy with which the Masters of Wisdom are supposed to surround themselves?" The answer is that they do nothing of the kind. The veils which hide them from us are of our weaving, as is the Veil of Isis. Masters do not weave illusions; they are the most childlike and transparent of human beings; our ignorance is the veil. Their lives are simple. Their words are simple. It is because they are so plain and direct that what they say is seldom understood. Hence an old alchemical author says:

"The Sages, then, do well to call their gold or earth water, for they have a perfect right to term it whatever they like. So they have frequently called the Stone their gold, their super perfect gold, their regenerate gold, and many other names. If anyone does not perceive their meaning at first glance, he must blame his ignorance, not their jealousy."

The two concentric circles are symbols of the fourth dimension. It is the *other way* around or through the stone wall. It is also shown as the children with their backs to the wall.

The nature of the Other Way is shown by the fairy ring in which they dance. The way of the spiritual man is not the way of the natural man. The spiritual man centers himself in the inner circle of manifestation. By repeated practice, they have made habitual their identification with the indwelling, Central Self.

Hence the children are of equal stature and stand on the same level, with one foot in the inner ring. In natural humanity, subconsciousness, the feminine aspect of personality, is subordinate. She is subjected to the misunderstandings and misinterpretations of the masculine or self-conscious mind.

In the life of spiritual humanity, subconsciousness is released from the bondage of erroneous suggestions. In the regenerated personality, the powers of subconsciousness are understood and unfolded by Law. By accurate observation, the Law of Suggestion effects changes to our mind and body. We become more and more confident that the five senses are a limited source of information. When we allow the idea that the world is full of unseen forces and centers of intelligence, the law of averages takes a walk.

For this reason, the first of the Tarot Keys is named "The Fool." The freedom possessed by spiritual humanity is knowledge gained by means beyond sensation. Such knowledge seems foolish to the uninitiated, and the world of sense bound humanity ridicules it. For the Way of Certainty is the Way of Non-Sense, even as St. Paul meant when he wrote that his doctrine was "sheer folly" to the Greeks.

Do not confuse this esoteric Non-Sense with ordinary "nonsense." It seems that the one sure way to get a popular hearing for anything purporting to be occultism is to make it as fantastically absurd as possible. The Inner School permits this to test the discrimination of those who seek to approach its portals.

The little girl gestures repudiation toward the wall, indicating that subconsciousness has been trained to accept the Other Way. The little boy holds the palm of his hand away from the wall in a gesture of acceptance that complements the girl. He is ready to receive the New Light on the Open Way.

These two represent the regenerated personality. Compare them with the kneeling figures at the feet of the Hierophant. Layout Keys 5, 12, and 19, as shown in the Tarot tableau given in Chapter 2. Taken together in this manner, the Keys have more power to evoke thought than when studied separately (displayed horizontally to save space).

Cube of Space

Key 19 and Resh (ר) are attributed to the direction south.

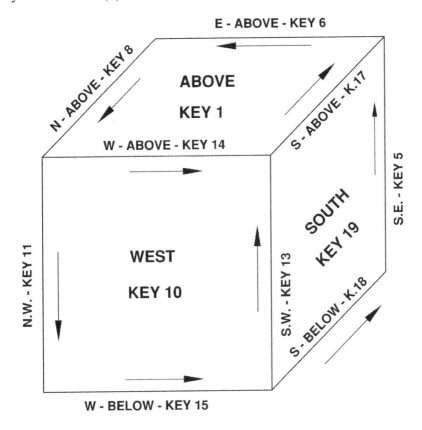

Usually, in a Tarot Key, to observer sits in the west and looks east. Key 19 represents the southern face of the Cube of Space. Therefore the observer is facing South, the observer's right is East, and the left is West.

This makes the girl and the two sunflowers, one with an unopened bud, correspond to the South-East. It symbolizes that it is only in humanity that the function of subconsciousness as *Intuition* is expressed. Subconsciousness is its agency of manifestation. Intuition cannot be manifest in the kingdoms of nature below humanity because Intuition is a conscious awareness of universal principles. This conscious awareness is not among the organisms' functions in the three kingdoms of nature below natural humanity.

In those three kingdoms, represented by the three sunflowers behind the boy, there is an ever-increasing consciousness development. In the higher animals, something very much like self-consciousness. Animals like dogs and cats have the most decided personalities, and do birds in captivity, like canaries and parrots.

These higher animals are not wholly identified with a group-soul; they have an identity of their own. They have personalities as distinct as those of human beings, including some persons who are very glib with their putter about animal group-souls, learned by rote from Theosophical primers. Humanity has a group-soul. Like animals, many humans are dominated by the group soul.

The little boy and the three sunflowers behind him represent South-West, Scorpio, and Key 13. Through the force's operation symbolized by Key 13, the development of higher states of consciousness is made possible. This force is the active principle of generation and reproduction, which provides the Life-power with the billions of physical vehicles necessary to the evolution of human personality at the natural man's level. This same force, directed purposefully by the regenerated consciousness, typified by the little boy, is what completes the Great Work.

The upper part of Key 19 corresponds to the top of the southern face of the cube. Therefore the Sun is a repetition of the Blazing Star of Key 17, which is brought into full manifestation in Key 19.

The lower part of Key 19 corresponds to the direction South-Below, and thus we learn that the fairy ring in which the children dance is another symbol of Key 18 teachings. The ring is the Ring-Pass-Not of the regenerated organism. The children clasp hands above its center. For the Other Way and the Way of Return are one, and that One Way leads within, or from the surface to the center. We shall see plainly expressed by the last two Keys of the Tarot series.

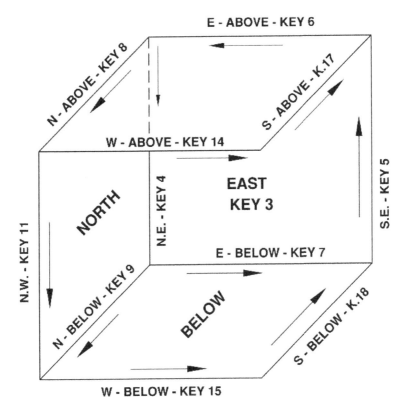

The student will do well to study the other Keys corresponding to the faces of the cube. Because the human mind never can get behind the plane of causes, the eastern face of the cube, corresponding to Key 3, must be viewed from the West. The right side of Key 3 is the South-East, and the left side is North-East.

Similarly, the lower face of the cube is viewed from above, so that:

The right side of Key 2 corresponds to South-Below.

The left side is North-Below.

The upper part of Key 2 corresponds to East-Below.

The lower part is West-Below.

381

North is the place of the unknown, so that we cannot get behind that. Therefore we look at Key 16 facing south, which puts North-East on the right and North-West on the left side, with North-Above at the top and North-Below at the bottom.

The wise student will take these hints and work out the correspondences. A complete exposition of the correspondences of Tarot with the Cube of Space would require many volumes. We advise you to give *some time* to it, recording your findings in your diary. However, we warn you that you do not become too preoccupied with this phase of Tarot at this stage of your work.

Chapter 43

REALISATION

Key 20 shows the sixth stage of spiritual unfoldment, in which the personal consciousness is verging of blending with the universal. At this stage, the adept realizes that their existence is nothing but a manifestation of the relation between self-consciousness and subconsciousness. The adept sees that self-consciousness and subconsciousness are modes of universal consciousness. The adept knows their personality has no separate existence. At the 6th stage, the intellectual conviction is *confirmed by a fourth-dimensional experience*, which blots out the delusion of separateness.

Number 20

Kaph (כ) is numerically 20. It is assigned to Key 10, Jupiter, and the Wheel of Fortune. As a pictograph, Kaph is an open hand ready to receive. Therefore the ideas associated with Kaph or grasp and comprehension of cycles.

From one perspective, Kaph and the number 20 are completing a cycle of manifestation represented by the Wheel of Fortune.

The majority of humanity is in the position of Hermanubis. The Great Work's completion consists of the extension of the light of intelligence through that segment of the wheel, which is marked by the letter Yod.

In other words, when humanity comprehends their true nature, they see that this nature is identical with the One Reality, the One Will, of which the universe is a manifestation. Then he says, "I have no will but to do the will of him that sent me."

Adept knows the Will to Good, joy, health is also the will to freedom. The consciousness associated with Key 20 comprehends that the WILL expresses itself in all activity. Here and now, the adept sees that Will expresses no lack, disease, failure, or poverty. The consciousness of Key 20 grasps the truth that whatever appearances of evil surround us; they seem as they do because we do not yet see the real relations.

For such a one, the daily experience is a succession of miracles. When we begin to see the light, it is like the lightning-flash of Key 16. While it lasts, it breaks down structures of error and shows all existence as it is. Then the darkness of ignorance closes in again, and we have to wait for the next flash.

In the state represented by Key 20, however, there is perpetual recognition of the power of Spirit. Thus 20, expresses the No-Thing operation (Key 0) through memory (Key 2). That is the working of the Fool's vision through the law of the High Priestess. Key 20 is freedom from the lapses of memory, which assail us earlier in work. Moment by moment, without cessation, we see the truth and live it. With this recognition comes a new kind of consciousness. We do not sleep anymore. Our bodies are put to rest, but we remain awake, able to function consciously in the fourth dimension so that we do "serve God, day and night."

This is one of the meanings of conscious immortality. I testify to my knowledge that it is an experience of normal men and women. To be unconscious eight hours out of the twenty-four is as unnecessary as to wear a gas-mask in ordinary air. *We are immortal*, and whether we know it or not, we can function consciously while our bodies are asleep.

Most people, however, do not recall their nocturnal experiences because they have not developed the physical instruments for recording them. Once this power of remembering your nocturnal journeys is established, it is possible to plan the whole night's work, and recollection will be part of your day's activities. Until this is known experimentally, no human language can convey the alteration it makes in one's life.

31ˢᵗ Path of Shin - ש

The 31ˢᵗ Path is Perpetual Intelligence (Sekhel Tamidi). It regulates all the cyclic forces that form the revolutions of the stars and planets (Mazloth).

Temidiy (ידימת) is derived from [דימת], *tawmeed*, signifying continuance, or indefinite extension, and often referring in ancient Hebrew to perpetual time.

T'mee.dee (ידימת) means continuous, constant, regular, permanent, persistent, and persevering. Therefore Key 20 is associated with the ideas of conscious immortality.

Shin - ש

As a pictograph, Shin looks like a row of teeth. The word shen (שן) means tooth, claw, jaw, ivory, and peak. Shin has the general meaning of *sharp* or sharp things like fangs or scissors. Teeth press down and chop up food. Therefore Shin also means press, eat and consume.

Shin looks like three tongues of flame rising from a fiery base (ש). The *Sepher Yetzirah* assigned the element Fire to Shin. In Chapter 2:1, it adds this:

"Three Mothers, Alef, Mem Shin (אמש)

Mem hums, Shin hisses

And Aleph is the Breath of air deciding between them."

A serpent hisses and are symbols of wisdom. They are *silent*, subtle creatures. Jesus told his disciples to be wise as serpents, thus emphasizing those who had ears to hear, the ancient doctrine of silence. Therefore, Shin is an admonition to silence.

Secret

Knowers of the Secret do not maintain silence because they are stingy with their spiritual possessions. Nor is the silence kept because an order of beings higher than man imposes a prohibition forbidding speech. Neither is silence observed because there is danger in the Secret.

Lao-tze thus phrases the reason for the silence:

"The Tao, which is the subject of discussion, is not the true Tao." This is identical with the statement of the alchemists, "Our matter has as many names as there are things in this world; that is why the foolish know it not."

The Great Secret *cannot* be told. Hence it is folly to try to tell it. The wise waste no time, invite no misconception, expend no energy, in vain efforts to tell. When they speak, it is not to tell the Secret, but to point the Way.

On the other hand, those who know the Secret are forever telling it, by their words and lives. Thus a correspondent writes: "How strange that though I had read the same statement hundreds of times, it is only now that I perceive it!" As when we learn a foreign language, so with the speech of the wise. At first, the words are meaningless noises. Presently we apprehend some of the meanings. If we persist in our study, soon, the dictionary definitions of the words are comprehended. Then a day arrives when the subtle connotations and implications are conveyed to us in *the very same words,* which meant nothing in the beginning.

So it is with your Tarot studies. The written word is combined with the more expressive language of pictorial symbols. This is how the mysteries are taught. You have been given keys that will open the doors of the prison of ignorance and admit you to the freedom of the True World.

The language of symbols is the speech of the inhabitants of that True World. All languages of humanity are but poor translations from it.

Some have asked, "Why not put this into plain English?" Wherever plain English will convey the meaning, we endeavor to use it. However, no translation from the mystery language can ever be adequate. You must learn that silent speech of symbols for yourself. Then you will find yourself in communication with others who know it.

Judgment

Key 20 is named *The Judgment*. On the surface, this refers to that day when all souls shall be judged. It is a veil for the real meaning. Judgment is the consequence of weighing the evidence. Hence Justice is always represented by the scales. In ancient Egyptian, the candidate's heart was put in the balances with Maat's feather of truth in the soul's judgment.

Judgment implies estimation or measurement. One might say that the Great Secret answers the question, "How much do you weigh?" That is to say, all that is real of us is *identical* with the One Thing. Therefore, our true weight must be the same. George Burnell has expressed it beautifully:

"The truth is that which is; there cannot be that which is not. Therefore that which is, or Truth, must be *all* there is."

When the heart's weight – the inner consciousness in man – corresponds to the weight of the feather of truth, then the scales of justice are balanced.

A judgment is a reasoned conclusion. Ageless Wisdom offers a reasonable doctrine. The sages forever say: "Come now, let us reason together." St. Paul says that giving up the false sense of personality a reasonable sacrifice. *The Chaldean Oracles* bid us join works to sacred reason. Thus in the symbols of Key 20, we find many references to the number 4, And Key 4 is particularly associated with reason.

Since a judgment is a reasoned conclusion, and reasoning leads to that conclusion, *judgment is the end of reasoning*. In Key 20, reasoning has come to its term, and a new order of knowing is manifested. Old things have passed away through the operation of the laws pictured by Key 13, the agency of the principle of right discrimination portrayed by Key 6. There is no more weighing of evidence, no more discussion of pros and cons, and no more argument for and against. That is all done with, and in Key 20, we find an abundant witness to this.

Finally, judgment is a decision. It has direct consequences in action. The word "decision" is a derivation from a Latin root meaning "to cut." Shin (ש) has the meanings of cut, sharp, and, therefore, separation. The Judgment cuts off forever our connection with the false knowledge of "this world." It puts an end to our limitation to three-dimensional consciousness. It forever ends our sense of mortality.

Thus, in Revelation 7:16, which is directly related to the doctrine of Judgment, we read: "They shall hunger no more, neither thirst any more."

To have done with all this misery. That is the promise, and to have done with it *forever*. This is not a temporary alleviation — a devouring flame of realization which consumes the whole unhappy brood of lies.

This week try to practice SILENCE. Speak as little as you can, keep your emotions under control, and above all, try to make your thoughts quiet. Notice that this conserves energy for useful endeavors. Continue this practice, the rest of your life.

COLORING INSTRUCTIONS

YELLOW: Bell of the trumpet, rays from clouds.

BLUE: Background, water, angel's dress. (The dress a darker shade.)

GRAY: Bodies of human figures, the coffins a darker tint.

WHITE: Clouds, banner (not cross), icebergs (blue highlights, very delicate.) collar edging on angel's dress.

GOLD: Trumpet.

Blonde: Hair of woman, child, and the angel.

RED: Angels wings, cross on the banner.

Chapter 44

THE JUDGMENT

The angel of Key 20 is Gabriel; he carries the trumpet which summons the dead from their coffins. Gabriel is the archangel of the moon. By theosophic reduction, 20 reduces to two (2 + 0 = 2). Recall that Key 2, the High Priestess, is attributed to the Moon. Furthermore, in Key 2, the robe of the High Priestess is the source of water for the Tarot.

The idea is that reflection is the presiding power in the scene, the root-power of Universal Memory. Gabriel means "Might of God." The scene suggests that human personality is raised from the "death" of the three-dimensional consciousness by a power descending from above, rather than by its efforts. The Spirit of Life in us never forgets itself, and when the Day of Judgment comes, we hear the trumpet call. Its vibrations proclaim our real nature and call us from the deathlike sleep of the belief in mortal existence.

Figure 8

In Key 20, care has been taken to enclose the angel in a design of two equal circles, filling a larger circle. The angel's head is in the small upper circle, his body in the lower one. This figure is an ancient symbol of the fourth dimension.

Clouds surround the angel because appearances veil the true nature of the Self. The substance of all appearances is the same as the stream of consciousness symbolized by the robe of the High Priestess. It is the flow of the stream of consciousness, which gives rise to our ideas of time. And these ideas are what partly veil from us the true nature of the One Identity.

12 Rays Pierce the Clouds

Twelve rays of light pierce the clouds. Twelve is the number of *Hu* HVA (הוא). *Hu* is the Hebrew third personal pronoun, "He." It is also the divine name of Kether, the Crown of the Primal Will. The intimation is that the rays piercing the veil of clouds is the light of the True Self, called "He" by Qabalists. Gabriel personifies one aspect of that light.

7 Trumpet Rays

Descending from the trumpet are seven rays. The horn is gold, a metal attributed to the Sun. As an instrument for amplifying sound vibration, the trumpet refers to the awakening of the higher consciousness is accomplished by specific sounds. These are represented by the seven little rays that also symbolize the seven metals or chakras.

Icebergs

The icebergs in the background refer to an alchemical dictum, to perform the Great Work, we must *fix the volatile*. The volatile is the stream of conscious energy, typified as water. Its flow gives rise to the illusions from which our delusions are derived. When we fix it or make it stable by arresting the flow, we are liberated from bondage.

Thus Key 12, the Hanged Man, or Suspended Mind, is attributed to the element Water. The state of Samadhi, or perfect abstraction, there pictured, culminates in the perpetual Intelligence symbolized by Key 20.

Higher consciousness arrests the flow of mental energy. It does this utilizing abstractions having their basis in mathematics. The stopped stream of consciousness is represented by ice, seen in Keys 0 and 9.

The sea is the end of the flowing of water. Thus it suggests the same ideas of termination and conclusion, which we found associated with the word "judgment."

The sea supports three stone coffins. This symbolizes the real support or basis for physical form appearances is the vibration of mental energy. The sea is the great sea of the race-consciousness, operating at the subconscious level.

This sea is the substance of all things in the human environment. There is no difference between the substance of an electron and the substance of thought.

Coffins

The coffins are rectangular to suggest the apparent solidity and impenetrability of three-dimensional forms. The human figures stand upright so that their bodies are at right angles to the coffins' bottoms. This intimates something impossible to draw — by definition, the Fourth Dimension as at right angles to all three dimensions of space, as we perceive them.

The three figures represent self-conscious awareness (the man), subconsciousness (the woman), and their product, the regenerated personality (the child). They also correspond to the Egyptian triad, Osiris the father, Isis, the mother, and Horus, the child.

L.V.X.

Each figure represents a Roman letter. The woman, by her extended arms, denotes L. The child lifts his hands over his head so that his arms make a V. The man, in the traditional posture of Osiris risen, crosses his arms to form an X. Thus the three persons symbolize L.V.X., the Latin for *Light*.

The man is in an attitude of passive adoration. In fourth-dimensional consciousness or Perpetual Intelligence, the self-conscious mind realizes that it does nothing itself. It is a channel through which the higher life descends to lower levels. It's one virtue, the mode of consciousness typified by the Magician, the Intelligence of

Transparency. The more transparent self-consciousness becomes, the less interference it offers to the One Thing's free passage. "Of myself, I can do nothing," is the meaning of the man's crossed arms. The X crosses out or cancels the idea of personal origination for any action.

The woman actively receives the influx of power from above. Her posture suggests the L, Lamed (ל) and Key 11. And Key 11 represents the Faithful Intelligence. Under the guidance of the right reason, subconsciousness expresses absolute faith.

Unreasonable faith is impossible; however, stoutly, men affirm that their creeds and dogmas deserve to be called "faiths." Thus the woman represents the purification following right reasoning, the subconscious response to correct estimates of the reality.

The child faces toward the interior of the picture. Thus he represents insight, the turning of the mind array from the false reports of external sensation.

His posture corresponds to V or Vav (ו). He is the type of intuition and Root Intelligence.

The three figures are nude to suggest a state of perfect innocence, a state of freedom from shame. Shame is a false emotion caused by our incorrect interpretation of the real nature of human life. Their nudity also suggests intimacy. This is one of the Perpetual Intelligence conditions, in which the right relations between the conscious and subconscious minds and their offspring, personality, are clearly understood.

The flesh of the figures is gray. Gray is the tint resulting from the blending of any two complementary colors, such as white and black, red and green, blue and orange, and so on. The figure's grey skin is a symbol that they have overcome all the pairs of opposites.

In the Sepher Yetzirah, Raavad version, the double letters have different traits. And each trait has two polarities.

	Planet		Key	Traits
1	Mercury	☿	1	Life & Death
2	The Moon	☽	2	Peace & Strife
3	Venus	♀	3	Wisdom & Folly
4	Jupiter	♃	10	Wealth & Poverty
5	Mars	♂	16	Beauty (Grace) & Ugliness
6	The Sun	☉	19	Fertility & Sterility
7	Saturn	♄	21	Dominion & Slavery

Therefore the gray flesh of the figures shows that the alchemical metals or chakras have been perfectly coordinated. The seven rays issuing from the trumpet suggest the same thing.

Mars Banner

The banner on the trumpet is a square, measuring 5x5 units. It is the magic square of Mars. A magic square is a square divided into smaller squares, each containing a number, such that the numbers in each vertical, horizontal, and diagonal row add up to the same value.

Mars Magic Square				
11	24	7	20	3
4	12	25	8	16
17	5	13	21	9
10	18	1	14	22
23	6	19	2	15

Geburah, the 5th Sephiroth, is attributed to Mars. In the magic square of Mars, the rows, columns, and diagonals add to 65. It is the number of Adonai (אדני), the name of God in Malkuth, the 10th Sephiroth. And so Malkuth is under Law (65 – Geburah).

Fire, the quality of Mars, predominates in Key 20. Mars is also active in Keys 4 (Aries), 13 (Scorpio), and 15 (Capricorn). In astrology, Mars rules Aries and Scorpio and is Exalted in Capricorn.

Equal Armed Cross

Since the banner is square and bears an equal-armed cross, they both are symbols of the number 4. Notice there are four figures in the picture. There are four principal elements in the scene: the icebergs, the sea, the group of human figures, and the angel.

Number 20

Twenty (20) is Key 4, the Emperor, multiplied by Key 5, the Hierophant (4 x 5 = 20). The Emperor stands for Aries, a fiery sign, ruled by Mars. The Emperor is also the Tarot symbol of sovereign reason, which leads to a decision or right judgment.

The banner corresponds to Key 20. Because it is a square with each side five units long so that the perimeter is 20 units, we may think of Perpetual Intelligence as the product of Reason's interaction (Key 4) and Intuition (Key 5). We must reason correctly before we receive the inner teaching of Intuition. Lazy minds do not hear the angel's trumpet call.

In the Cube of Space, the Shin (ש) line joins the north and south faces. This line moves from the center, as do all three coordinates. Therefore the cube is brought into manifestation from the central point.

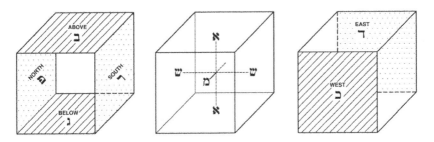

The Mother letter Aleph (א), its line extends from the center to Above (Beth, ב) and down to below (Gimel, ג).

The Mother letter Mem (מ), extends from the center to the East face (Daleth, ד) and West face (Kaph, כ).

The first coordinate line is Aleph (א) and the Fool, and the Life-Breath. Aleph represents spiritual consciousness or "superconsciousness." Remember, the terms "above" and "within" are interchangeable in occultism. Our thought habits were vestiges of ancestral thinking when "heaven" was identified with the sky, which appears to be above the earth's surface. But Masters of life know that the actual location of "heaven" is not *up*, but *in*. "The kingdom of heaven is within you."

Superconsciousness is *inner* consciousness. Thus in Key 18, the Path of Return *appears* to ascend, but really it leads *within*. Similarly, in Key 20, the little child faces the picture, as do the listening ministers in Key 5.

Hence each of the cube coordinates is a symbol for an aspect of superconsciousness or *awareness of the within*. In Key 12, this awareness is shown as a reversal of the average individual's mental attitude, concerned with outer appearances and emotional reactions. Key 12, through the letter Mem (מ), is related to the element of Water. Mem connects the East attributed to Venus, fabled to have been born from the ocean foam to the western face, attributed to Jupiter, the sky-father, ruler of rains and lord of the thunderbolt.

The third coordinate line, Shin (ש), is the mother of Fire and links the northern face (Mars) and the southern face (The Sun), a source of Fire in our world system.

The first coordinate that of Aleph is associated with Air and *life*. The second is Mem, associated with *substance* and symbolized as Water. The third coordinate is Shin and Fire, which has to do principally with *activity*.

Thus Key 0 is mainly concerned with the superconscious awareness of life. Key 12 with superconscious knowledge of the nature of substance. Key 20 with superconscious awareness of the true nature of activity. If you develop these hints, you will find many aspects of truth that will be all the more valuable to you because they will be your discoveries.

In each of these lines, there is a way from the center in two opposite directions. It is impossible to follow any of these lines from the surface back to the center.

How, then, shall one get to that center? By following one or other of the four interior diagonals.

These four interior diagonals correspond to four of the *five final forms* of letters in the Hebrew alphabet. When the letters Kaph, Mem, Nun, Peh, or Tzaddi come at the end of a word, they are in the final form.

		Final	Diagonal
Kaph	כ	ך	S.E to N.W
Mem	מ	ם	The Center
Nun	נ	ן	N.E. to S.W.
Peh	פ	ף	S.W. to N.E.
Tzaddi	צ	ץ	N.W. to S.E.

The four diagonals extend upward from the bottom of the cube, and they all pass through the center.

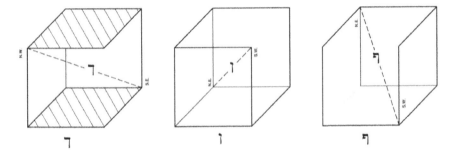

The final Kaph (ך) path begins at the south-east lower corner and runs diagonally upward through the center to the North-West upper corner.

The final Nun (ן) path begins at the North-East lower corner and runs up through the center to the South-West upper corner.

The path of final Peh (ף) is the diagonal uniting the lower end of the South-West line to the North-East line's upper end.

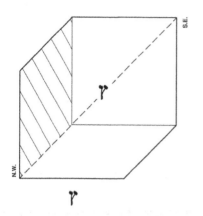

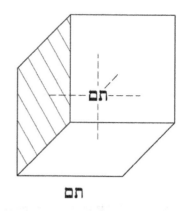

The final Tzaddi (צ) path joins the North-West line's lower end to the South-East line's top end.

The final Mem place is at the center of the cube, the point of perfect equilibrium, and the *point of control*. There final Mem (ם) is combined with Tav (ת), spelling ThM (תם), or *Toom*, signifying perfection and completeness.

The four final diagonals are Keys 10 (Jupiter), 13 (Scorpio), 16 (Mars) and 17 (Aquarius). Since the diagonals start Below and move upward, these Keys represent psychological and other responses originating at a subconscious level and then leading inward to the center. The upward movement along the diagonals is a consequence of a prior downward movement, originating at the conscious level represented by the cube's upper face.

For example, the shortest way to get to the beginning of the final Kaph (ך) diagonal is to descend through the line North-East (Key 4), then line East-Below (Key 7), and then upward through the final Kaph diagonal (Key 10).

The shortest way to reach the starting-point of the final Nun (ן) diagonal is to descend the N.E. Emperor line.

The shortest way to reach the beginning of the final Peh (ף) diagonal is to descend the north-east line, then west through North-Below, and thence south through line West-Below.

The shortest way to reach the beginning of the final Tzaddi (צ) diagonal is to descend the line North-East and go west to the end of line North-Below. This is the beginning of the final Tzaddi diagonal.

Note the first of these diagonals is the final Kaph. Therefore it cannot be crossed until the west face, corresponding to Kaph, has been bounded. None of the interior diagonals can be entered until one has passed through the line West-Below (Key 15). This is purely diagrammatic. What is meant is that one is not ready for the journey upward toward the center until one has faced one's Dweller on the Threshold.

Having arrived at the center by way of any one of the four interior diagonals, one may pass in any of ten different ways to the exterior.

Four lines lead to the upper *corners* through the diagonals. Six lines lead to the *faces* through the Mother letter lines. Thus, we learn that Keys 0, 12, 20, 10, 13, 16, and 17 represent the ways leading from the center to the cube's outer faces and corners.

All this is difficult at first reading, but it is included in the chapters because nothing in this whole system of Tarot symbolism, with the possible exception of the Tree of Life, is of greater value. Thus we advise you strongly to follow all these descriptions of the cube symbolism and directions. While you read, have your diagrams and Tarot Keys nearby.

We approach the end of this course. Now is the time to bring your diary up to date. Go back through the chapters, and make sure that you are carrying out the practical instruction.

The cumulative effect of simple tasks is most valuable. Do not be deceived by the seeming simplicity of some of this work. Nature operates by simple means, and the Great Work is an imitation of those simple methods whereby she accomplishes marvelous results.

Chapter 45

COSMIC CONSCIOUSNESS

The last card of the major Tarot Keys is *The World*. It is symbolic of the 7th stage of spiritual unfoldment, cosmic consciousness, or Nirvana. The identification with the One Power, which is the Pivot and Source of the whole cosmos. The adept at this stage experience firsthand through their personality the Power, which governs and directs the universe flows out into manifestation. This, of course, is always true. But experiencing such a thing is another matter.

Words fail to express the seventh stage of spiritual unfoldment. It is left to your intuition combined with the picture's suggestions with the meaning Tav (ת). Key 21 is a picture of what you are and of what the cosmos is. The universe is the Dance of Life. The innermost, **Central Self** of *your personality* is the Eternal Dancer. It always has been; it always will be.

Number 21

Twenty-one (21) is the sum of the numbers from 0 to 6 (0 + 1 + 2 + 3 + 4 + 5 + 6 = 21). The theosophic extension shows the completion or extension of the power of the principles represented by the seven Keys from Key 0 to Key 6.

There is an affinity between Key 21 and Key 7. Twenty-one (21) adds the digits from 0 to 6, so 7 *follows* 6 in the numerical scale. Also, Saturn is attributed to Key 21, and Saturn is the *seventh* planet known to the ancients. Saturn's name in Hebrew is *Shabbathai* (שבתאי), from this is derived the *Sabbath*, the day of rest or inertia, and the seventh day of the week. In the Tarot Tableau, Key 21 (3 x 7) is below Key 14 (2 x 7), and Key 14 is below Key 7. To save space, the three Keys are shown horizontally.

| 7 | THE CHARIOT | ח | 14 | TEMPERANCE | ם | 21 | THE WORLD | ת |

One Self

The principle at work in Key 21 is represented by Key 7, and the secret of Key seven is beautifully explained in the following words from *Light on the Path*:

"Stand aside in the coming battle, and though thou fights, be not thou the warrior, Look for the warrior, and let him fight in thee. Take his orders for the battle and obey them."

"Obey him not as though he were a general, as though he were thyself, and his spoken words were the utterance of thy secret desires; for he is thyself, yet infinitely wiser and stronger than thyself. Look for him, else in the fever and hurry of the fight you may pass him, and he will not know thee unless thou knows him. If your cry reaches his listening ear, then he will fight in thee and fill the dull void within. And if this is so, then canst thou go through the fight cool and unwearied, standing aside and letting him battle for thee. Then it will be impossible for thee to strike one blow amiss. But if thou look not for him, if thou pass him by, then there is no safeguard for thee. Thy brain will reel, thy heart grow uncertain, and in the dust of the battlefield thy sight and sense will fail, and thou wilt not know thy friends from thy enemies.

"He is thyself, yet thou art but finite and liable to error. He is eternal and is sure. He is eternal truth. Then once he has entered thee and

403

become thy warrior, he will never utterly desert thee, and at the day of the great peace, he will become one with thee."

Read this quotation carefully. See how the warrior, the rider in the chariot, is identified with speech, the function associated with Key 7.

In the quotation above, his "listening ear" is mentioned. Since the rider is the One Self, he is also the Hierophant, associated with hearing. Additionally, the two sections of the text are divided into twenty-one numbered paragraphs, preceded by an introduction bearing no number.

"He is thyself," The quest is for the SELF. The knowledge is knowledge of the SELF. The power of the infinite and eternal SELF is the only power. The SELF is the ONE, working through the mysterious activity of reflection and duality. All this is symbolized in Key 21, the last Tarot Key.

Tav - ת

Tav and its letter name (תו) means signature or mark. The original form was two crossed lines similar to the plus sign (+) in math. It is similar to the banner on Key 20 and the cross on the breast of the High Priestess. In Ezekiel 9:4, Tav is a symbol of salvation from death and a signature of eternal life.

As representing a signature, Tav implies security, pledge, guarantee, and so on.
A signature makes a business instrument valid. Thus Tav indicates the final seal and completion of the Great Work. The great secret of the letter Tav is the point where the two lines cross. This point represents the inner center, the abode of the One Identity.

According to the *Sepher Yetzirah* or *Book of Formation*, the central abode is described.

Ten Sefirot of Nothingness:
There measure is ten, which have no end.

A depth of beginning
A depth of end

A depth of good
A depth of evil.

A depth of above
A depth of below.

A depth of east
A depth of west.

A depth of north
A depth of south.

A singular Master, God faithful King, dominates over them all,
From His holy dwelling until eternity of eternities.

And so God's Holy Temple stands in the center. This innermost point is No-thing.

Read this quotation above several times with your Cube of Space diagrams in sight. Glace at the diagrams between readings. I recommend for your library *Sefer Yetzirah* by Rabbi Aryeh Kaplan.

Note that the abode of God is called the *heart*. It is also termed "That-which-is-not" because it has no physical form or fashion and symbolizes the zero sign, which we attribute to the Fool. By no means a non-entity, for this inner POINT is a positive metaphysical, intellectual reality. Hence, if you can grasp *the idea that this place of God, or Holy Temple that stands at the center, is necessarily everywhere, therefore, it must be the center of your being.*

The 32nd Path is Serving Intelligence (Sekhel Ne'evad). It repairs (Tikun) all the seven planets' operations and keeps them in their orbits.

Remember that the planets are the same as the interior stars or chakras. Recall from Chapter 37.

Please note that these diagrams and tables are shown several times. That's because they are important.

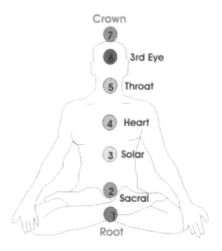

By LordtNis - Own work, CC BY-SA 4.0,
https://commons.wikimedia.org/w/index.php?curid=47747148

	Chakra	Planet			Chakra	Planet
1	Root	Saturn		5	Throat	Venus
2	Sacral	Mars		6	3rd Eye	Moon
3	Solar	Jupiter		7	Crown	Mercury
4	Heart	Sun				

Remember also that each of these planets corresponds to a Hebrew double letter and one of the six directions.

Key	Letter		Planet	Direction
1	Beth	ב	Mercury	Up
2	Gimel	ג	Moon	Down
3	Daleth	ד	Venus	East
10	Kaph	כ	Jupiter	West
16	Peh	פ	Mars	North
19	Resh	ר	The Sun	South
21	Tav	ת	Saturn	Center, The Holy Temple

Tav represents the point of control, at the CENTER, or the heart. Not the physical organ, but the heart in the sense of "midst, inmost, core." To get at the heart of your existence is to enter the Palace of the King. There the ONESELF is enthroned. There the Lord of the Universe has His abode. There is the central point of authority and rulership, extending its boundless influence throughout the cosmos. There, when the Great Work is accomplished, the Father and the Son are One, and the New Kingdom is established. Concerning this, an alchemical text says:

"The Son ever remains in the Father,
And the Father in the Son.
Thus in divers things
They produce untold, precious fruit.
They perish nevermore.

And laugh at death.
By the Grace of God, they abide forever.
The Father and the Son, triumphing gloriously
In the splendor of their New Kingdom,
Upon one throne, they sit.

And the face of the Ancient Master
Is straightway seen between them."
— Book of Lambspring.

That CENTER within. Seek it diligently, and you shall surely find it, and find there the
Stone of the Wise, described in the quotation you have just read.

Key 21 summarizes the whole Tarot and so summarizes in its symbolism the culmination of the Great Work. Stamp the symbols deep upon your subconsciousness as you color them this week.

COLORING INSTRUCTIONS

GREEN: Wreath.

BLUE: Background, (leave blank the ellipses round spirals in hands).

BROWN: Animals (as in Key 10).

WHITE: Clouds, as in Key 10. Rays should be painted white, extending from the ellipses around the spirals into the blue of the background.

BLONDE: Hair on man and dancer; beak of the eagle.

VIOLET: The veil around the dancer.

RED: Binding at top and bottom of the wreath; the cap-like wreath on the head of the dancing figure.

Chapter 46

THE WORLD

The title of Key 21, The World, suggests world-consciousness. When you attain this, you find yourself in tune with the whole universe. You discover that the center of life and power at the heart of your personal life is one with the Power which rules creation.

In this consciousness, the whole universe is realized as the body of the I AM. When you experience this, you will know that the directive Center of the entire field of cosmic activity is identical to your innermost SELF.

Taurus (♉), the Bull, and the element Earth

The four corners of this Key are the same mystical figures which appear on Key 10. There is a difference in one detail. In Key 21, the bull's face is turned away from the lion and away from the design's central figure. This detail follows a tradition observed in early versions of the Tarot.

The bull represents the element of Earth or that which gives form. In Key 10, this is turned toward the lion, and the center of the Key, where the symbol of Spirit is shown at the heart of the wheel. The mental activity pictured in Key 10 turns the mind away from form to the consideration of energy and away from the body to the consideration of Spirit. *The comprehension of the Law of Cycles (Key 10) is an act of mental abstraction, in which attention is turned away from the forms of things to their fiery essence (the lion).*

In Key 21, the bull faces away from the lion and the center. This detail emphasizes concrete manifestation. Therefore Key 21 is attributed to Saturn (♄), representing cosmic forces that limit energy in producing form.

The goal of the Great Work is not an abstraction. It is the demonstration, expression, and an orderly procession of energy into forms — the life-power's adornment with fitting garments.

The four living creatures are also related to the four fixed signs of the zodiac. These figures are Cherubim and are part of the Jewish angelic hierarchy. They are generally considered protectors. The lion is Leo, the eagle Scorpio, the man Aquarius, and the bull Taurus. The four fixed signs are also assigned to one of the Tetragrammaton letters and one of the four elements.

Leo - ♌	Scorpio - ♏	Aquarius - ♒	Taurus - ♉
Lion	Eagle	Man	Bull
י	ה	ו	ה
Fire	Water	Air	Earth

Also, each of the letters has a numerical value.

	Letter	Gematria
י	Yod	10
ה	Heh	5
ו	Vav	6
ה	Heh	10

Notice the value of the four-letter name of God or Tetragrammaton is 26. These creatures represent the Great Name, IHVH (יהוה). The four positions at the corners of the Key suggest that all manifestation is within this Name and the Reality boundaries.

The wreath is an ellipsoid figure with the long eight units, and the shorter is five units. It is a rectangle eight units high and five units wide. In the *Fama Fraternitatis*, a rectangle of 5 x 8 describes the walls of a vault of seven sides and seven corners. The area of this rectangle is 40 square units. And 40 is *Mem* (מ), the letter on the Hanged Man, Key 12. The perimeter of the rectangle is 26 (5 + 5 + 8 + 8 = 26).

Golden Ratio

In Chapter 13, I touched on the meaning of the Golden Ratio. Since it's an important concept, let's explore the number Phi (ϕ) in more detail.

The Divine Proportion is also called the Golden Mean, Golden Section, Golden Cut, or extreme and mean proportion.

One unique point exists that divides a line into two unequal segments so that the whole is to the greater as the greater is to the lesser.

It is paraphrased in the occult maxim: "Nature (the lesser part) is to Man (the greater part) as Man is to The All or IHVH (יהוה) if you prefer. By studying the golden ratio, we have a better understanding of our place in the cosmos. Please read through at least once the explanation below. I apologize in advance for the brain damage it may cause in the non-math oriented.

Consider the line segment A + B. If we divide it in just the right spot, we find that the length of the entire segment (A + B) is to the length of segment A as the length of segment A is to the length of segment B. If we calculate these ratios, we see that we get an approximation of the Golden Ratio.

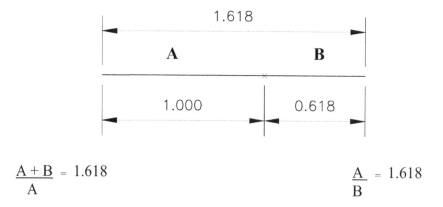

$$\frac{A+B}{A} = 1.618 \qquad\qquad \frac{A}{B} = 1.618$$

Please note that 1.618 is only an approximation of the golden ratio. The Golden Ratio is an irrational number. An irrational number has no *exact* decimal equivalent, although 1.618 is a good approximation. In mathematics, the Golden Ratio number is called *Phi* (ϕ). For the sake of convenience, I will use the term *Phi* (ϕ) exclusively.

Phi has many unique properties. It is the only number, which, when, subtracted from one (1), becomes its own reciprocal.

$$\phi - 1 = 1/\phi$$

By solving this equation, we find that the roots are

$$\phi = \frac{1 + \sqrt{5}}{2} \sim 1.618$$

$\sim$ Means approximately equal to

The Phi ratio can be approximated using the Fibonacci series. Briefly, these are the numbers 1, 2, 3, 5, 8, 13, 21, 34…

Noticed that by adding any to adjacent numbers in a series, you generate the next number. For example, $13 + 21 = 34$. To find the next number in the series,

$$21 + 34 = 55$$

Using single digits, $8/5 = 1.6$, which is the ancients' approximation for the phi ratio.

Logarithmic Spiral

The 5 x 8 rectangle is known as the "Rectangle of the Whirling Square." It is the basis of the logarithmic spiral, concerning which Claude Bragdon says:

"Now the generic or archetypal form of everything in the universe is naturally not other than the form of the universe itself. Our stellar

413

universe is now thought by astronomers to be a spiral nebula, and the spiral nebulae we see in the heavens, stellar systems like our own. The geometric equivalent of the nebula form is the logarithmic spiral. This is, therefore, the unit form of the universe, the form of all forms."

[Paul Foster Case has a doctor's degree in music. His writing style suggests that he assumes that everyone knows what he is talking about or has the time and patience to do research. I found that when it comes to math and geometry, few students do the research. So I add the explanation below.]

The spiral mentioned is constructed by nesting together squares using the Fibonacci series: 1, 2, 3, 5, 8, 13, 21, etc.

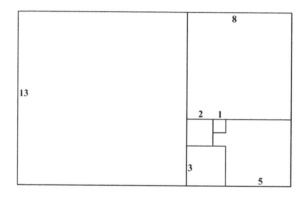

When you connect the corners, they from the logarithmic spiral

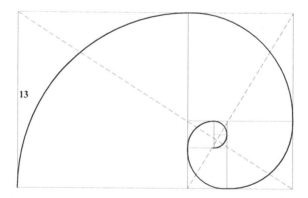

Organisms (whether plants, humans, and solar systems) organize their structures to the number Phi. The most well-known is the Nautilus shell.

Green Wreath

The wreath is composed of 22 triads of leaves. Every triad corresponds to a Hebrew letter and the conscious energy represented by the letters. Every mode of Life-power has three kinds of expression: 1. Integrative; 2. Disintegrative; 3. Equilibrating - balancing the other two.

Note that a wreath is a work of humanity. Nature provides the leaves. Humans weave them into a chaplet for the victor. Thus the wreath is a symbol for human adaptation of the forces of nature. It also suggests that cosmic consciousness is not spontaneously provided by natural evolution. It is the completion of the Great Work, and man is the Artificer.

At the top and bottom, the wreath is fastened with the infinity symbol (∞) similar to the one over the magician's head. All that is visible of this band makes the letter X. This is Tav's original shape (ת). It intimates that the power represented by Tav is used to bind the forces of nature into a wreath of victory. Tav is assigned the pair of opposites of dominion and slavery. Thus the wreath of victory is also a symbol that identical causes produce opposite effects.

The wreath rests on the bull and the lion because our power of giving form (the bull) to the formless, fiery, essential energy (the lion) is what enables humanity to weave together the 22 modes of force derived from that one energy.

Finally, the outline of the wreath is a zero sign. The ellipse of manifestation, woven by from the forces which play through us, is No-Thing. It has just as much power over us as we give it, and not one bit more. It does not bind us when we understand what it is. This world to a Master of life is a wreath of victory.

Thus the wreath represents the name, IHVH (יהוה), as the Fundamental Principle of form, of which the entire cosmos is the representation or manifestation.

World Dancer

The dancer in the wreath appears to be feminine, but the legs are masculine. The World-Dancer is the Celestial Androgyne. Her purple veil is in the form of Kaph (כ). Because Kaph is represented in Tarot by Key 10, the meaning here is:

> The mechanical appearance assumed by natural phenomena (Kaph, the Wheel of Fortune) veils their real character. The cosmos seems to be a system of wheels within wheels. It presents itself to our intellectual consciousness as a vast machine. Cause and effect seem to be rigidly and unalterably connected.

This is only *relatively* true. The Life-power is the author and master of the Law of Cause and Consequence. All laws are part and parcel of the drama of manifestation. *No law binds the SELF.*

The World-Dancer is entirely free, and this state of freedom is NOT. Hence the Dancer stands on nothing. She is self–supported and in perfect equilibrium.

The spiral in her right-hand turns toward the right. One in her left-hand turns toward the left. These spirals represent integration and disintegration. They are complements that turn simultaneously.

In the picture, each spiral has a definite beginning and end, but this is a limitation due to the impossibility of picturing the infinite. The processes the spirals symbolize has no beginning or end. Each spiral has eleven loops so that the two together represent the twenty-two modes of conscious energy symbolized by the Hebrew letters and Tarot Keys.

A person who enters into cosmic consciousness experiences what is symbolized by this Key. They know that every atom of the manifested universe is a living center of the One Reality, *within* that One Reality. They perceive that whatever is disintegrated is balanced simultaneously with integration. They know that the universe is conscious motion, consisting of infinite production sequences, destruction, and reproduction. Evolution is balanced by devolution, association by dissociation, integration by disintegration.

The Book of Concealed Mystery says: Before there was equilibrium, countenance beheld not countenance. This equilibrium hangs in that region which is NOT." Compare this with the quote "That-which-is-not" in the *Clementine Homilies*, in Chapter 45.

The Central Point

This region, which is NOT, is the central point in the Cube of Space, where the three coordinates and the four interior diagonals cross. It is the point of perfect balance, through which pass the thirteen axes of symmetry of the cube. At this point, the three Mother letters, Aleph (א), Mem (מ), and Shin (ש), are located. The lines corresponding to these letters radiate from this center.

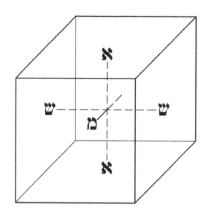
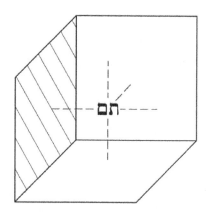

Also at the center is Tav (ת), the Temple of Holiness in the midst where final Mem (ם) is located. From these letters, form two words, *Emeth*, AMTh (אמת) meaning confirm, validate, certainty, and truth. Also, *Shem* (שם), meaning sign, token, memorial, monument, *name*. Ha (ה) Shem, means "the Name," and it is used to designate the Divine Name Jehovah IHVH (יהוה). Thus, the letters assigned to the cube's central point signify *the Truth of THAT, which was, is and will be.*

The same truth is the central reality, at the core of human personality. Therefore is the Name of God declared by Moses to be I AM. For the same reason, Hindu philosophers term this reality the Supreme SELF.

The central point is without form or dimensions. It is the region which is NOT or *Ain*, AIN (אין), the No-thing. This is the "First Veil of the Absolute." That is why The Fool is Key Zero (0); it symbolizes the Spirit that manifests the whole of creation. *No conditions of time, space, or quality limit the perfect freedom of the Central Reality. At this center is the focus of all possibilities, conceivable and inconceivable, known and unknown.*

Walt Whitman emphasizes the idea of equilibrium also, for he tells us that cosmic consciousness is an

> "Intuition of the absolute balance, in time and space, of the whole of this multifariousness, this revel of fools, and incredible make-believe and general unsettledness we call the *world*; a soul-sight of that divine clue and unseen thread which holds the whole congeries of things, all history and time, and all events, however trivial, however momentous, like a leashed dog in the hand of a hunter."

Leashed but ready to be let loose to fulfill the hunter's bidding. When the SELF is known, it is known as the Master of the Show of Illusion named the World. The name of this Master is *Eheyeh*, AHIH (אהיה), or I AM. This is the supreme Divine Name attributed to Kether, the Crown of Primal Will. It is connected with the last Key because *Eheyeh* is numerically 21.

Hebrew	Gematria
א	1
ה	5
י	10
ה	5

To summarize, states of consciousness are states of power. The Great Work goal is to know the Self, but not merely to witness or to be aware of something external. The knowledge which completes the Great Work is identification with the Central Reality of the universe. This knowledge is the acme of practical power.

Stone of the Wise

In alchemical books, this knowledge is the Philosophers' Stone—the mineral kingdom as the wise perceive it. The mineral kingdom is the basis of form-manifestation throughout the universe, and to see that kingdom as it really is, is to understand everything else. Hence the alchemists say that whoever knows the First Matter knows all that is necessary. In the *Fount of Chemical Truth*, Philalethes says, "Our appliances are part of our substance." Here is the secret, in plain sight.

In the consciousness of one who has reached this goal, Father and Son have become one and rule from the throne at the center of The ALL. This is the secret meaning of *Ehben*, ABN (אבן), Stone. Therefore it is written that those who possess the STONE have the means for preserving their youth, expelling disease, preventing suffering, and providing themselves with all they require. All this is true, without any metaphor whatever. Success in the Great Work unites the personal self with the One Identity that every detail of the personal existence is a conscious expression of the ALL POWER.

A life so lived is a life of perfect freedom, health, and joy. It is a life in which there is no trace of want or insufficiency. It is a life in which every circumstance of daily experience is an opportunity to demonstrate what is Tav and Serving Intelligence.

Such a life is the perfect fulfillment of one's real heart's desire. It is the actual and practical realization of heaven on earth, here and now. They who lives it ceases to be a bond-slave to appearances, a mere subject of the cosmic government. We enter into joyous participation in that government, as one whose life is a continual administration of the perfect law of liberty.

Make this your goal. Devote yourself with all your heart to it, and, like thousands who have gone this way before you, you shall be among those who tread the joyous measures of the Dance of Life.

* * *

Next week you will receive the Supplement to this course. It is a series of meditations to be used in conjunction with the Keys of Tarot. Be sure to follow the instruction given in this Supplement with full attention to all its details.

Chapter 47

A MONTH OF TAROT PRACTICE

Now you possess the fundamental knowledge required for your further progress. You know enough about each Key to understanding more advanced instruction. However, to make Tarot serve you as it should, you need to become better acquainted with it. In the hands of experts, it is a powerful instrument for self-transformation and self-mastery. Even the greatest adepts once knew less about the Tarot than you do now.

Do not make the mistake of trying to review *Tarot Fundamentals* at this time. You don't repeat the formula of introduction every time you meet a new acquaintance — every time you see him in a different set of circumstances. You get to know him better by hearing what he says and seeing what he does. So it is with Tarot. The best way to broaden and deepen your knowledge of it is to see it from as many different points of view as possible.

You can arrange the 22 Keys (using them all in each arrangement) One Sextillion Ways. The exact number is 1,124,000,727,777, 607,880,000.

There are innumerable other groupings in which only part of the series is used. Thus the total number of possible arrangements is practically infinite.

Every combination has a special meaning. Every combination calls forth its particular subconscious response. Every combination brings some fresh perception of relationships between ideas and things to the surface of your mind.

Therefore every combination helps you organize your mind and enables you to knit more closely the fabric of your thought.

In the following pages, you will find 24 combinations. Use one each day, six days a week, beginning the Monday after you receive this chapter. Do not work on Sundays, except for the recitation of the Pattern on the Trestleboard.

Begin by picking out the Keys selected for the day. Put them before you. Study them carefully in relation to each other. Then read the meditation aloud.

The meditations have strong suggestive power. A key sentence completes every meditation for the day, printed in capitals. Write this on a slip of paper, and carry it with you during the day. Repeat it at least three times as the day passes.

By carrying out this instruction carefully, you will accomplish several desirable results. You will charge your subconsciousness daily with seeds of creative thought. You will also review the entire series of Tarot Keys from a new point of view. You will begin to understand from experience how the Tarot can aid you in living a liberated life.

After you have completed the four weeks of practice, you will be ready to answer the Proficiency Test. This will enable you to check your grasp of *Tarot Fundamentals*.

The tools are now in your hands. You have learned what they are. You do the work which will enable you to be what you want to be, do what you want to do and have everything required to that being and doing. From now on, you begin to *live* your daily life by the principles and laws symbolized by the Tarot Keys. Your feet are firmly planted on the Way of Liberation.

MEDITATIONS

1st Day: Keys 0 and 1

Life limitless flows through me to complete its perfect work. The power which guides all things finds in me an open channel of expression. Receiving that power freely, I freely give it to all things and creatures in the field of existence surrounding me.

THROUGH ME LIFE ETERNAL TRANSFORMS ALL THINGS INTO ITS LIKENESS.

2nd Day: Keys 2 and 3

The law of truth is written in my heart; all my members are ruled by it. Through my subconsciousness, I am united to the Source of all wisdom, and its light banishes every shadow of ignorance and fear. I share the Universal Mind's perfect memory and have free access to its treasures of knowledge and wisdom.

THE PEACE OF THE ETERNAL AND THE LIGHT OF ITS PRESENCE ARE WITH ME NOW.

3rd Day: Keys 4 and 5

The Mind that frames the worlds is the ruler of my thoughts; I listen for its instruction. Through me, the One Life sets its house in order and makes known the hidden meaning of its ways and works. It arms me against all appearances of hostility, and by its revelation of truth, I meet and solve the problems of this day.

DIVINE REASON GUIDES MY THOUGHT AND DIRECTS MY ACTION, THROUGH THE INSTRUCTION OF THE VOICE OF INTUITION.

4th Day – Keys 6 and 7

The healing radiance of the One Life descends upon me; it fills the field of my whole personal existence with heavenly influences of strength and peace. All the force of my being is rightly disposed of, for I yield myself utterly to the sure guidance of the One Will which governs all things. I see things in their true relationships and proportions, and my words, expressing this clear vision, are words of power.

THIS DAY I THINK AND ACT WITH TRUE DISCRIMINATION, FOR MY PERSONALITY IS A VEHICLE FOR THE LORD OF LIFE.

5th Day – Keys 8 and 9

My strength is established, and I rejoice, for I am one with the Single Source of all power. Nothing is or can be my antagonist, for I am a perfectly responsive instrument, through which the Primal Will finds free expression. The subtle vibrations of cosmic energy work together for my liberation, and even now, the Hand of the Eternal leads me step by step along the way to freedom.

EVERY FORCE IN THE UNIVERSE IS AN OBEDIENT SERVANT OF THE ONE IDENTITY, MY TRUE SELF.

6th Day – Keys 10 and 11

One power spins electrons around the nucleus of an atom, whirls planets around suns, expresses itself in all cycles of universal activity, yet remains itself ever, and perpetually maintains its equilibrium.

The total of the great universe revolutions, is inseparable from the successive transformations of energy that make up my life history. Every detail of my daily experience is some part of a cosmic cycle of adjustment and transformation.

THE WHIRLING FORCE WHICH MOVES THE WORLDS IS THE MOTIVE POWER IN ALL MY ACTIVITIES AND ADJUSTS THEM ALL TOO RIGHT USES.

7th Day – Use only the Pattern today.

8th Day – Keys 12 and 13

I do nothing of myself. These thoughts and words and deeds are but the ripening of the seeds of past activities. Every phase of my existence depends utterly on the motion of the One Life. Therefore I am, free from fate, accident, even free from death since what I truly am can suffer neither decay nor change. By the knowledge of the truth, I reverse all former pain-bearing errors. The darkness of ignorance passes away, and the light of a new day dawns in my heart.

I SUSPEND THE ERROR OF PERSONAL ACTION AND THUS DISSOLVE THE LIE OF SEPARATION.

I recognize every detail of my life experience to be the operation of the One Life. I perceive that every appearance of adversity must be, in truth, a mask worn by that same One Life, to test my power to know it, even though the most forbidding veils.

Like a wise teacher, the One Life sets me problems that in the solutions I may receive renewed proofs that nothing whatever may be excluded from the perfect order of the Great Plan.

THAT WHICH WAS AND IS AND WILL BE IS THE ONLY REALITY. THIS DAY I SEE THE FACE OF THE BELOVED BEHIND EVERY MASK OF ADVERSITY.

10th Day – Keys 16 and 17

I am awakened from the nightmare of delusion, and now the truth that God, Man, and Universe are three names for the One Identity. It is clear to me. Fear makes some men build prisons that they call places of safety, but he who has seen the vision of the Beloved has in his heart no room for fear.

I NEED NO BARRIERS OF PROTECTION, FOR THE LIFE OF ALL CREATURES IS MY TRUEST FRIEND.

11th Day – Keys 18 and 19

My feet are set upon the path of liberation, which shall lead me far from the limits of the world of sense-illusion. I follow the Way of Return as a child turns its face homeward at the end of the day. I do not see the end of the road, for it goes beyond the boundaries of my present vision, but I know the sun shines there, and that joy is there, for I have heard the messages of encouragement sent back by those who have gone on ahead.

MY EYES ARE TURNED TOWARD THE HEIGHTS. I PRESS ON TOWARD THE NEW LIFE OF A NEW DAY.

12th Day – Keys 20 and 21

The life of the heavens is manifested here on earth. The fire of right knowledge burns away the bonds of illusion, and the light of real understanding transforms the face of the world. Through me, the Perpetual Intelligence, which governs all things, administers its Perfect Law.

MINE IS THE LIFE ETERNAL, TRENDING THE JOYOUS MEASURE OF THE DANCE OF MANIFESTATION.

13th Day – Keys 0, 1, 2

This "self-consciousness" of mine is the means whereby the One Life's cultural power may be directed to the field of subconscious activity. Its primary function is alert attention. As I watch the sequence of this day's events closely, their learning will be transmitted to my subconsciousness, there to germinate in forms of right knowledge and right desire.

TODAY I AM ON THE ALERT.

14th DAY – Use only the Pattern.

15th Day – Keys 3, 4, 5

My world is as I see it. If the images rising from my subconsciousness are consequences of my faulty perceptions of other days, the new knowledge I have gained will help me detect and destroy them. By being ever on the watch, I shall set my world in order. Therefore shall I make ready to hear the Voice of Intuition, which will enable me to solve my problems when I am face to face with appearances of disorder, which my reasoning will not set straight.

I SEE THINGS AS THEY ARE.

16th Day – Keys 6, 7, 8

Consciousness and subconsciousness work together in my life as harmoniously balanced counterparts. I yield my whole personality to the directive and protective influx of the One Life. The mighty forces of vibration below my self-consciousness level are purified and adjusted by the Master Power of which I am a receptive vehicle.

HARMONY, PEACE, AND STRENGTH ARE MINE.

17th Day – Keys 9, 10, 11

The Will of the Eternal guides me to perfect union with the One Identity. Every detail of my daily experience is, in truth, a revelation of that Will through the cycles of its expression. What I do now is inseparable from the cosmic sequences of manifestation, which establish the reign of justice throughout creation.

THE ONE POWER, MANIFESTING THE PERFECT ORDER OF THE UNIVERSE, KEEPS ME POISED THROUGH ALL CHANGES.

18th Day – Keys 12, 13, 14

Every detail of my activity is a part of the operation of cosmic life. Today I reap the fruit of thoughts and words and deeds of other days and pass on to better things. I am guided, moment by moment, by the overshadowing presence of the One Identity.

MY PERSONALITY DOES NOTHING OF ITSELF, PASSING FROM STAGE TO STAGE OF ITS GROWTH, BY THE POWER OF THE ONE LIFE, TOWARD THE GOAL OF FREEDOM.

19th Day – Keys 15, 16, 17

Every appearance of adversity and antagonism is evidence of impaired vision. Let me be freed today from the delusion of separateness, and let my eyes be opened to this white splendor of the Truth of Being.

I REJOICE IN MY PROBLEMS, FOR THEY STIMULATE MY CONSCIOUSNESS TO OVERCOME ERROR, THAT I MAY SEE THE BEAUTY OF THE DIVINE PERFECTION.

20th Day – Keys 18, 19, 20

The cosmic urge animates every cell in my body to freedom. I turn my back upon the past limitations and face courageously toward the new way that opens before me.

MY VERY FLESH IS THE SEED-GROUND FOR A NEW LIFE, FREE FROM BONDAGE TO TIME AND SPACE.

21st Day: Use only the Pattern.

22nd Day – Keys 1, 2, 3

The manifold illusions of sensation do not deceive me. I remember continually that these appearances are but reflections of a Single Reality. By its power of deductive reasoning, my subconsciousness develops the seed of accurate observation into an abundant harvest of wisdom.

ALERT AND CONCENTRATED, I SEE CLEARLY, MAKE CLEAR AND DEFINITE MEMORY RECORDS OF EXPERIENCE, AND THUS COLLECT MATERIAL FOR THE GROWTH OF TRUE UNDERSTANDING.

23rd Day – Keys 4, 5, 6

The empire of the Universal Order includes the little province of my existence. All experience teaches me the perfection of the Great Plan. Consciously and subconsciously, I respond to the perfect Wisdom, which rules all creation.

THROUGH ME THE ONE LIFE ESTABLISHES ORDER, REVEALS THE SIGNIFICANCE OF EVERY PHASE OF MANIFESTATION, RIGHTLY DISPOSES OF ALL THINGS.

24th Day – Keys 7, 8, 9

The One Life lives through me. Its vital fire permeates my being. Its unfailing Will sustains me continually.

THE MASTER PRINCIPLE OF THE UNIVERSE, DWELLING IN MY HEART, PURIFIES AND PERFECTS ME, AND LEADS ME TO THE HEIGHTS OF UNION WITH ITSELF.

25th Day – Keys 10, 11, 12

The revolutions of circumstance in the outer world are manifestations of the One Power seated in my heart. That Power maintains its perfect equilibrium through all sequences of cause and effect. My activities have no existence apart from that Power.

THE WHEEL OF LIFE REVOLVES AROUND THE CENTER OF PURE SPIRIT, PRESENT EVERYWHERE, AND THEREFORE CENTERED IN MY HEART. THIS UNMOVED MOVER OF ALL CREATION IS MY UNFAILING STAY.

26th Day – Keys 13, 14, 15

Out of the darkness of the unknown comes the power which sets me free. The Way of Liberation stands open and free. I face this day's tests with a joyful heart.

AS I DIE TO THE OLD PERSONALITY, FULL OF DELUSION, AND FACE THE UNKNOWN FUTURE BRAVELY, CONFIDENT OF SUPPLY FOR EVERY NEED, MY FEARS DISSOLVE IN THE CLEAR SUNLIGHT OF RIGHT UNDERSTANDING.

Let others imprison themselves in their towers of false knowledge. I will be free. Let others dread the workings of our Mother Nature. I will love all of her ways. Let others be servants of the body, which they hate because they are its slaves. I will make it my servant and love my body for its faithfulness in responding to my commands.

RENOUNCING EVERY ERROR, I SEEK TO GROW IN KNOWLEDGE OF TRUTH, AND WORK TO MAKE MY FLESH AND BLOOD A GLORIOUS EMBODIMENT OF LIFE ETERNAL.

28ᵗʰ Day – Use only the Pattern today.

You are now ready to check your progress using the Proficiency Test, given in the two pages following. This will help you summarize the results of your work with *Tarot Fundamentals*. It will also focus all your forces on the fascinating use of Tarot taught in the next course, *Tarot Interpretation*.

Chapter 48

TAROT FUNDAMENTALS

PROFICIENCY TEST

Do not copy the questions. Make your answers brief.

1. How does Tarot evoke thought?

2. What statement in *The Pattern on the Trestleboard* means most to you? Which seems most difficult?

5. Which number from 0 to 9 seems most important to you? Which of the 22 Keys is your favorite?

4. What is magic? The hidden forces of Subconsciousness.

5. How does one tap the Universal Memory?

6. What is the significance of the number Five and the Pentagram as symbols of man?

7. What do you understand by the Hexagram or a six-pointed star?

8. As symbols of consciousness, what are Sulfur, Salt, and Mercury?

9. What is the occult teaching about water as a substance?

10. What is the occult meaning of the Hebrew noun translated as wrath"?

11. What is the activity of the liberating aspect of the force symbolized by Key 15?

12. Why are the Yods in Key 16 suspended in the air?

13. Why does the woman in Key 17 rest her foot on the surface of the pool?

14. Upon what fundamental condition does the achievement of your purpose depend?

15. What is the significance of the saying, "Osiris is a black god"?

16. What is the goal of the Great Work?

17. After careful study of the chapters and the tables in the Appendix, construct from memory the Cube of Space. Use two diagrams and show the following attributions:

1. Directions,

2. Tarot Keys, by name.

3. Letters of the Hebrew alphabet.

4. The various ''Intelligences."

5. Alphabetical numeral values (not numbers of Keys).

6. Astrological symbols.

7. Symbols of elements.

Below your diagrams, write a short paragraph giving your idea of how this Cube helps interpret life using Tarot.

Appendix 1

Tarot Correspondences

Key	Title	Hebrew Letter	
0	The Fool	א	Aleph
1	The Magician	ב	Beth
2	The Moon	ג	Gimel
3	The High Priestess	ד	Daleth
4	The Emperor	ה	Heh
5	The Hierophant	ו	Vav
6	The Lovers	ז	Zain
7	The Chariot	ח	Cheth
8	Strength	ט	Teth
9	The Hermit	י	Yod
10	The Wheel of Fortune	כ ך	Kaph
11	Justice	ל	Lamed
12	The Hanged Man	מ ם	Mem
13	Death	נ ן	Nun
14	Temperance	ס	Samekh
15	The Devil	ע	Ayin
16	The Tower	פ ף	Peh
17	The Star	צ ץ	Tzaddi
18	The Moon	ק	Qoph
19	The Sun	ר	Resh
20	Judgment	ש	Shin
21	The World	ת	Tav

Many, if not all, of the Hebrew letters, have a correspondence with Ancient Egyptian Hieroglyphs. For those interested in learning more, I recommend Hieroglyphic Sign List by Bill Petty.

Key		Hebrew	Pictograph	Gardner
0	א	Aleph	Ox	F1, U6
1	ב	Beth	House, tent	O1
2	ג	Gimel	foot	D56, D58
3	ד	Daleth	Door	O34,
4	ה	Heh	arms raised	A28, D28, P6
5	ו	Vav	peg	M44
6	ז	Zain	sickle	U1
7	ח	Cheth	Tent wall, fence	O1, O4
8	ט	Teth	Coiled basket	V30
9	י	Yod	Closed Hand	D36, D49
10	כ ך	Kaph	Open Hand	D47
11	ל	Lamed	Shepherd staff	S38, S39
12	מ ם	Mem	Water	N35
13	נ ן	Nun	Seed sprout	M42
14	ס	Samekh	thorn	M44, R11
15	ע	Ayin	Eye	D4
16	פ ף	Peh	Mouth	D21
17	צ ץ	Tzaddi	Net, snare	T19, T24
18	ק	Qoph	horizon	
19	ר	Resh	Head	D1, D2
20	ש	Shin	Teeth	N37
21	ת	Tav	Mark	D42, Z9, O49, Z11

These correspondences are from, *The Ancient Hebrew Language and Alphabet*. They differ somewhat from Case.

Key	Hebrew		# Value	Color	Musical Note
0	א	Aleph	1	Yellow	E Natural
1	ב	Beth	2	Yellow	E Natural
2	ג	Gimel	3	Blue	G Sharp
3	ד	Daleth	4	Green	F Sharp
4	ה	Heh	5	Red	C Natural
5	ו	Vav	6	Red-Orange	C Sharp
6	ז	Zain	7	Orange	D Natural
7	ח	Cheth	8	Orange-Yellow	D Sharp
8	ט	Teth	9	Yellow	E Natural
9	י	Yod	10	Yellow-Green	F Natural
10	כ	Kaph	20	Violet	A Sharp
11	ל	Lamed	30	Green	F Sharp
12	מ	Mem	40	Blue	G Sharp
13	נ	Nun	50	Blue-Green	G Natural
14	ס	Samekh	60	Blue	G Sharp
15	ע	Ayin	70	Blue-Violet	A Natural
16	פ	Peh	80	Red	C Natural
17	צ	Tzaddi	90	Violet	A Sharp
18	ק	Qoph	100	Violet-Red	B Natural
19	ר	Resh	200	Orange	D Natural
20	ש	Shin	300	Red	C Natural
21	ת	Tav	400	Blue-Violet	A Natural

Astrological and Alchemical Correspondences				
Key		Modality	Element	Alchemy
0	Uranus		Mother of Air	
1	Mercury			Mercury
2	Moon			Silver
3	Venus			Copper
4	Aries	Cardinal	Fire	
5	Taurus	Fixed	Earth	Earthy
6	Gemini	Mutable	Air	
7	Cancer		Water	
8	Leo	Fixed	Fire	Fiery
9	Virgo	Mutable	Earth	
10	Jupiter			Tin
11	Libra	Cardinal	Air	
12	Neptune		Mother of Water	
13	Scorpio	Fixed	Water	
14	Sagittarius	Mutable	Fire	
15	Capricorn	Cardinal	Earth	
16	Mars			Iron
17	Aquarius	Fixed	Air	
18	Pisces	Mutable	Water	
19	Sun			Gold
20	Pluto		Mother of Fire	
21	Saturn			Lead

Only Astrological signs have modality. The planets take on the characteristics of the signs they occupy.

Cube of Space Attributions

Key	Hebrew				Direction
0	Aleph	א	F I	Mother of Air	Above-Below
1	Beth	ב	N		Above
2	Gimel	ג	A	double	Below
3	Daleth	ד	L		East
4	Heh	ה	S		North East
5	Vav	ו			South East
6	Zain	ז		simple	East Above
7	Cheth	ח			East Below
8	Teth	ט			North Above
9	Yod	י			North Below
10	Kaph	כ	ך	double	West
11	Lamed	ל		simple	North West
12	Mem	מ	ם	Mother of Water	East-West
13	Nun	נ	ן	simple	South West
14	Samekh	ס			West Above
15	Ayin	ע		simple	West Below
16	Peh	פ	ף	double	North
17	Tzaddi	צ	ץ	simple	South Above
18	Qoph	ק			South Below
19	Resh	ר		double	South
20	Shin	ש		Mother of Fire	North-South
21	Tau	ת		double	Center

Key	Intelligences	Other Attributes
0	Shining Intelligence	Super-consciousness, cultural power
1	Glowing Intelligence	attention, life & death
2	Unity Directing Intelligence	memory, peace & strife
3	Illuminating Intelligence	imagination, wisdom & folly
4	Stable Intelligence	reason, sight
5	Eternal Intelligence	intuition, hearing
6	Perceptive Intelligence	discrimination, smell
7	Intelligence of the House of Influx	Receptivity, will, speech
8	Intelligence of the Secret of all Spiritual Activities	suggestion, digestion, taste
9	Intelligence of Will	response, union of opposites, touch
10	Seeking Intelligence	rotation, wealth & poverty
11	Faithful Intelligence	equilibration, action, work

Key	Intelligences	Other Attributes
12	Sustaining Intelligence	reversal, suspended mind
13	Imaginative Intelligence	transformation, motion
14	Experimental Intelligence	verification, wrath
15	Regenerating Intelligence	bondage, mirth
16	Perceptible Intelligence	awakening, grace and sin
17	Natural Intelligence	revelation, meditation
18	Physical Intelligence	organization, sleep
19	Inclusive Intelligence	regeneration, fertility & sterility
20	Perpetual Intelligence	realization, decision
21	Serving Intelligence	Cosmic Consciousness, domination & slavery

The attributions of sight, smell etc., are from the short version (Raavid) of Sepher Yetzirah, p. 219. See also Appendix 1 of the same book.

Appendix 2

32 Paths in Hebrew

1st Path

The 1st Path is the Marvelous Intelligence (Sekhel Mufla). It is the Light of the Primordial Mind. It is the 1st Glory. No creature can attain its essence.

מופלא	שכל	נקרא	ה-ראשין	הנתיב
Marvelous	Consciousness	is called	The First	Path
פלא	Intelligence		1	
wonderful			principal	
Title of Kether			supreme	

קדמון	מישכל	אור	והוא	ו׳ס׳ע
ancient	Mind	light	It is	The highest
	Intelligence			crown

כל	אין	ראשון	כבוד	והוא
all	not, no	First	honor	It is
	nothing		respect	
	without			

443

בריה	יכולה	ל-עמוד
Briah	can	stand
Creation		platform
נברא		
living creature(s)		

על	מציאתו
on	essence
about	תמצית
to	summary
	essence, juice, lifeblood

קדמון - ancient, primitive, ancestor; eastern

מצת – igniter, spark, glow

444

2nd Path

The Second Path is that of the Illuminating Intelligence (Sekhel Maz'hir). It is the Crown of Creation. It is the Splendor of the Unity(s) and exalted above every head.

The Kabbalists call it the Second Glory.

הנתיב	ה-ב	הוא	נקרא	שכל	מזהיר
Path	The 2	It	is	Consciousness	Shining
	second		called	Intelligence	Radiant
					Illumination

ו-הוא	כתר	ה-בריאה	ו-זהר	ה-אחדות
& It is	*Kether*	*Briah*	*Zohar*	*Achad*
	Crown	Creation	Splendor	Unity(s)

השוה	ה-מתנשא	ל-כל	ל-ראש
It is	towering	to all	head
	exalted		top
			chief

ו-הוא	נקרא	כפי	בעלי
& It	is called	by	Masters
			Kabbalists
			Masters of Reception

ה-קבלה	כבוד	שני
קבל	glory	second
receive	honor	

The 3rd Path is the Sanctifying Intelligence (Sekhel MeKudash). It is the foundation of Primordial Wisdom. It is called the Faithful Faith. It is the basis of faith (Amen) and the Father of Faith. By its power, Faith emanates (*Atziluth*).

Atziluth – World of Fire.

הנתיב	השלישי	נקרא	שכל	ה-קודש
Path	3	is called	Consciousness	The Holy
			Intelligence	Sanctity

ו-הוא	יסוד	ה-חכמה	ה-קדומה
& It is	*Yesod*	*Chokmah*	The Ancient
	Foundation	Wisdom	Primordial
			Original

הנקרא	אמונה	אומן	ושרשיה
is called	faith	craftsman	& its roots
	confidence	educator	שירש
	trust	artesian	basis
	honesty		origin

ה-אמונה	אב	ו-הוא	אמן
Faith	father	& It is	*Amen*
trust			Faithfulness
			Firm
			found true

נאצלת	ה-אמונה	שמכחו
Noble	Faith	מכח
אצילות	trust	By virtue of
Atziluth		on the strength of
Emanation		

The Fourth Path is named the Fixed or Immutable Intelligence (Sekhel Kavua). From it, all spiritual powers emanate as the most subtle emanations. Their powers are from the Original Emanation.

הנתיב	הרביעי	נקרא	שכל	קבוע
Path	4	is	Consciousness	Fixed, constant
		called	Intelligence	regular, steady
				Permanent
				immutable

ונקרא	כן	שממנו	מת-אצלים	כל	חכתות
and	yes	From	Emanation	all	powers
called	so	which	masc. plural		forces

ה-רחניות	ב-דקות	ה-אצילות	שמת-אצילות
רחן	subtlety	Atziluth	
spiritualization	fineness	Emanation	

אלו	מאלה	ב-כח	ה-מאציל	ה-קדמון
These	From these	force	אציל	Ancient
They	those	power	Emanation	Primordial
	These ones	strength		Original

דק – thin, lean, fine, delicate, sensitive, minute (time); dust, fine cloth, heaven (poetical).

448

The 5th Path is called the Root Intelligence (Sekhel Nishrash). It is the essence of unity(s). Its essence of Binah (Intelligence, Understanding) that emanates from the refuge of the Original Wisdom (Chokmah).

הנתיב	החמישי	נקרא	שכל	נשרש
Path	5	is	Consciousness	Root
		called	Intelligence	Basis
				Foundation

ונקרא	כן	מפני	שהוא	עצם	ה-אחדות
and called	so	because	It is	essence	unity(s)

השוה	ו-הוא	ה-מיוהד	ב-עצם	ה-בינה
That	& It is	no word	essence	*Binah*
		מיועד		Understanding
		intended		
		designated		

ה-נאצלת	מגדר	החכמה	ה-קדומה
אציל	enclosure	Chokmah	Ancient
Atziluth	גדר	Wisdom	Primordial
Emanation	to fence, enclose		Original
	refuge		

מיועד – google translate suggested this word.

The 6th Path is the Differentiating Influx Intelligence (Sekhel Shefa Nivdal). It emanates its blessing in abundance, uniting everything in its essence.

הנתיב	השישי	נקרא	שכל	שפע
Path	6	is	Consciousness	influx
		called	Intelligence	

נבדל	ה-אצילות	ו-הוא	משפיע
to separate divide	*Atziluth*	& It is	influencing
discern	Emanation		giving in abundance
distinguish			
בדל			
to differentiate			

ה-שפע	על	כל	ה-בריכות	ה-מתאחדות
influx	on	all	blessings	unite, uniting
		everything	ברך	אחד
			To bless	One (1)

ב-עצמו
in its essence

להבדיל - to separate day from night. Genesis 1:4.

The 7th Path is the Hidden Intelligence (Sekhel Nistar). It is the splendor that radiates all intellectual powers that is visible to the mind's eye and contemplation of faith.

הנתיב	השביעי	נקרא	שכל	נסתר
Path	7	is called	Consciousness	hidden
			Intelligence	latent
				occult

ונקרא	כן	מפני	שהוא	זוהר	מזהיר
& called	so	because	that is	Zohar	Brilliant, bright
				Splendor	shining
				radiant	זהר
					To brighten
					shine

לכל	ה-כחות	ה-שכליים	ה-נראים	ב-עין
To all	Power(s)	Intellectual	visible	eye
For all	Force(s)	Rational	apparent, seen	

ה-שכל	ו-ב-רעיון	ה-אמונה
Intelligence	idea, concept	Faith
mind	thought	
	imagination	
	desire	

451

The 8th Path is called the Whole or Perfect Intelligence. It is the Original Plan. There is no root it can dwell on, except in the chamber of Gedulah (Greatness), which emanates from its essence.

הנתיב	השמיני	נקרא	שכל	שלם
Path	8	is called	Consciousness	whole
			Intelligence	complete

ונקרא	כן	מפני	שהוא	תכונת	ה-קדמות
&	so	because	that is	attribute	Antiquity
called			It is	trait	Days of Old
				quality	original
				plan	Primordial

אשר	אין	לו	שורש	ל-ה-תיישב	בו
which	no	to it	root	ישב	to it
that	not	if	basis	To sit	
who		Oh	origin	dwell	
where		that!			

כִּי	אָם	בְּ-חַדְרֵי
because	If	room
	except	chamber
		bridal chamber

הַ-גְּדוּלָה	הַ-נֶּאֱצָלִים	מֵעַצְּם
Gedulah	*Atzileem*	
greatness	Emanation	essence
Magnificence		

שָׁלֵם – whole, entire, intact, complete, integral, unhewn, full, perfect, total; safe, unharmed, healthy true, faithful; peaceful.

כִּי – for, because, yet, but, as, if, in case, while, when, through, although, since, only.

The 9th Path is Pure Intelligence (Sekhel Tahor). It purifies the Sephiroth (numbers). It tests the law and repairs the pattern. They are unified without any curtailment or separation and bestowing favor (or giving heat).

הנתיב	התשיעי	נקרא	שכל	טהור
Path	9	is	Consciousness	pure
		called	Intelligence	clean
				purified

ו-נקרא	כן	לפי	שהוא	מטהר
& called	yes	because	that is	purifier
	so		It is	purifies
				to be
				cleansed

את	ה-ספירות	ו-מבחין	ו-מבהיק	גזירת
	Sephiroth	מבחן	מבנה	גזרה
	numbering	test	structure	decree
	counting		building	law

את – This word indicates that the next word in the sentence is a direct object.

תבניתם	ו-תוכן	אחדותם	שהן
תבנית	תכן	their unity	to glow
pattern, image	design	oneness	שחן
בנה			grace, favor
establish			
to repair			

מיוחדות	מבלי	קצוץ	ו-פירוד
unity	without	cut	נפרד
אחדות		chopped	separate
unity		curtailment	

10th Path

The 10th Path is Scintillating Intelligence (Sekhel MitNotzetz). It is exalted and sits on the throne of Binah (Understanding). It illuminates the splendor of all the lights and causes an influx of increase from the Prince of Face.

הנתיב	העשירי	נקרא	שכל	מתנוצץ
Path		is called	Consciousness Intelligence	Shining מתצנץ Scintillating

ונקרא	כן	שהוא	מפני	מתעלה	ו-יושב
and called	yes so	that is	because	העלה exalted rise above p. 1282	resident ישב sits

על	כסא	ה-בינה	ו-מאיר	ב-זוהר
on	seat כס throne	Binah Intelligence Understanding Intellect	illuminate shine brightness	Zohar splendor radiant

456

ה-מאורות	כולם	ו-משפיע	שפע
אור	everyone	influx	influx
fire		influence	abundance
illumination		motivate	wealth
lights			

ריבוי	ל-שר	ה-פונים
רוה	Prince	פנים
multiply	ruler, noble	face
increase	captain	front
		appearance

457

The 11th Path is the Shining Consciousness. It is truly the essence of the veil which arranges the sequence of the stars. It assigns the Paths to their relationships. And (it) stands before the Cause of Causes.

The Cause of Causes is a title of Kether, the Crown – the 1st Path.

הנתיב	אחד	עשר	נקרא	שכל	מצוחצח
Path	1	10	is called	Consciousness	shining
				Intelligence	glaring
					scintillating

ונקרא	כן	מפני	שהיא	עצם	ה-פרגוד
& called	rightly	because	that is	essence	the veil
	true			bone	curtain
	base			substance	screen
	here			mighty	
				numerous	

פרגוד is related to פרכת, *parocheth* (curtain of the Ark of the Law).

458

ה-מסודר	ב-סדר	ה-מערכה	ו-הוא
the arrangement	in succession	the array, arrangement	and it
the ordered	sequence	row, battle-line	and he
	series	subkingdom	*Hu* – divine
	section (Seder)	disposition of the stars	name of Kether

יחס	ה-נתנת	ל-עמוד	ב-פני
assign	the paths	to stand	in front
attribute		pole	before
attach		pagination	to face
pedigree		make-up	
relationship			

עילת	ה-עילות
cause	the causes
	of causes

12th Path of Beth - ב

The 12th Path is the Glowing Consciousness (Sekhel Bahir). It is the essence of the Great Wheel (the zodiac). It is called the Visualizer (Chaz.chaz.it). It is the source of vision of the prophets and those who see apparitions.

הנתיב	שנים	עשר	נקרא	שכל	בוער
Path	2	10	is called	Consciousness	glowing
				Intelligence	burning

מפני	שהוא	עצם	ה-אופן
because	that is	essence	The wheel
		bone	*Ophan*
		substance	

ה-גדלה	ו-נקרא	חזחזית
the great	and called	Visualizer
magnificence		*Chaz.chaz.it*
increase		חזית
		Seeing, prophecy revelation, aspect

פי	מקים	מוצא
transitive verb	place, spot	way out
	dwelling-place	origin
	seat	source
	location	fountain
		utterance, edict

חזיון	ה-חוזים	ב-מראה
vision	prophets	appearance, vision
		sight, view, seeing
	חוזה	mirror
	prophet	shown, displayed

באיר – No such word. Rabbi Kaplan translates, "Glowing." In Alcalay's *English to Hebrew*, p. 1582, glowing is בוער.

Transparent is ברור.

Prophets spelled with two Cheth (ח) in the original text. I changed it to Heh (ה).

A **transitive verb** has two characteristics. First, it is an action **verb**, expressing a doable activity like kick, want, paint, write, eat, clean, etc. Second, it must have a direct object, something or someone who receives the verb's action.

The 13th *Path* is the Unity Directing Consciousness (*Sekhel Man.hig Ha.Achdut*). It (*Hu*) is the essence of Glory and the reward of the spiritual ones.

The Thirteenth Path is named the Uniting Intelligence and is so-called because it is itself the Essence of Glory. It is the Consummation of the Truth of individual spiritual things.

הנתיב	שלשה	עשר	נקרא	שכל	מנהיג
Path	3	10	is called	Consciousness	leader
				Intelligence	director
					directing

ה-אחדות	מפני	שהוא	עצם
the unity(s)	because	that is	essence
harmony		It is	bone
uniting			substance

ה-כבוד	ו-הוא	תשלום
the glory	and it	payment
honor, respect	and he	reward
majesty	*Hu* – divine name	completion
importance	of Kether	consummation

אמתת	ה-רוחניים	ה-אחדים
truth	spiritual	the others
prove right		things
verify, confirm		beings
authenticate		"the ones"
		unity (s)

The 14th Path is Illuminating Consciousness. It is the essence of electricity (Chashmal). It teaches the fundamentals of the secret mysteries of the Holy Sanctuary and its plan.

הנתיב	ארבעה	עשר	נקרא	שכל	מאיר
Path	4	10	is	Consciousness	brightness
			called	Intelligence	luminous
					light
					Illuminating

מפני	שהיא	עצם	ה-חשמל
because	that is	essence	Chashmal
	It is	substance	shining, amber
			substance
			electricity
			speaking silence - Kaplan

ו-ה-מורה	על	רזי	יסודות
teacher	of	mysteries	basics
instruction		secret(s)	foundations
		רז	fundamental
		secret	

ה-קדש	ו-תכונתם
the sanctuary	and their plan
holy	תכונה
to be consecrated	quality, character, trait
Holy Temple	plan, astronomy
	Treasures (biblical)

על – on, upon, over, near, to, unto, towards, against; with, together, because; yoke, burden, servitude.

15th Path of Heh - ה

The 15th Path is Stable Intelligence (Sekhel Ma'amid). From the pure darkness, it stabilizes the essence of Creation (Briah). The Masters say, "wrapped it in thick darkness." – Job 38:9.

הנתיב	החמשה	עשר	נקרא	שכל	מעמיד
Path	5	10	Is called	Consciousness Intelligence	stand base support

ו-נקרא	כן	מפני	שהוא	מעמיד
is called	because	because	It is	stability

עצם	ה-בריאה	כ-ערפלי	טהור
essence substance	Briah - creation בריאה	foggy gloom, darkness misty	pure

ו-בעלי	העיון	אמרו	כי	הוא
masters	Theory עיוני Theoretical Deep study	they said	because	Hu It, he

ה-ערפל	ו-זהו	ו-ערפל	ה-תולתו
the mist darkness gloom fog	and that is this is	fog	curly band wrapped it in thick darkness Gloom is its cocoon - Kaplan

ערפלי – According to Alcalay, Lower Sky in the Kabbalah

The 16th Path is the Eternal Intelligence (Sekhel Nitz.chi). It is the pleasure (Eden) of the Glory. There is no Glory like it (beneath it). It is called the Garden of Eden prepared for the Merciful Ones (Saints).

הנתיב	ששה	עשר	נקרא	שכל	נצחי
Path	6	10	is	Consciousness	eternal
			called	Intelligence	perpetual
					infinite

ו-נקרא	כן	מפני	שהוא
is called	because	because	It is
			as it is

עדון	ה-כבוד	שאין	כבוד
Eden	The glory	There	glory
garden, pleasure	honor	is no	
Delicacy, delight			
time period, era			

ל-מטה	הימנה	כמו	שהוא
down	There	same as	It is
lower		Like, as, thus	
beneath		honored	

שם	והוא	הנקרא	גן
name	and it/he	called	garden
Renown	*Hu*		
Memorial			
Divine Name			

עדן	המוכן	לחסדים
Eden	ready	reward, favors
	prepared	חסד
		grace, love
		benevolence

The 17th Path is the Perceptive Intelligence (Sekhel Ha.Her.gesh). It is prepared for the Faithful Ones (Saints), so they are clothed with the Holy Spirit. It is called the Foundation (Yesod) of Beauty (Tiphareth) and is placed among the Supernals (upper realms).

הנתיב	שבעה	עשר	נקרא	שכל	ה-הרגש
Path	7	10	is called	Consciousness Intelligence	feeling sentiment
					perception, senses

ו-הוא	מוכן	ל-חסידי	ה-אמונה
and it	prepared	Merciful Ones	faith, belief
Hu	ready	Saints	Confidence, trust

ל-ה-תלבשא	בו	ב-רוה	קדושה
to dress	with	Rauch	holy, blessing
clothed		Wind, breath	purification
		soul, spirit	sanctification

ו-חוא	נקרא	יסוד	ה-תפארת
and it	is	Yesod	Tiphareth
Hu	called	foundation, basis	Beauty, glory, honor
		element, source	

ב-מעמד	ה-עליונים
place	upper
standing, erected	height
candidate	supremacy
nominee	supernal

The 18th Path is called Intelligence of the House of Influx. From investigations (through seeking), a secret is transmitted/attracted to all who dwell/cleave to its shadow. Those who walk the 18th Path bind themselves to investigate the substance (reality) transmitted (emanating) from the Cause of Causes.

הנתיב	שמונה	נקרא	שכל	בית
Path	8	is	Consciousness	house
		called	Intelligence	dwell

ה-שפע	ו-מתוך	חקירותו
influence	from, of out of	probe, investigate
abundance	since	חקר
influx	whereas	search, inquiry

מושכים	רז	ו-הירה	ה-מתלוננים
attracting	secret	?	?
משך	mystery	העבר	יתלוננים
attract		transmit	he-will-rest
			Ps. 90:1

ב-עלו	ו-הדבקים	ב-חקירות
in its (shadow)	and cleave	probe
p.3323²	cling, glue	investigate
	bind, join	

ממשותו	מעילת	העילות
reality, effect	cause	the causes
Substance, materialize		of causes

ה-קירותו 1 – It's walls. Notice the change of mean from Heh (ה) to Cheth (ח). Walls – seeking.

² Alcalay *English to Hebrew*

The 19th Path is the Intelligence of the Secret All Spiritual Activities (Sekhel Sod HaPaulot Haruchniot Kulam). It is the influx that permeates from the Supreme Blessing and the Glory of the Most High.

הנתיב	תשעה	נקרא	שכל
Path	9	is	Consciousness
		called	Intelligence

סוד	ה-פעולות	ה-רוחניות	כולם
secret	the actions	Spiritual	all
	activities	רוח	everyone
	accomplish	*Rauch,* spirit, wind, breath	

מפני	שהוא	ה-שפע	ה-מתפשט	בו
because	It is	influx	spread, pervasive	from
		abundance	permeates	with
		18th Path	פשט	
			stretch, extend	

מהברכה	ה-עליונה	ו-ה-כבוד	ה-מעולה
blessing	the height	and the honor	the excellent
ברך	top	respect	מעלה
to bless	supreme	glory	rise, elevated
thank	eminence		עיל
			height

The 20th Path is the Intelligence of Will (Sekhel HaRatzon). It is the trait from which everything is formed. Through this consciousness, everyone can know the essence of the Original Wisdom.

הנתיב	העשרים	נקרא	שכל	ה-רצון
Path	20	is	Consciousness	the will
		called	Intelligence	goodwill
				desire

מפני	שהוא	תכונת	כל	ה-יצורים
because	It is	attribute, trait	all	fabrication, form(s)
		quality		imaginative
		characteristic		creatures
		plan, astronomy		יצירה
				Yetzirah - Formation

כולם	ו-ב-זה	ה-שכל	כל
all	And-in-this	Intelligence	all
everyone	Through this	Consciousness	
	This is		

יודע	מציאות	ה-חכמה	ה-קדומה
know	reality	Chokmah	the ancient
knowing	existence	wisdom, intelligence	original, primordial
	essence	knowledge, insight	ancient
			קדם
		science	Ancient Days

קדמון - ancient, primitive, ancestor; eastern

471

The 21st Path is the Seeking and Delightful Intelligence (Sekhel HaChafutz HaMevukash). It receives the divine influx to bless all, everyone.

הנתיב	אחד	ו-עשרים	נקרא	שכל
Path	1	& 20	is	Consciousness
			called	Intelligence

ה-חפץ	ה-מבוקש	מפני
wish, desire	בקש	because
delight, find pleasure in	to ask, desire	
have affection for	seek, to search	

שהוא	מקבל	שפע
It is	receives, recipient	influx
	accepted	18th Path
	customary	

ה-אלהות	כדי	ל-חשפיע	מברכת
divinity	in order to,	to influence	bless
divine	so that	to bestow	ברק
	so as to, to the extent	שפע	To bless
		18th Path	

472

ל-כל	הנמצאים	כולם
to all	found, to be found	all, everyone
	available, present	
	discovered	
	Root - מצא	

מצא – to find, find out, guess, catch, reach, overtake; to discover, come upon, reveal, meet, encounter, happen, befall, and be sufficient.

22nd Path of Lamed - ל

The 22nd Path is the Faithful Intelligence (Sekhel Ne'eman). It causes spiritual powers to multiply. Through it, the Spiritual Ones are drawn close, and all find shelter in its shadow.

שנים	ו-עשרים	נקרא	שכל
2	20	is	Consciousness
		called	Intelligence

נאמן	מפני	שבו	מתרבים
faithful	because	It is	multiply
trustworthy		of	רבה
Loyal, firm; sure			to increase, enlarge, bring up, raise, cultivate

כחות	ה-רוחניות	כדי
כח	Spiritual	through it
Resource, power	רוח	
force, strength ability, wealth riches	Rauch spirit, wind, breath	

להיותם	קרובים	ל-כל
to be	close	to all
היה	near, at hand	
exist, come to pass	relation, about	
become, remain	approximately	

ה-מתלוננים	ב-צילו
? - dwell	in his shadow
יתלוננים	צל
he-will-rest	shadow, shade
Ps. 90:1	shelter, protection

The 23rd Path is the Sustaining Intelligence (Sekhel Kayam). It is the power sustaining all the Sephiroth.

הנתיב	שלשה	ו-עשרים	נקרא	שכל
Path	3	20	is called	Consciousness
				Intelligence

קיום	מפני	שהוא	כח
sustaining	because	It is	Resource, power
subsistence			force, strength
existence			ability, wealth
observance			riches

קיום	ל-כל	ה-ספירות
sustaining	to all, for	Sephiroth
subsistence	all	numerations
existence		numbers
observance		

The 24th Path is Imaginative Intelligence (Sekhel Dimyoni). It gives a form to the imaginations of all Living Creatures.

הנתיב	ארבעה	ו-עשרים	נקרא	שכל
Path	4	20	is	Consciousness
			called	Intelligence

דמיוני	מפני	שהוא	נותן
resemblance	because	It is	נתן
likeness		It	gives
imaginative			provides
fantasy			dispense

דמות	ל-כל	ה-דמיונים	נבראים
likeness, image	to all	imaginations	Living
figure, character	of all		Creatures

477

The 25th Path is Experimental Intelligence (Sekhel Nisyoni). It is the primary test through which all the Merciful Ones become skilled.

הנתיב	חמשה	ו-עשרים	נקרא	שכל
Path	5	20	is	Consciousness
			called	Intelligence

נסיוני	מפני	שהוא	ה-נסיון
Experimental	because	It is	the test
נסיון			
trial, probation			
test			

ה-קדמון	שבו	מנסה
ancient,	through	experience
primitive, primary	which	skilled, tried out
original		tested

ל-כל	ה-חסידים
to all	Merciful Ones
	Saints

The 26th Path is the Regenerating Intelligence (Sekhel MeChudash).
By it, the Blessed Holy One regenerates the World of Creation.

הנתיב	ששה	ו-עשרים	נקרא	שכל
Path	6	20	is	Consciousness
			called	Intelligence

מחודש	מפני	קב "ה	ש"ה
renewed	because	Blessed Holy One	
regenerate			

מחדש	בו	כל	ה-חדשים
Innovator, inventor	By it	all	renew, revive
rejuvenation			invent
Title of God			establish a new interpretation

479

ב-בריאת	ה-עולם
in creation	the world, universe
making	humanity, space
world	existence, surroundings
cosmos	eternity, ages
	distant future

ש"ה - שם המפרש - The Ineffable Name (God).

קב "ה		
קודשא	בריך	הוא
The holy one	Blessed be	He (*Hu*)

The 27th Path is the Perceptible or Felt Intelligence (Sekhel Murgash). Through it, the senses of all living beings under the zodiac are excited.

הנתיב	שבעה	ו-עשרים	נקרא	שכל
Path	7	20	is	Consciousness
			called	Intelligence

מורגש	ו-הוא	חומר	מפני	שממנו
מרגש		חמר		from which
felt,	& it	material	because	through
perceived		element		
perceptible		matter		

נבראו	ה-נבראים	כל	מתחת
were created	נברא	all	below, under
his creatures	living creature(s)		beneath
humanity			

גלגל	ה-עליון	ו-ה-רגשותם
revolve	high, exalted	feelings
to cause	The Most High	רגש
bring about	Title of God	To be excited, to rage
		Emotion, sense

The 28th Path is called the Natural Intelligence (Sekhel Mutba). It completes and perfects the nature of all that exists under the revolution of the Sun.

שכל	נקרא	ו-עשרים	שמנה	הנתיב
Consciousness	is	& 20	8	Path
Intelligence	called			

טבע	נשלם	שבו	מפני	מוטבע מטבע
nature	completed	It is	Because	Innate, Inborn
character				
element				natural

ה-חמה	גלגל	מתחת	ה-נמצים	כל
The Sun	revolve	under	נמצא	all
warmth	to cause	below	existing	
heat	circuit of the sun		available	

ב-שלימות
In perfection
שלום
peace, complete
perfected

The 29th Path is Physical Intelligence (Sekhel Mugsham). It depicts and establishes the growth of all physical bodies incorporated under the Zodiac.

The Zodiac is an allusion to the Celestial Spheres of the ancients. The seven planets plus the 8th sphere of the fixed stars.

שכל	נקרא	ו-עשרים	תשעה	הנתיב
Consciousness	is	& 20	9	Path
Intelligence	called			

כל	מתאר	שהוא	מפני	מוגשם
All	Described	It is	Because	physical
every	Depicted			corporal
	Portrayed			

תכונת	תחת	שית-גשם	גשם
כון	Under, below	incorporated	physical
established	Instead		body

483

ה-גלגלים	ב-גידולים
the revolutions	In Growth
cycles, spheres	development
the zodiac	

שׁית – to place, put, set, lay, fix; to appoint, foundation, bottom, pit.

כון – to be correct, proper, firm, established, clear, determined, ready, prepared.

גדול – growth, raising, rearing, development.

אשׁר – that, which

Joining Hod to Yesod

The 30th Path is called the Collective or Inclusive Intelligence. By it, astrologers study the Laws that govern the stars and the zodiac and perfect their knowledge.

[Stars include the seven planets known to the ancients.]

נתיב	שלשים	נקרא	שכל	כללי
	30		Consciousness	General
Path		is	Intelligence	Collective
		called		Universal
				common

מפני	כוללים	הוברי	שמים
because of	comprehensive	Astrologers	Heavens
	inclusive		Starry
	including		sky
	embracing		

ב-משפטיהם	ה-ככבים	וה-מזלות	עיונם
Justice	to shine	*Mazloth*	theoretical
Laws	ככב	Zodiac	speculative
Statues	star	Lucky	deep study
	Mercury	Fortunate	theory

תשלומי	ידיעתם	ב-אופני	גלגלים
completion	*Da'ath*	Ophan	Wheels
payment	knowledge	wheels	sphere
reward			to revolve
			to cause

The 31st Path is Perpetual Intelligence (Sekhel Tamidi). It regulates all the cyclic forces that form the revolutions of the stars and planets (Mazloth).

הנתיב	אחד	ו-שלשים	נקרא	שכל
Path	1	& 30	is	Consciousness
			called	Intelligence

תמידי	מפני	שהוא	כלל	כחות
continuous	Because	It is	rule	Power(s)
consistent			whole	Forces
persevering			principle	

כל	ה-גלגלים	ו-מזלות	ו-ה-צורות
all	wheels	*Mazloth*	shapes, form(s)
	sphere		צור
	to revolve		to mold, form
	to cause		to bind, wrap
			rock, fortress, refuge

ו-משפטיהם
משפט
Justice, judgment
Law
theorem

486

The 32nd Path is Serving Intelligence (Sekhel Ne'evad). It repairs (Tikun) all the seven planets' operations and keeps them in their orbits.

נתיב	שנים	ו-שלשים	נקרא	שכל
Path	2	& 30	is	Consciousness
			called	Intelligence

נעבד	מפני	שהוא	מתוקן	לכל
work	because	It is	repaired	To all
serving			תוקן	
slave			fixed	
worship			repair	

המשתמשים	ב-עבודת	שבעה
?	work(s)	7
תמשים	operations	
realize	*p. 2556*	

כוכבי	לכת	ל-חבלם
planets	to go	orbits, orbiting
stars		חבלים
		ropes
		rigging

חבלם - The ideas of ropes and rigging are linked with the planets and stars. Therefore I translated the word as "orbit."

Appendix 3

Hebrew Letter Names

	Hebrew Letters Spelled in Full	
	Letter Name	Meaning
א	אלף	1,000. To teach, tame. Domesticate.
ב	בית	House, household; wife and children.
ג	גמל	Camel, mature, requital, compensation, remuneration.
ד	דלת	Door, portal, gate
ה	הא	Lo, Behold!
ו	וו	Hook, peg, nail
ז	זין	Arms, weapons
ח	חית	No entry
ט	טית	No entry
י	יוד	No entry
כ	כף	Spoon, palm of hand, sole of foot, handle, scale, branch
ל	למד	To learn, study, be accustomed to
מ	מים	water
נ	נון	fish, to shine, to flourish, sprout, spread, to be established
ס	סמך	to rely on, trust in, support, aid, assist, to draw (make), close; to graduate, to lean upon

Hebrew Letters Spelled in Full		
	Letter Name	Meaning
ע	עין	Spring, fountain; to be hostile, antagonistic; to hate; to consider, go into a matter, think over, look carefully at, to weigh carefully, reflect, study, meditate, ponder
פ	פא	Edge, border, side, lock of hair, region
צ	צדי	Lateral, side,
	צדיה	evil design, malice, an afterthought,
	צדה	to lie in wait, ambush, lurk, do by design, scheme, intend maliciously
ק	קוף	Monkey, ape; the *eye* of a needle, *hole* for an ax handle.
	קף	circle, go around
ר	ריש	poverty; head, principal
	רישה	beginning
ש	שין	urine
	שן	tooth, jaw, claw, ivory, peak
ת	תו	sign, line, feature; note
	תה & תו	Aramaic: again, further, more and no more, and nothing else, and that's all
	תוא	plotter, designer

Cube Figures

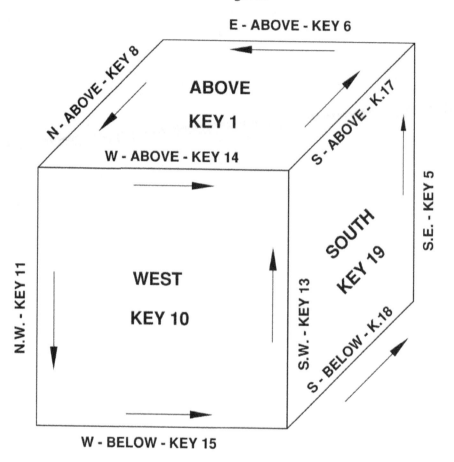

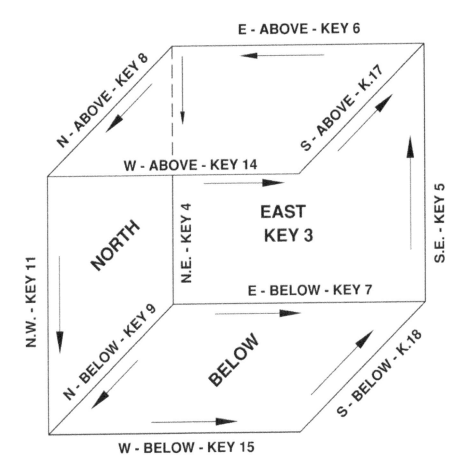

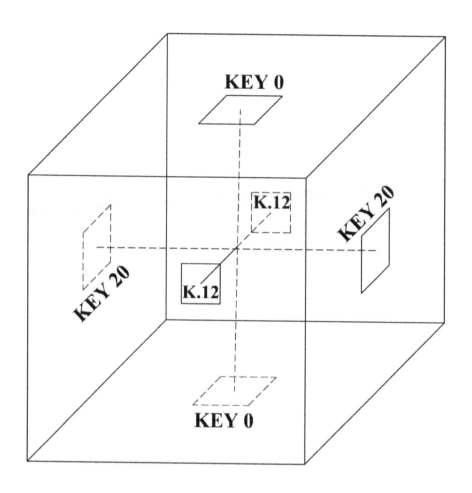

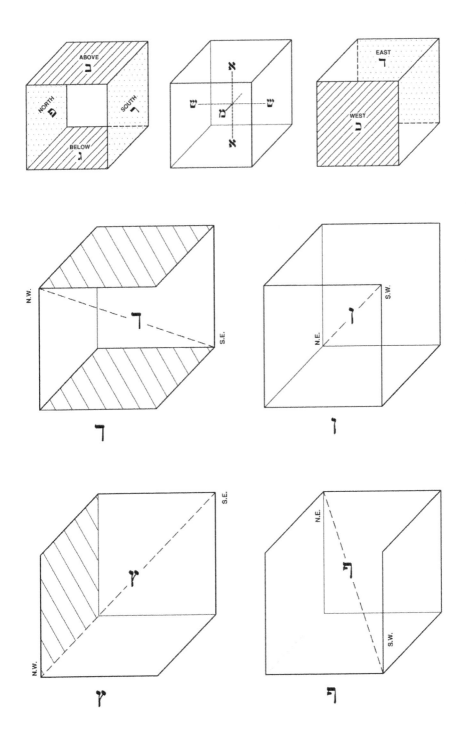

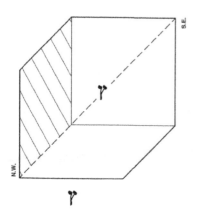

צ

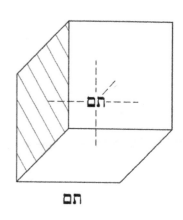

תם

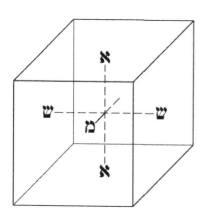

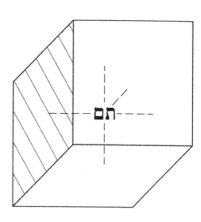

494

Made in the USA
Monee, IL
15 February 2021